THE DOG AGGRESSION SYSTEM
EVERY DOG OWNER NEEDS

THE
DOG AGGRESSION
SYSTEM

EVERY DOG OWNER NEEDS

From Leashes to Neuroscience
A dog owner's journey through the treatment of dog aggression

Jackie Ferrier

Written by Jackie Ferrier
Published by K9aggression.com

ISBN 978-0-9917295-2-4

DEDICATION

To all misunderstood dogs that suffer because of our arrogance and ignorance.

THE DOG AGGRESSION SYSTEM EVERY DOG OWNER NEEDS

DISCLAIMER

Dealing with aggressive dogs is risky. Always consult a qualified professional before beginning any treatment program to deal with dog aggression. Never disregard professional advice from a qualified dog behavior specialist or delay in seeking it because of something you have read in this book. All content and information provided in this document is as is and provided for informational and educational purposes only and any use of thereof is solely at your own risk. The author shall not be liable for any injury, cost, or damage arising directly or indirectly from the use of this book. It is solely your responsibility to evaluate the accuracy, completeness and usefulness of all opinions, advice, services, merchandise, and other information provided either directly or indirectly through this book or on the Internet in general.

The information contained herein is not intended to be a substitute for professional advice, diagnosis, or treatment in any manner. Always seek the advice of a qualified dog behavior specialist with any questions you have about your dog's behavior. By reading the information and content in this book, the reader and/or viewer does hereby acknowledge that it is your sole responsibility to review this disclaimer.

The site and this book may be hyper-linked or point to other sites, which are not maintained by, or related to author of this book. Hyper-links to such sites are provided as a service to the reader and are not sponsored by or affiliated with the author. The author is not responsible for the content on those sites. Hyper-links are to be accessed at the user's own risk and the author makes no representations or warranties about the content, completeness or accuracy of these hyper-linked sites, or the sites that are hyper-linked to this site. The author provides hyperlinks as a convenience, and the inclusion of any hyper-link to a third party does not necessarily imply endorsement by the author of that site or any associations with its operators.

THE DOG AGGRESSION SYSTEM EVERY DOG OWNER NEEDS

WHO IS THIS BOOK FOR?

This book is for you if you are just starting out; looking for help; on a waiting list to see a professional, or you might be a little further down the road: either on a successful training program, or having gone around the block with people who weren't much help at all.

If you have a really good trainer or have seen a veterinary behaviorist, my hope is that this book is acts as an adjunct to your program. Perhaps it will remind you of some things you have forgotten; give you some new ideas or even prompt you to ask your professional questions you hadn't thought of.

Maybe you are just starting out, or perhaps in the process of realizing that things like alpha rolls and leash corrections aren't working. My hope is that this book provides you guidance and gives ideas you can use right now. Plus, will help demystifying the treatments for you. If your dog has the potential to hurt someone – you should find a qualified professional who has expertise in dog aggression. This book gives you some ideas on how to find the right person. But there is plenty in this book that can help you.

It is the kind of book that I wish I had when I was starting out. And, it is the kind of book that answers some of the more in depth questions I have many years later.

Although most of the book assumes your dog has an aggression problem, it can be adapted for dogs that you are not sure about or think might develop a problem. These include rescued dogs with unknown histories or those dogs that have been the victims of dog attacks. There is plenty here that can make a normal dog's life better.

ABOUT THIS BOOK

I envisioned this book as a blue print for a treatment program, with a particular emphasis on setting you and your dog up to succeed. This book offers steps for building a treatment program, but it is not meant to be a do-it-yourself guide. No book can diagnose your dog or understand your unique situation. Anticipating when the aggression might occur is essential in treatment. But even qualified experienced professionals can only suggest specific treatment for your dog and situations that might trigger the aggression when you provide them with complete information surrounding past aggressive events. Trying to treat dog aggression on your own can be dangerous.

In addition, most dog owners are not trained to read the language of stress and anxiety that dogs display that is essential for behavior modification. We describe signs of stress/anxiety, how to get better at looking for and reading these signs. A seasoned and qualified professional can help teach you what to look out for, especially as they often happen quickly.

At the same time, there are reasons why *behavior modification* goes wrong, and this book tries to address that. One of the reasons why this book was written is because of the number of people who found their way onto the K9aggression support group that were making the same kinds of mistakes over the years.

And because over the years we have seen the need to treat the human issues around dog aggression, this book was also written with the intention of helping you cope with dog that behaves aggressively just as much as helping you help your dog.

Part One is the system. It is like a broad view blueprint of a treatment and response plan that could be applied to a typical case of dog aggression with modifications for four broad categories: dog aggression towards people in the family, aggression towards strangers, aggression towards dogs in the family, and aggression towards strange dogs.

While it provides some explanation for why the recommendations are made and in some cases information to motivate you, part one is meant to get you started without weighing you down with the detail in part 2.

When it comes to *Targeted Behavior Modification* (step 5), you will likely need someone to help you develop a specialized plan for you and your dog. They can help you understand what behavior you need to be aware of in your dog, and how fast or slow to proceed. Outside of this, and the *Emergency Response Plan*, the other recommendations are intended to be safe practices you can get started on now *as long as you are ensuring your dog is not becoming stressed or anxious.*

Part Two goes into further detail about dog aggression, touching on genetics to how dogs learn. It also expands on many of the areas in part 1. This section is meant to provide you with a deeper understanding of the aspects that lead to or are involved in dog aggression and treatment of it. The more you learn, the easier it is to ask questions and understand the answers. It will help you to understand when or why to make modifications to the treatment plan because you understand *why* it's happening or what you can do about it.
But, it is included in a separate section so not to overwhelm those who are new to treatment and who want to get started right away.

Part Three includes a collection of myth busters, trouble-shooting tips, tools and resources, and discusses professionals you might want to consult.

A word on gender neutrality: He, she, or it?

While it might make sense to use the pronoun *it* when referring to a dog; that would bother me as a reader, since my dog is a real being with a personality that has a special place in my life. She is not an it.

As an attempt to cover both genders, or be gender neutral, in this book we have referred to the dog(s) as *he* or *she*, or to avoid excessive wordiness, also used the incorrect plural *they*, even when referring to a singular dog.

 WHO AM I

I have spent more than a decade tracking scientific and academic research related to dog aggression, treatment, and psychology as it relates to both people and dogs. I have consulted a variety of trainers (covering all spectrums from excellent to terrible), board certified veterinary behaviorists, as well as other vets, breeders, those in the dog show circuit, and even psychological professionals. I had the opportunity to assist a dog trainer for a short period of time although I didn't learn much about aggression. I did learn a lot about people, though.

I've lived with dogs that have shown aggression to dogs and people, both familiar and unknown. My journey with my own dogs is what initially led me on the search for factual research that is credible, repeatable and could be verified. This was after discovering the hard way that there is a lot of bad advice disguised as good in the dog training industry. The more I learned, the more I realized just how many smart dog owners are vulnerable to following advice or making choices that can make their dogs worse. Knowing the fate of many of those dogs, I was compelled to make a difference.

In 2002 I founded K9aggression.com anonymously with a group of similar minded people. A year later I started the K9aggression support group where I have witnessed countless stories and reports by people just like you.

When the site was created, we provided information and challenged people to do their research so they wouldn't fall into a trap of falling under the spell of a trainer who promised magic but who really had no idea what they were doing. I am honored to say we have had many positive responses to our online efforts, not only from dog owners, but also from experienced professionals.

But we, as web users, have changed now that we spend more and more of time online and search engines have allowed us to search so easily. "Research" has now evolved to collecting a bunch of snippets from a variety of forums and web pages. Most of us really don't know whether the information is truly legitimate.

So we collect the pieces that seem right and only half believe it all. We're experimenting but not committing to any of it wholeheartedly.

I cringe when I see or hear people are still "correcting" their dog's aggression with a leash "pop", or are considering a shock collar or when I hear that their dogs are being pushed into situations they are just not ready to cope with. But you just don't know what you don't know.

So I was compelled to write a book that addresses the gaps that are left over from the "pick-your-own-adventure" style of treatment approaches people cobble together for their dogs. Some of the information is widely held or has come from personal experience. I have also included a good number of references so that you can determine for yourself if the research is legitimate.

If your dog has the potential to hurt someone you really need to find a qualified professional. But I also believe there are many, many things you can start doing now while you are in the process.

Improving the lives of aggressive dogs and those around them is a passion of mine. If you find yourself with the time and curiosity to learn more, an account of my story is at the end of the book. But at the moment, I think you might have other priorities!

So for now, let's move on!

 **BONUS MATERIAL**

In addition, these resources are only available to the purchasers of this book. Simply go to this web page to access them. Your password is: eZv5je45

http://k9aggression.com/e-book-bonus-materials/

They include:

1. Core Behavior Training Guide. A 30 page booklet to teach basic core behaviors needed for this treatment program using clicker training.
2. A History Form
3. Behavior Modification Progress log
4. Emergency Response Plan Cheat Sheet

In addition, we have collected other resources that are in online and available to the public that you might find useful. Here are a few you should read:

1. Dr. Karen Overall's Protocol for Deference
2. Dr. Karen Overall's Protocol for Relaxation
3. Dr. Lore I Haug's Desensitization/Counterconditioning for Vet visit
4. Dr. Lore I Haug's Desensitization for Muzzles and Head Halters

We are also collecting links to videos that you might find useful for your convenience in this area too.

If any links in this book no longer work by the time you try them, try finding the updated links on the K9aggression.com site in the Resources instead.

IS MY DOG REALLY "AGGRESSIVE"?

Aggression only defines behavior. It is not a diagnosis because all dogs are capable of behaving aggressively. While we would like our dogs to like all people and all dogs, many of them never will. So, how do you know there is actually a problem?

Any time that aggression occurs, it should be cause for concern. But, the challenge is in determining whether the behavior is abnormal. In some cases, dog aggression is quite normal and appropriate within a context. For example, it's normal for a dog to be afraid of an unknown thing. If that unknown thing starts to approach the dog, then that dog might growl to encourage the thing to back off if the dog feels threatened.

It's also normal to show aggressive behavior when confronting other animals or people that are perceived as a threat in a situation, especially when there is no escape such as while on leash, in a room, or in a car.

It's also normal for puppies to cause adult dogs to growl or even pin puppies during interactions where the adult has perceived that the puppy has gone too far or bitten too hard. In that case, the growls serve as warnings and communication. They are not intended to cause harm.

BUT MY DOG HARDLY EVER ACTS AGGRESSIVELY!

You would not be alone if you were saying right now, "He (or she) is so sweet and good 95% of the time; it's just that 5%..."

Dogs with aggression problems can often appear to be just fine most of the time. Some might go weeks, even months without an incident. They might always be aggressive towards strangers, or they might seem to react arbitrarily occasionally.

You may have a problem when any of these situations occur:

- The aggressive situation or response intensifies over time.

- The reaction is extreme given the context.

- There is no threat to the dog.

- The intent is not to resolve conflict but to cause harm.

- There is a risk that the target of the aggression will be hurt.

- You are frightened or anxious.

- The dog gives no warning signs (although, it's possible you may not know what to look for yet).

- Biting is not inhibited (i.e. there are punctures, bleeding, etc.).

- There are other behavior problems, concerns, or unusual behavior habits.

You will need a qualified professional that is an expert in dog behavioral problems to determine if the behavior is abnormal and provide you with a diagnosis.

YOUR DOG'S PROBLEM MIGHT BE HARD TO ACCEPT

When you first wonder if there may be a problem, the realization does not always happen instantly. There is a process associated with coming to terms that your dog does have a problem that needs to be addressed. It is similar to a grieving process. Part of this process is realizing that we have to let go of the hopes and dreams of the life we imagined with our dog and recognize that things are not as rosy or easy as we wanted them to be. However, we often experience denial before we get come to that conclusion and it manifests in different ways.

People in denial sometimes deny the issue outright, while others downplay it. In fact, probably one of the reasons why we hear about dog aggression happening so often is that the dog owners have not come to terms with the problem. We just don't want to believe that something might happen.

It is not a black and white experience, though. Denial can shift and change over time. People might think an aggressive event was a strange, mysterious one-time thing or perhaps something that is limited to a particular situation (i.e. "my dog is only afraid of big black dogs"). It may be that the aggressive episode(s) did not actually result in damage, so it gets swept under the rug. Or, people simply get used to it and see it as a personality quirk. Denial even happens with people whose dog has improved with work and they mislead themselves into thinking their dog is more rehabilitated than he or she actually is. Some might even want to believe their dog is cured.

It is not just that it's hard to accept that our dog behaves aggressively at times; there are social costs associated with having an aggressive dog, too. Not only can it shake the faith and trust we have in our dog, but it can affect our relationships with others, as they fear our dog and judge us for our dog's behavior. It can lead us to feeling conflicted or guilty.

The reality is there are many reasons for aggression issues, from poor socialization to abuse, but often the dog is predisposed to having a behavior problem develop. And while you may have accidently made the problem worse, it may have happened even if you did everything right.

However, denying that your dog may be aggressive is very problematic. We end up exposing them to these situations that cause the anxiety/aggression sequence again and again. This increases their anxiety and making the situation worse. In so many cases where a dog causes harm, the dog was already recognized as having aggressive tendencies in that situation. This makes everything worse when the victims involved in the incident realize that the situation could have been prevented.

Even if you think the problem might not be that bad, it is still worth taking precautions and lowering stress levels, rather than keeping up the exhausting task of hoping for the best. While many of us can recover well enough from a scare, it is deeply upsetting when another dog or person gets injured. It's compounded when a dog is euthanized because of a bite or even an attack.

One assumes that if you are reading this book, you are coming around to the idea that you might have a problem on your hands (unless you are in the dog behavior industry, in which case: "Hi!").

 ## MY DOG MIGHT HAVE A PROBLEM WITH AGGRESSION.

Once you start to realize your dog might actually have a problem, determining what to do - determining the right thing to do - can be a real task because in the dog training industry there are a lot of different methods, theories and techniques for training dogs in general.

To make things more confusing, there is actually conflict between trainers and specialists. Just when a dog owner is convinced one way is right; another professional puts those ideas down. No group of professionals, or self-called experts, seems to be able to agree on the way to treat dog aggression.

Unfortunately, some trainers simply see dog aggression as a behavior to correct or punish, rather than an actual problem that has cognitive, physiological, and bio-chemical implications. This confusion often leads dog owners to try to make sense of it all on their own.

Some behavioral techniques are good for all dogs, regardless of the kind and intensity of the aggression. Normal dogs will tolerate some behavioral techniques while others will cause the aggression to become worse, resulting in a more unpredictable, dangerous dog. Other techniques may work for dogs that have aggression for certain reasons, but will have little effect on others. Some dogs will find it impossible to learn anything without pharmaceutical interventions.

 ## WHAT TRAINING IS RIGHT?

Knowing which information is legitimate is difficult for us - consumer reports have made an industry in this. As soon as we see someone in the media, on TV, on National Geographic or Animal Planet for example, we immediately assume the individual has some kind of credibility. But the reality is that broadcasters and news publishers are primarily interested in attracting audiences (and I know this first hand as someone who has worked in media and marketing for a number of years). Any person selling services and products might be thinking of their business first, and the right thing to do to help your dog, second. But, consumers don't know the difference. And, how should they?

A vet is trusted because there is a license required. Unfortunately, the average vet does not specialize in behavior and may actually know a lot less than some good trainers. And sadly, in addition to many good trainers, there are a lot of bad trainers.

This book aims to answer these questions and explain why some methods are good and why some are dangerous, or just ineffective. It won't be able to answer all your questions, because no book can, but it will provide you with a very good base: one that is based on science and not charisma and personalities.

WHAT IS MOTIVATING MY DOG TO REACT?

This is a loaded question of course, since we can't get into those brains too well, and they aren't telling us! But, it's a key question in helping you determine exactly how you approach treatment.

A big picture view holds that there are primary and secondary emotions. Anger is considered to be a secondary emotion. The primary emotions that lead to anger are: pain, fear, and frustration. When you examine the motivations behind the aggression, which of these emotions may have developed before the aggression? One, two, or all three may play a factor.

ANXIETY

Scientists generally believe that some form of anxiety precedes or underlies almost all aggression in dogs. Anxiety is the natural response to stress, which is activated in any situation where we feel threatened on some level. The anxiety actually serves a purpose. It motivates us to do something to cope with it. It's what causes us as students to study for an exam, or finally stop procrastinating to write that essay. It's what causes us to prepare before we have to give a presentation. It's also what we feel walking home late at night when there is someone approaching who is behaving erratically.

The problem develops when the stress or anxiety becomes excessive, prolonged or occurs when there is no actual threat.

PAIN

Your dog is more likely to react when he or she is experiencing pain. A medical check-up is important. Bad teeth, sore joints or any other medical condition can contribute to aggression. Also, if you are pulling your dog out of a fight, he or she may bite you. The adrenaline has kicked in and your dog is not quite feeling the same pain as they might ordinarily but they could bite from redirected aggression or pain. Attacks from dogs that are experiencing pain are more likely to be snaps than vicious bites.[1] They are also more likely to display fewer warning signs.

FRUSTRATION

Your dog may be frustrated for a number of reasons. A common one is related to people's use of the leash, and how the leash or fence is used to restrict their natural desires or behaviors. For example, dogs may become frustrated when trying to meet other dogs and the person is pulling on the leash and not letting them show their normal body language. As mentioned before, interfering with fighting may cause a dog to lash out at you or the other dog. This is considered to be re-directed aggression.

Another situation is when dogs come to expect something they desire. When they are not given the thing when they expect it, they can become frustrated. Frustration can lead to stress. And stress, depending on how reactive your dog is, how acute the stress is, the stress load your dog already experiences, or how chronic the stress is, can lead to aggression.

A dog may also grow frustrated when he or she is unable to deal with their anxiety as well.

DETAILED HISTORY TAKING

Put together a history of all the situations that caused your dog to react, and note as objectively as you can all the factors involved. There is a list to get you started in the Management chapter, under the "Anticipate and Avoid" section.

Keep in mind that aggression progresses. This changes the nature of the aggression, not just in terms of how your dog responds, but how quickly he or she responds, and what else they start to respond to.

ANTHROPOMORPHIZING

It's natural for us to ascribe human tendencies and motivations to dogs. While we share many things with dogs including similar brains, social systems, the desire to play, etc. there are some fundamental differences.

Our morals are not the dogs' morals. You may feel that your dog has torn up something when you left the house because he or she was angry at you for leaving. If they look guilty when you scolded them on your return, this is an example of anthropomorphizing. Dogs look guilty because *we* see guilt, not because they feel guilt. What they see is a human who might behave in a threatening way. If we have a habit of scolding our dogs when we return for destructive behavior, all the dog has come to learn is that sometimes when we return, we behave threateningly. The look on their face is designed to appease us so that we don't hurt them or scare them any further.

We have a tendency to punish our dogs the way we punish our children. It is very hard not to ascribe moral qualities to dogs that make us feel they deserve our rewards or punishment. But, dogs don't behave aggressively because they are inherently evil or bad.

Understanding that there are similarities but also some fundamental differences may help us from getting so emotionally tied into the aggression problem. Of course, we should be concerned and do everything to prevent people from getting hurt. But, we don't need to feel betrayed the way we often do.

IT'S OUR WORLD, NOT THEIRS

It also behooves us to remember that dogs are living in our world; we are not living in theirs. Not only are we their guides to this foreign world, but also we need to make sure that our dogs are being allowed to live in a way that satisfies them in a species-typical and breed-typical way. The number of people over the years I've seen that insist their dogs walk in a perfect heel and grow frustrated when the dog wants to stop and sniff on walks is really unfortunate. Dogs should be allowed to smell their environment – it's their most dominant sense. Stop being in such a rush to get down the street and back before you go to work; the degree to which he or she can smell is stimulating their mind. Stimulate your dog in ways that would be interesting to your dog – not just to you. You might love a snuggle on the couch, but your dog might need a game of hide and seek with their favorite toy just as much. Get a sand box for digging for your terrier, play fetch with your lab, or do scent work with your hound. Let them experience new things, but aim to keep their world safe and predictable.

CAN MY DOG BE CURED?

No dog can be cured, because all dogs have the potential to behave aggressively. In addition, once behaviors are learned, they won't be "forgotten" (see the section in Part two about *extinction* in *Behavior Modification* explained). What we seek instead is a new behavior that is incompatible with the aggression. As well, we are looking to cause a change in the underlying emotional states that cause your dog to behave aggressively. So no dog can be cured. But the majority of dog aggression cases can be controlled and improved. How much really depends on many factors. We do know from the data reported by various veterinary behavior clinics that with treatment, dogs can be controlled and improved to the extent that the owners are happy to keep their dog. And, that's pretty darn good.

BEHAVIOR MODIFICATION: ISN'T THERE A FASTER WAY?

The quick way to prevent aggression is just that: prevent it. Avoid the circumstances that cause it to happen. In fact, you should be doing this anyway for a number of very good reasons that we talk about in the prevention and management section of the book. I would go so far as to say if you could actually avoid the circumstances that cause the aggression, the idea of *behavior modification* becomes far less intimidating because your stress load has been reduced and things don't seem so out of control.

Behavior modification is not as scary as it may seem and here is why I recommend it: it's better for the dog long term (if you can do it properly). A less stressed, calmer dog is a happier, safer dog.

But more importantly, accidents happen. You cannot foresee every possible accident that might happen. Gates get left open or opened by people who don't know any better. Leashes break. Sometimes people approach regardless of your requests to stay back. Off-leash dogs appear where they shouldn't.

There was a sad story told by one of the members of K9aggression.com support group on Yahoo. One woman had her dog behind a glass front door. There was a child outside on the other side of the door. The woman thought the situation was managed safely, until the dog actually leapt right through the glass to attack the child. The dog was euthanized shortly after this incident.

On the flip side, my dog, who was very aggressive towards all other dogs, managed to get out of the backyard on one occasion after someone had left a gate open. I found a woman in the front yard holding my dog by her collar. The person she had been walking with was standing nearby with their dog. My heart was pounding as I led my dog – who seemed oblivious to this other dog - back inside. I asked the woman if there had been any problems. The woman seemed mystified and simply said she had seen my dog off leash, and thought she had got out by accident. I was grateful for all the *behavior modification* I continued to do with my dog while we went for walks.

If you can reduce your dog's reactivity, it might make the difference between keeping your dog and losing your dog.

MEDICAL ISSUES

Book an appointment with your vet to rule out any medical issues or problems as soon as you realize there is an aggression problem. Medical issues can contribute or lead to or aggravate aggression.

However, if the aggression has been going on for a period of time, your dog will still need a *behavior modification* program to deal with the learning component that occurs in aggressive episodes, even when the aggression is entirely caused by a medical problem.

BEHAVIORAL MEDICATION

In serious cases of aggression, behavioral medication may be needed as an adjunct to a behavior modification program. See your vet to get a referral to a veterinary behaviorist. Medication is not a quick fix – it only allows *behavior modification* to be effective. If your dog needs medication, he or she will have difficulties learning, as well as inhibiting their reactivity without it. See the section on Medication in Part Two for more information about medication.

There are not a lot of board-certified veterinary behaviorists available unfortunately. But if you can get to see one, it's usually worth it – even if it's a long drive. Alternatively, your vet can consult one on your behalf – many veterinary behaviorists do consultations with other vets. If your dog needs medication, it's best to start this right away; otherwise, all work you do with your dog will be an uphill battle.

If you are in a country where this kind of service or professional is not available, you can contact Tufts University in the USA to use their remote service called PETFAX. Your veterinarian can use their veterinarian service called VETFAX on your behalf.

BLUEPRINT FOR TREATING DOG AGGRESSION

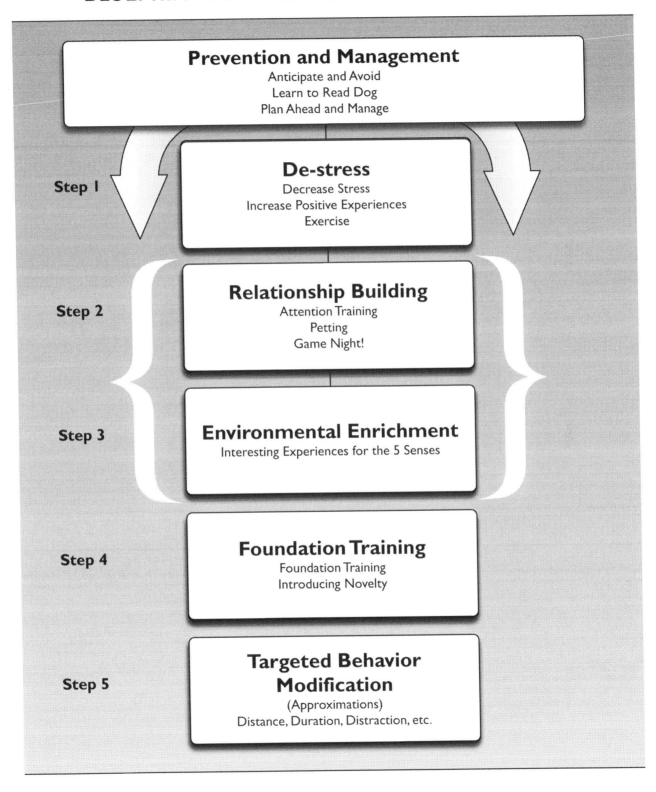

Prevention and Management
Anticipate and Avoid
Learn to Read Dog
Plan Ahead and Manage

Step 1
De-stress
Decrease Stress
Increase Positive Experiences
Exercise

Step 2
Relationship Building
Attention Training
Petting
Game Night!

Step 3
Environmental Enrichment
Interesting Experiences for the 5 Senses

Step 4
Foundation Training
Foundation Training
Introducing Novelty

Step 5
Targeted Behavior Modification
(Approximations)
Distance, Duration, Distraction, etc.

Treatment Plan Goal

The overall goal of this treatment plan blueprint is to improve dog aggression problems by helping you understand what is involved and how to succeed.

Always consult an experienced and *qualified* dog aggression expert to help you with your specific situation.

The aim of this treatment plan is to make things easier and more successful for you by preparing your dog properly. There is a lot of information here but don't let it overwhelm you. The information will give you more confidence and a better relationship with your dog.

But first, a word on *behavior modification*. Some people are put off or intimidated by the phrase *behavior modification*. There is no need to be. Although some people think that behavior modification refers to a specific set of techniques (most commonly referred to as *desensitization* and *counter conditioning*, which we will go into detail about later), *behavior modification* is simply a systematic approach to changing the way an animal (or person) reacts to a particular situation (or *stimulus*).

Note, in this book, we refer to *Targeted Behavior Modification* as a way of communicating that it is *behavior modification* that directly deals with a *stimulus* target. There are other ways to modify behavior that are not so direct, and many of the suggestions in this book deal with that. For example, doing the *SAW* program may go a long way to reducing dog aggression towards a dog's owners. It does not specifically *desensitize* and *counter condition* the dog towards the specific situation the dog is reacting to, but indirectly has a positive effect.

From experience, we regularly see do-it-yourselfers (and frankly, some trainers) just jump right into *desensitization* and *counter conditioning*, i.e. *Targeted Behavior Modification* - Step 5. It is the most challenging, trickiest (and rewarding) part of any treatment program. It is often the step people start with because people feel that it is addressing the problem directly.

Unfortunately, jumping in without adequately preparing your dog is one of the biggest mistakes dog owners make. Your dog needs foundation training in order to be successful. Don't jump in just yet: give your dog a chance to learn what he or she needs to first.

In addition to *Targeted Behavior Modification*, the treatment of dog aggression should incorporate a number of strategies to give your dog every chance to improve. With the right treatment approach, and with patience and perseverance, the *majority* of dogs can improve *substantially*!

This treatment blueprint is set up to give your dog every opportunity to succeed by modifying their environment and teaching them things in such a way that he or she is a happier, more well-adjusted dog.

However, your dog can't *unlearn* what he or she has learned. Their brain has been programmed (for lack of a better word) to emotionally respond the way it does in certain situations, and aggression has been one way he or she has learned to cope. However, it is possible for your dog to learn new behaviors that compete with the old undesirable ones. It is possible to change your dog's attitude about some situations and for your dog to become less sensitive to the things that set him or her off in the past.

This book should not replace professional help. Dealing with aggression is risky and complicated. Where possible you should always consult a professional to help you. The benefits are that you will have a treatment hand crafted for your particular situation. You will have the opportunity to ask questions about your dog, and provide an individual history so that the professional is equipped to modify and adapt a program that will work for you. In addition, the average dog owner is likely to miss cues and signals that an experienced professional will pick up on.

In the section on professionals in the book, we describe the kinds of professionals you can consult and what their roles or approaches might be. In the meantime there are things that you can start doing right now. Read on!

BLUEPRINT FOR TREATING DOG AGGRESSION

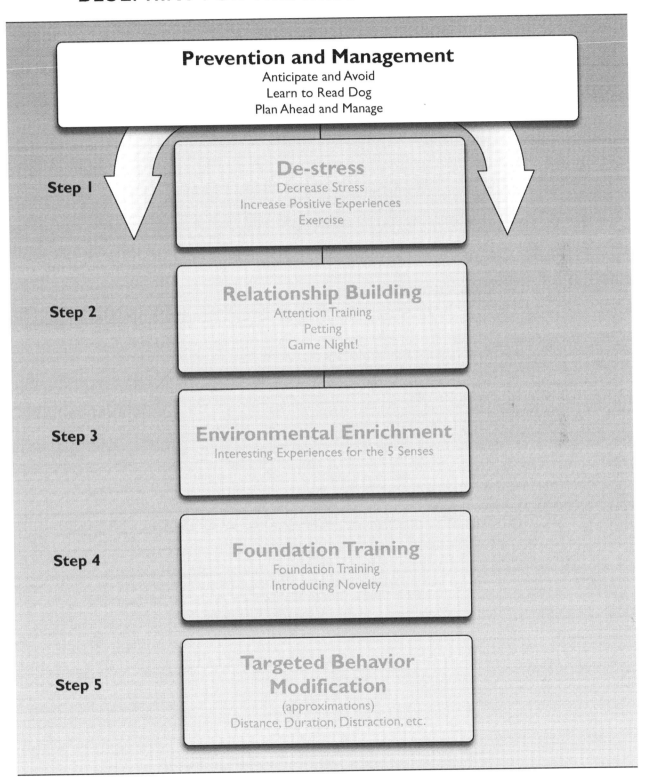

Prevention and Management
Anticipate and Avoid
Learn to Read Dog
Plan Ahead and Manage

Step 1

De-stress
Decrease Stress
Increase Positive Experiences
Exercise

Step 2

Relationship Building
Attention Training
Petting
Game Night!

Step 3

Environmental Enrichment
Interesting Experiences for the 5 Senses

Step 4

Foundation Training
Foundation Training
Introducing Novelty

Step 5

Targeted Behavior Modification
(approximations)
Distance, Duration, Distraction, etc.

Management and Prevention Goal:

The goal of management and prevention is to avoid the situations that cause your dog to behave aggressively so that your dog's brain does not become better and more efficient at relying on aggression as a coping response.

In time we will teach your dog other more preferred ways to deal with the situation. With practice those preferred behaviors will compete with the aggressive behavior.

But until then, we need to weaken the neural networks responsible for the anxiety/aggression sequence as much as possible to give those preferred behavior options a chance to become the more dominant neural network in the brain later on.

Otherwise the good habits will have a very hard time competing with the bad habit of relying of aggression as a coping strategy.

PREVENTION AND MANAGEMENT PROGRAM

Prevention and Management is truly the most important section of the book! In a full-fledged treatment program, prevention and management is used at *all* times except when you are working with your dog in a controlled *behavior modification* program that directly deals with the targets of the aggression.

Most people who want to start working to improve an aggression problem usually rush their dogs into situations the dogs are simply unable to cope with yet. This makes their issues worse. This is one of the biggest reasons why good treatment programs fail (outside of not following through with it).

It's understandable. An aggression problem creates a great sense of urgency. Nonetheless, we all need to learn how to walk before we run, learn how to count before we multiply, and learn the alphabet before writing a novel.

Proper prevention and management takes the pressure off of you to push your dog into situations he or she is not ready for. When it comes time to change your dog's attitude about the circumstances that cause them to be aggressive, your dog *needs* to be ready. That development will take some time. In the meantime, if your dog does not get the chance to behave aggressively, this reduces your sense of urgency substantially.

While good prevention and management could theoretically solve your problems, it is recommended that you follow through to *Targeted Behavior Modification* where it is safely possible. Why? If you missed it earlier it is because accidents happen. You want your dog to be a safer dog. And of course, you want them to be a happier, healthier dog, too.

BUT, if you do nothing else, you should prevent and manage aggression. There are a number of reasons why. Read on.

PRACTICING AGGRESSION MAKES IT WORSE

Initially, your dog is going through tremendous stress every time he or she is exposed to the situation that prompts the aggression. I say initially because some dogs learn to react more and more quickly to the event once they learn that the aggression works to help them cope. The aggression can evolve into a reflex-like behavior.

Imagine that you had a deep-rooted fear of public speaking or a fear of snakes. What if someone were to force you into that situation again and again, meaning you are unable to avoid it? Not only would you dread the event, but also you would even start to dread the circumstances that predict the event is going to happen: the phone call that tells you it's coming, walking into the room where it's going to happen, and so on. Dread makes us feel terrible.

YOUR DOG GETS BETTER AT BEING AGGRESSIVE

The more opportunities your dog has to behave aggressively, the worse the problem will become and the harder it will be to improve the situation. There is more detail on this in Part Two, but the more you do something, the better you get at it.

That message and practice makes those neural pathways in the brain better at the thing you are doing: more efficient, faster, and stronger. A dog that has the opportunity to behave aggressively will get better at it.

But, there is more: those neural pathways *compete* with the neural pathways of other alternative behaviors! That means all those other behaviors you are trying to teach are going to have a tougher time sticking because the aggressive behavior is bullying it out. It's for the same reason it can be so hard to break bad habits.

AGGRESSION CAN CAUSE TRAUMA

The victims of dog aggression probably experience far more acute stress than you will, and you will experience a lot. When another person or animal is bitten, or there is some kind of dogfight or attack, the victims or the owners of the victims have a whole number of feelings from helplessness to rage, (never mind the physical discomfort from the actual injuries if recovery is possible). The victims will often be deeply upset long after the fact, and may have problems eating or sleeping, etc. It also makes them fearful in similar situations in the future.

Proper control is a must. Not only can a bite result in getting sued, but also there are long lasting social and psychological effects on the victims. In a study looking at 22 children who were victims of dog bites, more than half had symptoms of posttraumatic stress disorder 2 to 9 months after the bite. [2]

It's not just the victims either. Many dog owners don't even realize until it happens to them, that the victims are not the only ones who experience long lasting social and psychological effects. When a dog attacks, you, as the owner of the dog, are witnessing violence. That is traumatic. It is not uncommon for us to get people on the K9aggression Yahoo support group complaining of being exhausted and at the end of their rope. Of course they are. Acute, prolonged, uncontrollable stress has that effect on people (and dogs). It affects our bodies and it affects our abilities to think and has emotional impacts. Of course, few people in the general public have much empathy for owners of aggressive dogs.

AGGRESSION INCREASES THE RISK OF EUTHANASIA.

It may seem obvious, but in most cases euthanasia is considered just after an aggressive event has occurred. That means the decision is made when people are emotional. It's hard to be calm and rational about what decisions should be made under those conditions.

It sounds obvious, but euthanasia is hardly ever considered when the dog has no opportunity to behave aggressively.

YOU ARE RESPONSIBLE.

I have been on both ends of a dog aggression problem. The victims rarely have any empathy for you, *especially* if the situation could have been prevented. They are often more than ready to have you reported to authorities or find some other way of attaining justice.

Even in the case where someone has their dog off leash and they shouldn't have or a person approached your dog when they shouldn't have, you will be the party in the wrong because *your* dog caused harm. It may not seem fair, especially when you are doing your best to keep people away, but it is a reality. If you are on the receiving end of aggression, fairness goes out the window. In many areas as the owner of an aggressive dog, you are responsible for damages or can be sued without anyone needing to prove that you were negligent in any way. It can also negatively impact other things such as your home insurance and the relationships you have with those around you: neighbors, friends and family.

So, it is your responsibility to ensure that the utmost care is used when dealing with aggression. Muzzles, head-halters, and crates should be used for safety purposes in any situation where you cannot avoid the circumstances that cause your dog to behave aggressively. For example, your dog might behave aggressively at the veterinarian's office, but you still need to take your dog there. In this case you need to make sure your dog is muzzled and well controlled. But in all cases, until you have a very controlled treatment plan with safety measures in place, avoiding the circumstances altogether is the safest and most humane thing to do, for everyone involved.

DO I HAVE TO AVOID THE TRIGGERS FOREVER?

Minimizing your dog's exposure to anxiety producing situations that trigger aggression will prevent the anxiety from worsening. It will also improve their quality of life tremendously. In this program, when the time comes to actually work with your dog on the *stressors* (the things that cause the anxiety/aggression sequence to start), you will have a plan on how to approach these situations without overwhelming your dog and causing the anxiety/aggression sequence to start. Right now, your dog has no way to cope except by acting aggressively.

So, the answer is yes and no. Yes, in that you don't want your dog to become aggressive ever again. If you can manage your dog's life in such a way that it doesn't occur again by avoiding your dog's triggers, management might even be enough to improve both your lives (depending on your situation). Although as said earlier, accidents are possible in the best managed situations.

Yes, in that whenever you are *not* working in a systematic and controlled way to change the response your dog has to a given situation-*once your dog has the tools to cope* - you should avoid the situation that is making them anxious, let alone aggressive.

No, in that should you choose to work with your dog rather than straight out manage the problem, you will, in time, approach the situation again only under much different circumstances where your dog is kept below threshold, or working sub threshold. In other words, we work with our dogs when they are calm or can easily become calm. Everything in part 1 is a blueprint for a plan to help you and your dog get to that point so that your dog is a safer, less reactive and happier dog.

HOW TO MANAGE YOUR DOG

Overview:
- Anticipate and avoid
- Learn to read *Dog*
- Management strategies
- Management after successful *behavior modification*

ANTICIPATE AND AVOID

Your dog has things that trigger their aggression. It might be people, other dogs, a particular situation, etc. These are the things you want to avoid from now on until it is time to do *Targeted Behavior Modification*, near the end of the program. Prolonged exposure to distressing events over which your dog has no control causes changes in the brain and leads to impairment in certain kinds of memory, as well as increases aggression.[3]

Again, avoiding the circumstances that cause aggression in your dog *is the most important aspect in treating aggression*. If you do nothing else at all - do this.

OBSERVE

To fully understand what triggers your dog's aggression, you should make a list of all the aggressive episodes that you can remember.

- What was occurring at the time? (On a leash, in a car, lots of people around, etc.)
- Where did it happen?
- Who was involved?
- What was going on before?
- Behavior (stiffening, growling, lunging, etc.)
  - The more you observe your dog, the better you will get at reading their behavior. When you start on relaxation work later in the book, you will get even better at it. Check out the section on Speaking Dog in Part Two of the book
- What happened after the event?
- Look at the progression of episodes: did the behavior change over time?

This will allow you to plan ahead and avoid the episode or *stressor*. Most people get caught in a reactive mode. In other words, they are often surprised by the aggression when it happens. Knowing when your dog typically is going to become aggressive allows you to anticipate future situations, so plan ahead.

This information will also be valuable information to present to a qualified professional, and in all likelihood, they can ask further questions in response to your answers to get a more detailed picture of what is going on. They will be looking for patterns and departures from normal behavior.

NOTE: In many cases, undesirable behaviors can be *overlearned* (the process where continual practice results in habit). Practicing aggression can cause a dog to use fewer and fewer warning signs once he or she has learned the aggression works to drive away the thing they are afraid of. It is important to look at the initial incidents for clues. If you have a rescue dog with an unknown history, you will have to do your best at being a detective.

BRAINSTORM

Once you have your list, you can now brainstorm other future challenges and figure out ways that you can avoid those situations. Get creative; imagine the worst.

Examples

- If your dog is protective when you approach their food, feed them alone in the other room.

- If your dog gets protective about the garbage, hide the garbage in a place where he or she can't get it, and put your dog in another room when you are emptying out the garbage. He or she may also have food or possession aggression.

- If your dog is aggressive towards other dogs, walk him or her in areas where there aren't any dogs; walk them at times of the day when other dogs are not around, for an example.

- If your dog is aggressive towards dogs that live with him or her in the home, for now, keep them separated in all situations that predict an aggressive outburst or tension. For example, this could include greetings with humans. In this case, if ignoring the dogs when you come in helps this, try it. This means don't pet, look at, or talk to your dogs until the greeting period is over. Keep a can of pennies or some other startle tool nearby in case you notice the characteristic stiffening up.

- If your mere presence is enough to get your dogs fighting or they tend to jump up, consider or putting one behind a sturdy metal gate or in in a separate room when you leave so that when you return, both dogs are not competing for your attention.

- If there is tension between household dogs over food and feeding times, toys, raw hides, etc., make sure all the toys are picked up. Feed dogs in separate rooms from each other.

- If your dog is aggressive around their bowl, put the dog away in a room when preparing their meal. Place the food in another room, and then go get the dog and lead him or her into the room. Leave the door open so he or she can come out on their own. Collect the bowl later.

- If your dog *fence runs* in the back yard, supervise him or her when they are out. Bring them in at the first sign of their focusing on the fence.

- If your dog is aggressive to someone in living in the home, note when these occasions are most likely to occur. Pay attention to behaviors and who was there at the time. Look for patterns. It might happen when someone pushes the dog off a bed or couch, or perhaps steps over the dog. It might even happen when a person reaches out to pet the dog. Discontinue these activities. Use a *drag line* if you have to pull the dog away, or better yet, teach a very solid *come when called* behavior, and reward with a treat.

- If your dog growls when you push him or her off the couch, have them go somewhere else, such as touch your hand or go to a mat on cue, and use this as a way to get them off the couch. Their aggression might be conflict aggression (owner directed), territorial, or fear.

- If your dog growls when you are on the bed together, don't let them on the bed. Keep them out of the room if you must, or put them in a crate.

- If he or she growls when you step over them, don't step over them. Call them out of the way instead.

- If your dog is aggressive towards visitors entering your home, then tell your visitors to wait before you open the door. Put your dog in another room. Only let your dog out once he or she can be calm. Be aware that if your dog is aggressive towards visitors entering your home, your dog may also behave aggressively towards people approaching or entering other areas where they feel like they have to protect, such as your car.

TIP

If your dog is aggressive towards you

Read the list of human behaviors that are common triggers of owner-directed aggression. It includes affectionate behaviors such as hugging as this would be considered a challenge if it were a dog doing it to another dog.

- Touching your dog on the head
- Touching your dog on the back
- Putting a collar on
- Stepping over your dog
- Pushing, bumping into or shoving your dog (i.e. to move them out of the way or get off furniture)
- Extended direct eye contact (this can be one of those loving gazes)
- Scolding
- Attempting to move a dog while he or she is resting
- Lifting a dog
- Hugging a dog
- Touching sensitive areas such as feet or ears
- Jerking on a leash or collar
- Raising an arm or object over their head
- Performing an alpha roll, which is essentially physically trying to place a dog on their side or back
- Grooming the dog (can include toweling, wiping the dog's face, trimming their nails, etc.)
- Taking a toy away
- Taking food away
- Taking a stolen object away
- Moving the dog away from something desirable (like garbage, for instance)
- Pushing on a dog's behind to get them to sit
- Going through entrances/exits such as doorways, hall ways, or stairways at the same time as the dog

These are all just examples, but if you are prepared ahead of time, you can manage to avoid most of the scenarios.

QUESTION

If my dog has snuck up on a couch where he doesn't belong, isn't it cheating to trick a dog to get off the couch? He wasn't even supposed to be on there, so why does he get a treat? Doesn't this reward the dog for getting up on the couch in the first place?

ANSWER

When a dog shows aggression towards you, it's always far better luring a dog to where you want him to be with a treat than it ever is confronting a dog and causing more stress by scolding, grabbing or shoving.

A better way is to teach your dog to touch your hand, or go to a mat when asked. When your dog gets on the couch again, ask them to touch the target or your hand or go to the mat. That way, you are rewarding the dog for doing what he is asked, not for the undesired behavior.

LEARNING DOG LANGUAGE

It's common for many people to think their dog's aggression is sudden or unpredictable. When they start to read about how serious sudden, unpredictable aggression is, they start to panic.

But true sudden and unpredictable aggression that doesn't have specific triggers is relatively rare. More often than not, people haven't been taught to recognize the signs that lead up to the aggression.

It's also possible that as the aggression occurs more and more frequently, the early signals, like growling, start to disappear. This does not mean your dog has rage syndrome. But it does mean that the risk that someone will get hurt is much higher.

It pays to learn. If your dog is aggressive, there may be many signs and signals of anxiety that your dog is displaying. If you know your dog is anxious, you can avoid doing anything that will make the dog worse (such as scolding them or grabbing their collar as mentioned earlier). You can also do something to help change their emotional state. Or, remove them from a potential bad situation.

Lessons from the trenches: If you have young children under the age of six, or children who will not follow your instructions to the letter, or you have friends of your children coming to visit, you need to be aware that you are putting those children into a risky situation. You need to keep them separate from your dog, and this is a challenging job. Children can be curious, willful and forgetful. Your attention will be split. Things happen when you aren't looking.

A dog that is sitting, lying down, and/or taking treats may still be ambivalent or anxious about a situation. It is worth learning as much as you can about dog body language and practice looking out for it.

 ## SIGNS OF STRESS

Some of the more obvious signs dogs can show under mild stress can be misinterpreted or overlooked. It's important to look at the context of the situation. For example:

- Lip licking or nose flicking with the tongue - but there is no food around.
- Yawning, but the dog is not tired – the yawns sometimes appear to be snappy and tight - not as wide or as long as true sleepy yawns (sleepy yawns in dogs are more rare than you might think).

So, look at the behaviors in context. You often will see them as a sequence of behaviors, rather than one thing in isolation. Is there some kind of social interaction or anticipation of social interaction that might be causing the dog to feel this way?

See More in Part 2 in the *Speaking Dog: Reading And Interpreting Dog Behavior* **section**

Examples of signs of stress	Examples of escalation of arousal
• Yawning • Licking lips • Sweaty feet (as seen by paw prints on a floor) • Pupil dilation (often goes unnoticed in dark brown eyes) • Tense facial features, including tight lips and furrowed forehead • Panting • Drooling in some dogs • Fast tail wagging • Hyperactivity	• Hackles are up • Standing tall • Holding their breath (or appears not to breathe) • Moving very slowly • Stiff body • Staring (dog will sometimes look away just before attack)

It's hard for the new learner to know if the dog is just being *doggy*. Therefore, look for a sequence of behaviors in a stressed dog.

Other behaviors that are indications of stress are sometimes called displacement behaviors such as scratching, pacing, or sniffing the ground, etc. It may be a way to cope with stress. A resting dog that previously had their head on their paws or floor may lift their head until the stressful thing goes away. That doesn't mean the dog is going to attack, but it does represent a kind of wariness on behalf of the dog and that is good to know. If the dog is uncomfortable around children or adults, you might see a dog do this until he or she can be certain that they can relax.

You might see an increase in energy or hyperactivity. This is similar to people when they get nervous, and adjust their hair or clothing, make an inappropriate joke, or avoid eye contact, etc.

If the dog can't escape the stressful situation, the behaviors can escalate. The dog's ears may turn to the side or be pulled back from their normally relaxed position. Moving more slowly is a big indication; staring or stiffening may indicate the dog is seconds away from striking. It is better to move the dog out of a stressful situation before this happens.

The more you are able to learn body language in dogs, the better! This skill is not only essential in treating your aggressive dog; it will allow you to avoid situations from escalating. But behaviors happen quickly. Video recording will help you learn.

 ## VIDEO MATERIALS TO INTERPRET DOG BEHAVIOR

Books like this one can be helpful, but no book will be able to communicate what these signs look like and the context in which they appear nearly as well as a video can. If you are inexperienced with reading stress in dogs or simply want to learn more, there are a number of video materials that can help. Although there is often some disagreement about actually what the behavior means, or whether a behavior is actually a calming signal (lots of controversy around that), here are some good ones:

- *THE LANGUAGE OF DOGS - UNDERSTANDING CANINE BODY LANGUAGE AND OTHER COMMUNICATION SIGNALS DVD SET* by Sarah Kalnajs

- *Canine Behavior, Body Postures and The Behaviorally Healthy Dog*, By Susanne Hetts, PhD & Daniel. Estep, PhD

Pick up a camera

In addition, pick up a video camera. Start recording your dog when you are working with them or interacting with them. Review the video footage and see if you can learn what behavior predicts different actions and responses. In *The Dog Trainer's Resource 2: The APDT Chronicle of the Dog Collection*, Daphne Robert-Hamilton, who runs K9 Partnership, asks clients to view *Canine Body Language* by Dr. Suzanne Hetts and provides the workbook. Then, homework is assigned. You can do the same.

1. Video their own dog for five minutes and write up what they see with ONE body part.

2. As they get proficient, add a new body part and continue to build their observational skills.

PLAN AHEAD AND MANAGE

Once you know the situations where your dog is likely to become aggressive you can plan on how to avoid those situations. But sometimes things will come up that you haven't anticipated or can't completely avoid. How will you reduce risk? There are strategies and tools that can help.

OBEDIENCE TRAINING FOR MANAGEMENT

While training your dog to sit or to come when called does not treat the aggression, teaching your dog how to perform certain behaviors at your request could help you manage potential problems. Asking your dog to do something else to avoid an anxiety-producing situation can help. Distracting or redirecting your dog when he or she is anxious or starting to fixate on something, can help prevent aggressive sequences from developing.

This will not work in every situation. You need to use redirection very early in the anxiety sequence for it to be an effective avoidance measure. Again, the more you learn to read your dog's body language, and knowing when the aggression is likely to occur, the better you will be at identifying when there may be a potential problem brewing.

In the earlier example, if your dog growls at you when you try to push them off the couch, rather than forcing to get them off, you may teach them to go to a spot instead (see more later in this section and the Core Behaviors Training Guide) as discussed earlier. A spot could be anything – a crate, a mat, or even a portable spot like a laminated bulls-eye graphic. For those dogs that are not aggressive towards their owners, it can even be your own hand. This way, your dog doesn't feel threatened; a conflict over the couch is easily avoided.

Another situation might be when your dog starts to fixate on another dog or grows anxious about a person he or she has to pass by; you ask them to pay attention to you or come to you, where you can play with them or lure them past with something your dog finds desirable.

Commands that can help you out in a variety of situations:

Look

When you have seen something you know your dog is going to react to, you might distract them by having them look at you, while you lead your dog away. Simply having their head orient toward you and eyes on your head may be enough. Direct eye contact may bother some dogs.

"Targeting" your hand

I say "Here!" and snap my hand out and my dog will come over and press her nose against my hand. It is good for recall, but also handy for maneuvering a dog in a small space or even around your body, as I can move my hand where I want her to be. It can also be trained without the dog being a distance away from you, which makes it easier to incorporate practicing it into your daily life. In addition, this can be used for distraction purposes, or to get your dog to move away from a potentially stressful situation. It is easy to teach.

Go to your mat

This is a very handy command to teach your dog and can be used to move your dog off of a couch, out of a hall, or away from a door without physically confronting them.

This could be a request to go anywhere: a mat, a bed, or a crate, for example. The nice thing about a mat is that a mat is portable and you can put it anywhere. It helps to use a clicker to train it, however, so you can let your dog know when they have done the right thing. Without a clicker or some kind of communication signal that *immediately* tells your dog he or she has done the right thing, it is harder for your dog to learn. People find that just relying on rewards is harder when the dog is a distance from you because the treat delivery doesn't occur quickly enough for the dogs to understand what they earned the treat for.

People have used *go to your mat* as a way to manage moderate barking when visitors come. There are different ways to teach this, but one way is to actually reward the dog for the initial bark to begin with. Once the dog links the two things together: 1) doorbell rings and they bark and 2) they then run to their mat for a treat (so keep treats nearby

> **TIP** If your dog is aggressive at the door, they may be uninterested in treats and requests. Dealing with aggression at the door uses a different approach. One way is to *counter condition* your dog to the knock on the door or the doorbell only *without* anyone coming in. This training should continue until your dog no longer responds. Only then do you move to the next step towards *counter conditioning* for the next part in the sequence. More about *counter conditioning* in the last step of the program.

this spot), you stop giving a great treat and then no treat at all for the bark and give extra great treats for going to their spot. What people start to see is the barking becomes shortened because dogs start to get a little lazy and take the easy route. Dogs will often do the minimum amount of activity they can get away with for a treat, and if then the treat starts to not appear, they get lazier about it. Great! A lazy barker!

Just make sure you are continuing to reward when he or she goes to his mat and stays on it because let's face it, when the door bell goes, it's a whole lot more interesting to hang out at the door than to go lie down. Putting a sign outside your door explaining that it may take you a minute or two to get to the door takes the pressure off you to open the door immediately, and allows you to reward your dog.

TIP Dogs are highly discriminatory - meaning that they will learn something within a very specific context. They don't generalize well. If you train your dog to come by saying, "Come" in your regular voice, and then one day you shout it at them, he or she might not understand what you mean. If you have a tendency to hunch over and reach out your arm when you call "Come," but one day you are sitting or standing upright, he or she may become confused or ignore you.

Come

Yes, having your dog come to you when you call can be very useful! But if your ability to call them to you is not very good and you have yelled or scolded your dog for not coming, you're better off training it again and using a different word. Like the previously mentioned cues, having your dog come to you is a good way to get them away from the other scary thing.

Sit

This is a good thing to teach because you will want to incorporate it into your *behavior modification* program. But, it is not always the best thing to ask for when your dog is faced with something he or she is threatened by. It may cause them to feel trapped. They will feel in conflict between what you have asked them to do and reacting to the thing that is worrying them. On the other hand, far enough away, sitting can be used to help calm other dogs and people. It's also a naturally deferring behavior. It is simple to teach with a treat lure. Simply put a treat in front of their nose and slowly move it up and back over their head so they need to sit to keep focused on it. Once sitting give them the treat.

Cue words (also called commands)

People use different cue words for the same actions. That's ok, although you might want to use words that come naturally to you to say or remember ("sit" comes to mind).

Be aware that your dog may get them confused in regular conversation, but also that they may learn to only respond when you say them in a certain way.

In time, train your dog to respond to your recall word (the word that gets them to come to you) even if you shout it (work up to that though – increase the loudness slowly). When you are stressed and you need to get your dog out of a situation – you might not be thinking about how you say this word and it may come out as a shout. Best to have your dog respond to your cue words said in a variety of ways.

Hand Signals

Some feel that you should not use hand signals because your dog will ignore cue words. This is a correct assumption, because dogs are more naturally inclined to read body language than they are to attend to the nuances that determine the sound of one word from another. Also, using hand signals relies on your dog looking and paying attention to you.

On the other hand, I prefer using a combination because I feel the communication is easier for the dog to understand. Also, hand signals come in handy when my dog lost her hearing. In addition, you can give hand signals without alerting your dog to the fact that you are stressed out as your voice might indicate. It can also be done without alarming your guests.

 Teaching your dog certain behaviors could help you avoid potential problems.

Train an *Emergency Cue*

The *Emergency Cue* is designed to get your dog's attention and hold it in an emergency situation.

Unless you already have a rock-solid cue that already does this, the *Emergency Cue* word should be a new word that is designed to catch your dog's attention and have them come over to you and follow you. If your dog shows aggression towards you, it should also include a *sit*. It should be so well trained and practiced that the dog does this automatically in almost any situation. Practice saying or shouting this cue in a number of ways by imagining you are anxious or stressed and practice this in many different situations.

Once the *Emergency Cue* is given, he or she must keep paying attention to you, until you *release* them (telling them it's okay to pay attention to other things). They should be rewarded for responding appropriately with their most highly valued food, paired, if possible with other high value rewards (such as lavish praise, fun play, walk outside, etc.). It should be regularly practiced and practiced at times when your dog is most likely to respond immediately, such as when they are interested in food and not right after they ate! You want this cue to be so hard wired that your dog always thinks – *I HAVE to pay attention to this!* However, research has shown that dogs learn best when they are fed (i.e. 30 minutes after a meal) so make sure they feel good when you are *teaching* them so they can focus. But *practicing* before dinner (or naps) is not a bad idea.

Don't use a word that does not currently work that well to get your dog's attention. Resist using the *Emergency Cue* to get your dog's attention when they are ignoring you or if you can't immediately reward him or her with a high value reward. You don't want to do anything to reduce the effectiveness of this cue. You are better off teaching your dog to come by using different words altogether than the *Emergency Cue* in that case.

 SAFETY TOOLS

These tools are not meant to be a Band-Aid solution to aggression. Each time your dog becomes aggressive, it will make the problem that much harder to deal with – this cannot be stressed enough. You should do everything you can to avoid the situation that triggers the aggression. However, you may not be able to predict every situation and safety needs to come first. These tools will help to prevent or minimize harm.

If you know how to properly use a head-halter, use it

These are NOT as safe as muzzles, as dogs can still bite with them on. They allow much more control of the head, allow you to give treats easily, and will provide you with the control to prevent your dog from lunging. Head-halters can be so beneficial when doing *Targeted Behavior Modification*. They allow you to feed your dog but close their mouths if necessary, and make even a relatively small adult capable of preventing a large, strong dog from lunging.

Some dogs do try to paw these off, but research has shown that their cortisol levels do not go up, and cortisol is produced as part of the stress response. Make sure you teach your dog how to accept wearing one first. Like *desensitizing* your dog to wearing a muzzle, the same techniques work for *desensitizing* your dog to wearing a head-halter; you can find these instructions in the bonus area on the site.

- Head-halters should fit snuggly, allowing just one finger underneath the neck strap at the back of the head. The nose loop can be loose.
- Head-halters should never be used with a spring or retractable leash.
- Work towards a goal of always having a loose leash. A good trainer can help you with this.

Use a muzzle for safety (but avoid their aggression triggers)

Sure, some dogs hate them. But, you are going to hate it if your dog bites someone even more. Do NOT expose your dog to their triggers regardless of the muzzle. This is for safety measures only in case you get surprised.

Make sure you condition your dog to wearing one first. You can find instructions in the bonus areas on the site. But, sometimes you aren't sure what is going to happen. You may have to take your dog to the vet for example. You vet might be willing to allow you to keep your dog in the car until you are called in, but you still have to get your dog in and sometimes you can't avoid what you would like to.

- Choose a basket muzzle type that allows your dog to open their mouth and pant.
- Try to choose one that will allow you to give them a treat, perhaps stick in something covered with cheese or peanut butter if you can.
- Ensure the dog can't paw it off.
- Check all fittings, latches, and fastenings each time before you go out.
- **Remember: dogs can still cause injuries even if they can't bite.**

Drag lines, leashes, or tethers

Drag leashes or long lines that are light and won't catch on anything in the house will allow you some control over the dog in a conflict situation but not get too close to them. A cat leash with the handle cut open can be helpful. Tethers can be used to tie a dog to a solid object, (i.e. a set of stairs for example).

Baby Gates

These can be used to keep your aggressive dog away from their triggers. For example, your dog's triggers might be another dog in the house or family members. Keep in mind that larger dogs can jump over some gates, and other gates can be pawed open or chewed through. The E'longate Gates are good for wider areas, and can be adapted with the use of an extension panel. They are also metal, which means they are not as easily destroyed as wooden or plastic gates. You can find these at Pet Edge http://www.petedge.com/. Baby gates that are not actually installed can also be used to get in between two fighting dogs in the house.

Bells

It can't hurt to know that your aggressive dog is on the move. Sometimes, we get lost in our own worlds. Having your dog wear a bell may help you stay a little more alert to what is happening in your house.

Distracters

It is best to use something like food or anything positive the dog will be distracted by IF you have interrupted early enough in the sequence when your dog is becoming anxious. Even if you have a resource guarder, you can show the dog the attractive distracter item and throw it away from the thing he or she is trying to guard.

If you are in a situation where it is too late, you need to discontinue the aggression as soon as possible. You may find treats or toys are not distracting enough.

Noisy things such as clanging pots and pans, tin cans with coins, air horns, etc. can help startle and distract a dog from the escalation of the aggression sequence. Other things such as spray bottles of water and even high value food may also help to distract a dog from becoming aggressive if you catch them early enough in the sequence. We go into this a little bit more in the Emergency Response section. In order for the dog to learn from this, it needs to be within 30 to 60 seconds of the anxiety/aggression sequence – around 2 or 3 seconds into actual aggression.

Unfortunately, **anything that startles the dog can have a punishing effect and cause unintended stress, and will potentially add to the aggression** if it is not distracting enough, or the dog is highly anxious about the trigger. So, think of this saying: never use a hammer where a feather will do.

Have a variety of food, toys, and other items stored in various locations where your dog might be. But it can't be said enough, do everything you can to avoid these situations.

Dog Gloves

You can find dog gloves where groomers buy their supplies. Unfortunately, you may not be thinking about putting on gloves. But if two dogs get into a fight, wearing these gloves may protect you from a redirected bite.

Citronella Spray or Pepper Spray

As a last resort, use this for preventing two dogs from fighting with each other.

Break stick

Break sticks are wedged-shaped sticks designed for inserting into the gap behind the teeth at the back of the mouth and then turned to pry the jaws open. They are more appropriate for those breeds whose bite style is to hang on and hold, (such as certain kinds of terriers) than they are for other breeds that tend to be bite multiple times during an incident. Be aware that they are used in the dog fighting culture and while they are generally not considered illegal in some states of the US, they are considered dog-fighting paraphernalia. Be responsible, but be discreet about owning one.

Do NOT use a choke chain, Martingale, prong collar, e-collar (shock collar), or a collar that provides any kind of electrical stimulation.

You may have been told to use one by a trainer, but research has repeatedly shown that collars that elicit irritation or pain cause problems.[4][5][6][7] Not only can they damage the relationship between the handler and dog, but also they can add to their stress level in training situations[8]. As stress increases, your dog is more likely to behave aggressively, plus your dog's tolerance for pain[9] also increases. When in an aggressive episode, your dog may be willing to trade off any pain from a collar.

Do NOT use invisible fencing

Electric invisible fencing is also problematic. Invisible fencing is designed to give the dog a shock via a collar when they cross the boundary. But at first he or she may not recognize that going through the fence line causes the shock. Instead your dog may associate it with whatever happened to be passing by at the moment: a child, a car or a dog perhaps. This can result in your dog becoming fearful and possibly aggressive towards whatever he or she associates with the shock. If your dog has trouble associating it with anything, he or she can become abnormally sensitive, tense or nervous about anything in the environment. For example they might startle when the wind blows or a neighbor appears. They might bark at things they used to ignore, or refuse to go into the space altogether.

Let's assume your dog does eventually recognize that it is the fence line that is causing the shock. The dog knows that there is something unseen that makes part of the area unsafe making him less secure. Invisible fencing does nothing to keep any other animal or person out, either. Your dog may respect the boundaries, but go after that animal or person as part of redirected aggression (this is when a dog behaves aggressively towards something other than his *stressor*). This is particularly a risk for dogs that already have anxiety or aggression problems. And like shock collars your dog may be willing to withstand the pain if they feel threatened enough. And as well as regular shock collars, shock collars used for fencing can malfunction.

Dogs and Kids

Dogs and kids can be a disaster even with what seems to be the best dogs. Prognosis can be guarded whenever there are kids or people with certain disabilities in the house. The risk dramatically increases with children under the age of 6.

In some cases, dogs are more threatened by children because they are unpredictable and unlike adults. Sometimes they are less threatened by children than they are by adults simply because they are smaller and less threatening. But, an anxious dog is an anxious dog. Young children typically have poor impulse control and may thwart their parents' wishes, unknowingly causing danger to themselves.

Children in particular like to try to test and control their environment and this often includes animals. What they do when you are watching may not be the same as what they do when you are not. Children must be supervised at all times. Children also like to hug and kiss dogs, and even crawl on them. This can be disastrous. It can be very difficult for a child to resist this impulse no matter how much you try to control them. If the situation is safe, and the child is old enough, including a child in training a dog can go a long way to provide a safe outlet for interaction. However, be aware of the human tendency to be in denial about how dangerous a situation actually is.

Babies, in particular, should never be left alone with dogs. Dogs can move faster than the time it takes for parents to get across the room.

It is really important that kids are educated about dogs in general. The following are some rules:

Before they touch the dog, there are *three permissions* they must get first:

1. Their parents: a simple ask
2. The dog's owner or handler: a simple ask
3. The permission of the dog: the child must wait for the dog to approach them; they do not approach the dog.

Children should be taught:

- Touch the shoulders (not the top of the head).

- All dogs are not the same: some like people, some are afraid of people.

- An aggressive dog is not a mean dog but a fearful dog.

- Always respect a growl and move away slowly.

- Never hit or yell at a dog.

- Dogs should not be teased with food.

- Dogs should not be stepped over.

- Dogs need a lot of personal space. Instruct children not to hug or grab an unknown dog. While humans love to hug, this can be an aggressive gesture for dogs and can make many dogs anxious or aggressive.

- When dealing with dogs, face the same direction as the dog so that they are side by side. Keep their face well away from the dog's face.

> **WARNING**: If you are in a situation where you are living with an aggressive dog and young children, and you have any concerns about your child's safety, you should talk to a professional about your options.

- Kids like to get dogs to do things like bark or growl. This is dangerous.

- Never approach a dog when he or she is eating or try to take their food.

- Children can be taught how to properly ask a dog to sit and once taught, should ask the dog to sit before they interact with them. Keep in mind that a dog may feel anxious if he or she doesn't like kids and he or she is asked to sit when a child approaches. It is important that the dog comes to learn positive associations and can be relaxed when someone approaches.

- Review dog behavior signaling with your kids: A particularly good video is *The Language of Dogs, Understanding Canine Body language and Other Communication Signals* by Sarah Kalnaks, although there is some slightly mature content and the DVD should be reviewed before showing children.

Another online resource for older kids is doggonesafe.com. This article encourages the child to be a Dog Detective, which is a great way to capture a child's imagination: http://www.doggonesafe.com/dog_detective.

MANAGEMENT AFTER BEHAVIOR MODIFICATION

Even when you have been successful with *behavior modification*, you always have to be aware that fear can resurface, especially under stress. That is because extinguishing behavior is not the same as forgetting. Your dog may have learned an alternative way to behave and may have learned to be calm under the circumstances. But under stressful enough situations, part of the brain (the amygdala) may override what he or she has learned.

Make sure you plan management into your life, even after the successful *behavior modification* to ensure everyone can live safely and happily. It is easy enough to make a habit.

WHAT TO DO IF YOUR DOG BECOMES AGGRESSIVE

I cringe writing this, I really do. Because **if you put your dog in the situation where he or she becomes aggressive, you are helping to train them to be aggressive.** You undo so much of the good you may have accomplished already. At a minimum, you have just made your dog's brain that much better at behaving aggressively, and it is that much harder to make a positive change in your dog's negative behavior.

But, this was the question I constantly asked of anyone who claimed to be an expert at one point. Surprisingly, I never got much of an answer. Mostly, I got advice on what I should do to prevent it from happening next time. But I was saying – it just happened – what do I do?! Punishment?? Treats?? Nothing??

Ok. So, unfortunately accidents happen. What do you do?

FORGET PUNISHMENT.

You WILL get recommendations from a certain type of trainer to punish (note that a veterinary behaviorist who bases their knowledge on actual scientific peer reviewed research may recommend this in a very rare situation). You might want to do this, in fact, you might even experience social pressure from others to do this; but it will not help. The aggression that he or she has used to cope with the anxiety preceding it is the reward that the dog is going to feel. In other words, you can try to punish the aggressive behavior, but the aggression itself dealt with a bigger problem the dog had. In addition, you risk having the dog associate the punishment with the thing they are being aggressive towards, such as a child.

If you feel there should be some kind of justice, check out the punishment area in Part Two of the book. It is natural to want justice, because we are hardwired to feel this way. If you were punished as a child, this will be even more of an inclination for you. However, there are many reasons not to including the potential escalation of aggression and the suppression of the signs that indicate it's coming.

IIR (Interrupt, Interfere, Rewrite)

Interrupt
- Interrupt the behavior sequence as soon as possible.

Interfere
- Interfere with the consolidation of memory formation.
- Keep awake: If possible, do not let your dog have a nap afterwards.
- Introduce novelty right away

Rewrite
- Rewrite history.

FIRST: INTERRUPT THE BEHAVIOR SEQUENCE

When you are there with a child

The first thing you want to do is interrupt the sequence, but if your dog has just growled at a child and you are right there, stand between the two, pick the child up if they are small enough, and move them to a place where the dog can't reach. This is because a child may continue to do whatever it was he or she was doing that elicited the growl from the dog. You do not want to add anything on top of the anxiety or frustration the dog is already feeling. DO NOT punish (as tempted as you might be), and DON'T grab the collar, as this may cause the dog to lunge. Remove the child. Otherwise, proceed with the following steps.

Always use the least invasive way to interrupt.

Whenever a dog is starting to become stressed and anxious, there are always risks that he or she might react badly and someone gets hurt. Dr. Karen Overall wrote in her book, *Clinical Behavioral Medicine for Small Animals* that in order for dogs to learn from an correction (like a startle), it needs to occur within 30 to 60 seconds of the anxiety/aggression sequence – no later than around 2 or 3 seconds into actual aggression. However, the suggestion of interfering with the consolidation of the memory related to this event may affect that learning. Talk to your qualified professional about what is right for your unique situation.

Interrupt with your Emergency Cue or something positive

If possible, you want to interrupt with your Emergency Cue or a command that gets them to focus on you and come to you if they are not aggressive towards you. Reward them for doing so – no, this is not rewarding for aggression, this is rewarding for them paying attention and responding to you.

If this doesn't work, there are probably other things you can use to get your dog's attention, such as your suggestion to play or go for a walk, the sound of a can opener or kibble bag opening up, a knock on the door or a door bell ringing.

When you start to understand your dog's behavior and notice signs of stress or hyper-vigilance, it is possible to interrupt that sequence before it erupts into aggression - provided you interrupt early enough in the sequence. See the sections on learning to read and interpret signs of stress and anxiety in dogs to help you act on these early signs.

If they are showing aggression towards you, stop what you are doing immediately. Back off and take a moment to think and cool down. Do not confront your dog!

Interrupt and redirect with food

If you don't have an *Emergency Cue* established well enough, then use whatever way results in the dog paying attention to you. You can lure them away with a treat. You can get their attention with the food and throw the food down on the floor away from the conflict. Make sure you use your happy voice, even if you are feeling angry because you have a chance at changing the dog's emotional state. Be careful with two dogs that are competitive over food, or those who have food aggression issues.

Interrupt with a startle

Dogs may be impossible to interrupt once they reach that level where the neurons in their brains are rapidly firing. Their body and brains have been flooded with various chemicals that prepare them to act in the face of a threat. Some dogs can't turn off the aggressive sequence easily and will continue to be fired up and reactive. Make note if they continue to be reactive even after the conflict, because it's often these kinds of dogs that may need medication.

It's important that you get your dog out of the situation as fast as possible. That is why anticipation of anxious behaviors that signal early concern is *essential* if treatment is to be effective. But don't forget - interrupting at any stage can cause you to get bitten.

You can use some of the ideas in the Management section under the *Safety Tools* as discussed earlier to interrupt. For example, you might interrupt them by dropping a book; ringing bells; clanging together pots and pans; using New

Year's Eve noise makers; using musical instruments such as a horn or drum; showering the dog with water from a hose; shouting, yelling, or screaming (unless they are showing aggression towards you); shaking a noisy can of pennies; sounding a bull horn; setting off an alarm such as a car alarm if outside; spraying something unpleasant such as an animal deterrent spray, citronella or bitter apple towards their nose. Pepper spray may work as well, although may not be legal in some areas. You can keep some of these items nearby just in case.

Loud sounds in particular send an alert to the brain that they need to be on guard. But keep in mind, anything that causes further stress, whether it is because they are alarmed or frustrated, can backfire.

Interrupt physically

Physically handling an aggressive dog or dogs **dramatically increases your chances of you or your dog being injured.** At the same time, you may need to physically separate fighting dogs to ensure that one or both do not get severely injured. Nevertheless, it can be incredibly difficult to interrupt an all out fight. **It is best to talk to a qualified and experienced professional about what methods are right for your situation.**

If you know your dog is aggressive towards others, you might consider keeping a leash or drag line on them to pull them away. Pulling a dog out of a conflict by his or her collar could simply increase the aggression, or may have them turn on you. A leash provides some distance between the person on the end of the leash and the dog's teeth. Throwing a blanket, a sheet or even coats over the dogs may help.

Some recommend pulling the dog up by his or her hind legs and then moving either forward or back or in a circular motion for dogs that are fighting. I have never done this and is likely dangerous. I've seen people hit the muzzles of the dogs to get them to let go, but again, it is a dangerous practice, it often needs repeating and someone or the dog could get injured.

Moving the dog or dogs towards an entranceway where you can then use a door or gate to wedge between and physically separate them may help. It may require pulling on a collar to move them, which could make things worse.

A break stick, again, as mentioned in the *Safety Tools* section helps release the jaws of a dog that has a bite style of holding on, but there needs to be a way to prevent the dog from trying again.

Some dogs, even after being separated, continue to be worked up for some time after the conflict so make sure you keep them away from the target because the aggression could erupt again at any time. Continued arousal after an aggressive episode may be an indication that there is a biochemical problem at work and a need for medication.

Again, it is best to talk to a qualified and experienced professional about what methods are appropriate for your unique situation.

 ## SECOND: INTERFERE WITH THE MEMORY FORMATION

You would like your dog to forget as much as possible about this situation because you don't want him or her making associations around the event that triggered them or further learning that aggression was a good way to deal with it. You won't be able to get them to forget all of it, especially if it has progressed to the point where you had to get physically involved. But you want to do the best you can – after all this is damage control, now.

Consolidating is the encoding of learning to memory. It is a process that continues after an event or where learning has occurred. It starts minutes after the event, and can continue for hours. It is within the first 6 hours that the memory is most vulnerable to interference from other learning. This means you have a window to provide experiences that will interfere with putting that experience fully to memory. Make these interferences a pleasurable activity. Again, this is not about rewarding aggression, but trying to do damage control.

Just to repeat – check with your qualified and experienced professional to determine if this is a good strategy for your particular situation.

Do not let your dog have a nap afterwards

It is common to put your dog in a crate or a room by him or herself to remove them. Sometimes, we just leave them there because we are too upset to want to deal with them. That's not a bad plan. However, if your dog goes to sleep, there is absolutely nothing at all to interfere with the memory consolidation. It's not always possible to avoid sleeping; some of us have to work in the morning or need to attend to the victims, but if you can, or someone can, keep them awake and do the next step.

Introduce novelty right away

Novelty does not cause forgetting exactly. But, research indicates that continuous exploration of novelty for approximately 30 minutes in rats reverses the strengthening of communication between cells that is needed for memory[10] – in other words, novelty introduced right after a learning event can erode memory of that learning. In addition, it can reduce the effects of stress after an acutely stressful experience.[11] Your dog will remember any stressful event very well, but it is the best we can do under the circumstances.

Later on in the book, I recommend discontinuing training for a period of time to de-stress your dog if your dog is experiencing chronic stress before starting the training part of treatment. This is the exception.

Introduce your dog to new, highly relevant experiences or training where he or she has to learn something new. The important thing is that they must pay attention and be interested, whether because it's terribly exciting, fantastic fun or even quite uncertain (but be careful with this one). Here are some ideas:

- Introduce non-stressful novelty: take them to a very novel location with new sites, sounds, and/or smells that is as unrelated to the situation you were in as possible.
- Introduce new puzzle toys or unusual foods and smells to them.
- Train them to do something he or she has never done before if possible.
- Use the highest value treats you can find so they are motivated to pay attention (freeze dried liver worked wonders for my dogs; cheese, cooked chicken, and other meat are good too – all depends on your dog).
- Get them excited about something – this might be excitable play or

chasing mice in a field, but be cautious if he or she is still stressed.

- If he or she is aggressive to people, take them out to meet new dogs or if he or she is aggressive to dogs, take them to meet new people but be cautious about this if there is any concern they are uncomfortable around either, as he or she will be more reactive as a result of the stress.
- Do the above for as much time as you can fit in – make a day of it.

It's best to have a plan set up before it happens. If your dog becomes aggressive in the evening, you might be unprepared to interfere with the consolidation of the memories, so have a number of things on hand and a plan.

 THIRD: RE-WRITE HISTORY

Return to the scene of the crime later and try to provide as many of the cues as possible (**without re-enacting the aggression**) and then have something different – and interesting - happen. Do this the next day if possible, and then again a few weeks later if you remember.

Although emotional memories tend to be recalled much better than neutral memories, when we bring a memory out of storage, that is, we remember something; it's fragile and can be interfered with especially if the interference is very similar to the original memory.[12] This can work for us. The point of this is to have them recall the earlier memory, but then interfere with the reconsolidation of that memory.

Unfortunately, all this is just damage control. The best you can do is to ensure he or she retains as little as possible of the experience. The brain tends to remember highly emotional experiences, especially those that have to do with fear because they are the most relevant. So with that said, let's have a look at the next stage of the systematic treatment program for dog aggression in the next chapter.

BLUEPRINT FOR TREATING DOG AGGRESSION

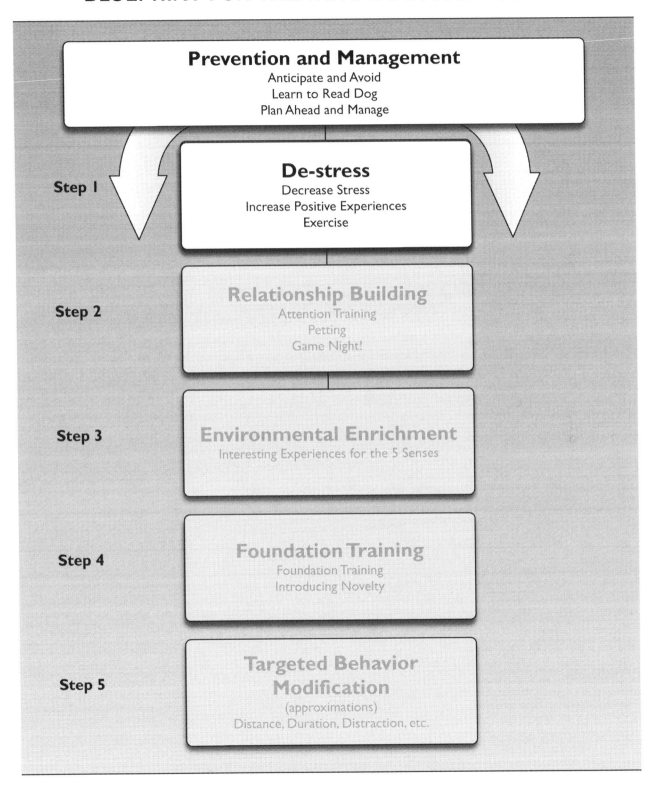

Prevention and Management
Anticipate and Avoid
Learn to Read Dog
Plan Ahead and Manage

Step 1
De-stress
Decrease Stress
Increase Positive Experiences
Exercise

Step 2
Relationship Building
Attention Training
Petting
Game Night!

Step 3
Environmental Enrichment
Interesting Experiences for the 5 Senses

Step 4
Foundation Training
Foundation Training
Introducing Novelty

Step 5
Targeted Behavior Modification
(approximations)
Distance, Duration, Distraction, etc.

STEP 1 – **Goals**:

Not only do our dogs and we experience stress in our regular lives, but also any aggressive episodes are highly stressful. Chronic or acute stress can cause mood disorders to worsen and can make us unable to regulate and respond to future stressors through emotional and cognitive changes in the brain.

Stress can make your dog more likely to react, and can contribute to aggression to escalating and worsening in the future. If we are to change our dog's reactivity, we need to get body and mind back into balance so that our dog is less reactive; can remain calmer with less effort; and is more prepared to learn. This will help us prevent aggression from worsening and encourage your dog to learn new things.

In addition to getting your dog's mind and body back to a healthy balance, reducing your own stress will enable you to: more easily cope with the situation; experience less frustration; and be empowered to make change happen.

Stress is a natural part of life, and in many cases, it's a positive thing. It can help us meet challenges; it can help us learn better, improve our memory, etc. It pushes us to grow and adapt. It keeps boredom at bay, and without it, we have a lack of motivation and often, lowered self-esteem. The issue is when stress becomes chronic or is so intense or prolonged that it impairs the brain to adapt to future stress.

When the body undergoes acute stress, various physical changes occur to make the body ready to cope with a threat. When the dog is no longer in a stressful situation, the various changes in the body eventually return to normal. This is called *homeostasis*. You don't need to know the term unless you want to do more research, but essentially it returns the dog to a normal balanced state.

How long does it take a dog to de-stress?

Unfortunately, there are so many factors that we don't know exactly how long it will take for any given dog to recover from acute stress because there are several factors that influence recovery. Here are some of the factors:

- Duration of the stress
- Intensity of the stress
- Age
- Genetic make-up of the dog
- Health status
- Experience of the dog
- Size of the dog, etc.

In addition, some physiological changes normalize quicker than others. Research on rats demonstrated this. The test rat was introduced into the territory of a larger rat, which then attacked him. The test rat was then removed immediately after showing submissive postures so that the test rat was not hurt or exposed to the larger rat again. The results were that some changes return back to normal in a couple of hours, some take at least four hours, others days and weeks, and some may be permanently altered.

In looking at animals that have been transported (a *stressor*), some of the primary mediators of stress returned to normal in 24 hours. Most physiological changes in the immune system and in the endocrine system, which is instrumental in regulating mood, can take one to seven days to normalize. Reproductive performance could require up to a month to normalize. [13] However, this research primarily looked at transport, which is likely not as intense as stress that a dog might experience in an aggressive episode.

CHRONIC STRESS

Chronic stress develops when stress persists or continues to occur. If your dog has generalized anxiety, or has been behaving aggressively on an ongoing basis, it's very likely that he or she is experiencing chronic stress. This can lead to serious health problems in dogs. In addition, it makes it very difficult to learn other ways of coping appropriately.

Some dogs will be better at coping than others, but the more the balances of certain neurochemicals get out of whack, the more stress the dog will experience, which of course, means recovery will be more difficult.

One result of chronic stress over time is the dog starts to interpret and learn from events in a skewed way. Eventually, the dog starts becoming anxious about being anxious. The original situation that triggered the dog's aggression in the first place becomes linked with the different events and occurrences that predict the trigger each time and in time, these other associations also cause anxiety in your dog.

What we need to do for dogs is facilitate learning, and lay down another set of rules for dogs so that they can develop positive associations with the events that are causing the anxiety. This will enable dogs to respond more appropriately.

But before that, we need to allow the dog to recover as much as we can from chronic or repeated stress.

 DE-STRESSING YOUR DOG

TEMPORARILY DISCONTINUE TRAINING

That's right! Do nothing. You will want to work with your dog later, but for now, let them be. Training doesn't cause a lot of stress the same way a fearful event would, but it does cause stress. For now, treat your dog like he or she is the patient, and needs to recover. The same way bed rest helps those recovering from surgery; your dog needs some psychological and probably physiological rest too. Again, play this by ear. The next stage in relationship building requires you teaching your dog how to sit. Not challenging, and he or she may already know how to do this. However because you will incorporate their sitting and looking to you to get whatever he or she wants, it will cause some change in their environment and this can be a little stressful.

How long should I discontinue training?

This depends on you and your dog. It's difficult to determine just how long will be beneficial since every dog and situation is different. Older dogs, just like older people, take longer to recover from stress. The amount of change in the brain will be difficult to gauge.

A minimum, wait at *least* a week since the last stressful experience your dog has had before returning to training. It would not be unreasonable to wait as long as a month as long as you can manage the situation and avoid your dog getting worked up. Obviously there needs to be some flexibility here. But take a break!

If your dog is unable to settle down eventually, visit the vet.

There is one exception:

- If your dog has just had a recent aggressive episode, you may wish to implement the *Emergency Response Plan.*

But if your dog is very stressed, my suggestion is to try a one-month break and see how that goes if possible.   In order to determine when to move to the next phase, start by making some notes and video recording. Note:

- How vigilant your dog is at the window or door
- How vigilant is he or she as people move around the room
- How much yawning or lip licking they might do
- Note their energy levels. Are they changing?
- What is he or she like when he or she goes outside? Always on guard?
- How do they lie down: uptight with their tails and paws tucked in perhaps?   Or loose and sprawled out?
- How jumpy are they; does he or she startle easily?

This behavior recording is going to be your behavior baseline that you are going to compare against later. Again, if your dog is unable to settle down eventually, visit the vet.

While it's possible to control a fear response, it takes very little to bring it back. Avoiding aggression should be practiced for the life of the dog.

CONTINUE TO CONTROL LIFE AROUND YOUR DOG

Continue to avoid the circumstances that cause your dog to become anxious. This is part of management of course, but it is also part of reducing stress in your dog.

CREATE A PREDICTABLE ENVIRONMENT

- Create predictability. When dogs can't predict what is going to happen next, *whether positive or negative*, they can become stressed.[14]
- Have the dog sleep in the same place every night and be fed at the same times during the day.
- Try to maintain your same schedule on days off from work; otherwise devise a plan to calm the dog when that's not possible.
- Build in signals that indicate when a change is going to happen.
- Use reward markers when you return to training. A clicker, or a well-timed "yesss," can act as a reward marker that indicates a treat is coming and exactly what the dog has done that has earned it. The sound says: what you are doing *right now* is right. The more distinct it is from regular conversation, the better, which is why a clicker is good for this. But also consider using non-reward markers. A simple calm "wrong" can work when the dog is not getting it right. Reward/no-reward markers are good for general training. Saying "wrong" when a dog is starting to freak out will likely be ignored by your dog.

CREATE A CALM ENVIRONMENT

- If you must have an argument with someone, go to another room to do it. Dogs pick up the stress of the humans around them.[15]
- Restrict guests for as long as you decide the focused de-stress period should be.
- Avoid leaving the dog alone for lengthy periods of time if possible. Isolation is stressful for dogs.

INCREASE POSITIVE EXPERIENCES

This may be as simple as giving your dog a treat from time to time (when he or she is being calm), increasing praise, play, or scratching them on the neck if they like that. Note what your dog likes (opposed to what we think he or she should like) and provide a little more. Allow them to sniff to their heart's content, lay in the sun with them, spend a little more time with them (if he or she likes it), and so on.

Be aware that what we think is positive might not be for your dog. For example, some dogs may feel anxious towards their owners. Excessive petting and neck scratches may just irritate your dog. He or she might prefer you hang out with them, but at a reasonable distance. That's ok.

ELIMINATE INAPPROPRIATE PUNISHMENT

Forget everything you ever learned about *alpha rolls*, leash pops, leash correction, scolding, hitting, pushing, or anything else that is punishment based. This may be a controversial topic in the unregulated dog training industry, but it's not in the science community where there is rigorous testing and peer reviewed academic papers. We will go more into punishment later, but for now - just stop. It makes things worse.

> **What is no-reward marker?**
>
> Imagine the children's game of Hot and Cold. Saying "cold" lets the player know that they are getting farther from the goal. The word "cold" in this case is considered a "no-reward marker" (or an NRM for short). While some trainers use this method, others are concerned that there may be problems using it. Check with your professional if it is right to use for your dog.

QUESTION

My dog growls at me when I tell them to get off the bed. I've decided that he will no longer be allowed up on the bed. How do I deal with this situation?

ANSWER

1. Keep a light leash or a drag line on them. A cat leash is ideal with the loop cut open so it doesn't snag on anything in the house. That way if your dog goes places where he or she shouldn't, rather than confront them, push them, or grabbing them, you can pick up the leash and lead them away.

2. If he or she already knows how to touch a target or go to a mat and special place, ask them to do this instead and reward them for it. You may want to punish them instead, but don't do it. This will only increase the problems. Then train them to sleep elsewhere. Redirect them before they get on the bed and reward them when they go to their sleeping place.

3. Keep them out when unsupervised.

Later, in time, when you start working with him or her again, you can teach your dog to touch a target. This could be your hand, or if you don't want their mouth so close to your fingers, you can use a target such as a target stick.

 EXERCISE

Calm aerobic exercise can be beneficial at combating stress

Exercise can also increase stress, but it has been proven that short-term stress such as exercise can actually alleviate chronic stress.[16] [17] Research also indicates that exercise is the critical factor in creating cell growth in the hippocampus. This means that cells that transmit information in the brain are being created.[18]

The challenge is if you are unable to exercise your dog easily outside because of a potential trigger (i.e. if you dog is aggressive towards strange dogs or people, and you can't walk your dog during a time where you can avoid these). If you can't control your dog's exposure to their *stressors*, you should avoid exercising during this phase, and instead pick it up during the Novelty phase, by taking your dog to new places.

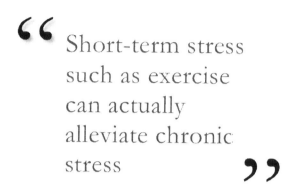

> " Short-term stress such as exercise can actually alleviate chronic stress "

Meanwhile, consider exercising your dog in the house or yard if you can. You can do this by:

- Throwing a ball or Kong

- Having them chase a rope or even a string

- For dogs who don't display possession aggression, a *flirt pole* (no, surprisingly this is not a brass pole on a stage; enter *flirt pole* on YouTube's search and you will see examples). They are relatively inexpensive to make.
  http://www.youtube.com/watch?v=SmlGbeIbemw

- If your dog knows how to touch more than one target, race them around the house or up and down stairs from target to target with rewards for each one (but not too long - they may get bored with this).

Increase Exercise but temporarily discontinue Agility or Fly-ball

Not all people do agility, but if you are doing it competitively, agility competitions could be potentially stressful for your dog.[19] You might consider still working with your dog if it's not competitive – especially with agility, if you are using positive methods, and your dog does not get too wound up.

TIP

If walking your dog is a challenge because of aggression

- People don't often walk their dogs around 9am. Stay-at-home people have just dropped their kids off to school and are starting their day's activities. Others are in transit or at work.

- 3:30pm until dark are typical times to walk dogs. You might have better luck after dark or late at night. However keep in mind, that everyone is a little on edge at night.

- Consider around the house exercises that keep your dog stimulated, including fetch, looking for hidden items, scent games, and the clicker game known as 101 Things To Do with a Box.

- If your dog is not food aggressive, consider making them work for their dinner and feed them small tidbits at a time for sitting and relaxation exercises. Have fun tossing kibbles for your dog to catch in the air. Have fun sliding kibbles across the floor for them to chase.

- When you do take your dog out, consider taking them to novel places to sniff and check out. These trips do not have to take very long. Places like shopping mall parking lots and fields can be full of interesting smells for dogs.

The Environment Enrichment section to come has more ideas.

DE-STRESSING THE HUMANS

We get stressed, too. Dog aggression can cause us to feel fearful and apprehensive, frustrated, confused, betrayed and angry, and not just with our dogs, but often with other people as well. The aggressive experiences themselves can be violent and traumatic just to witness, let alone experience. Dog owners also often feel judged and defensive. In many cases, the aggression leads to conflict within the family, with friends, neighbors and/or strangers. And, it also causes problems with our relationships with our dogs.

We usually have to deal with people offering us advice, and by the time the majority of people get to a professional such as a veterinary behaviorist, they will be told to euthanize their dog. In some cases, when people consider another home for the dog, they find this is next to impossible as rescuers find it challenging to place even non-aggressive animals.

Here are some results of chronic stress on us:

- Difficulty learning and remembering
- Feeling at the "end of our rope"
- Feeling hopeless
- Lack of control over our emotions
- Poor decision making
- Fatigue or exhaustion
- Broken relationship with our dog

Some of the earlier recommendations for dogs will also serve us, such as creating a calm environment, exercise, etc. Read on.

CREATE A CALM ENVIRONMENT

This will help our dogs and us. But, you have to make a conscious effort to make this happen. In other words, it's not enough to read this, you need to think about it, and then act on it. Unless we have it in our awareness, we will forget and revert back to old habits.

TEMPORARILY DISCONTINUE TRAINING AND OTHER ACTIVITIES THAT MAY CAUSE YOU STRESS

Sometimes owners get into the *training for perfection* trap especially if they have been trying to work on aggression for some time. This leads them to feel chronically unsatisfied with their dog and this breaks down the human-animal bond. Ironically, this can also allow denial to continue as you try to make your dog become that perfect dog you always dreamed of having. If your dog isn't being aggressive to you, it's possible that you already have that dog. He or she just doesn't like others.

Sometimes, people feel compelled to continue to take their dogs out for walks even though the experience is usually a stressful one because exercising your dog is what the good dog owner is supposed to do (if only we were as good at exercising and eating the right foods ourselves). But it isn't a great idea if the person and the dog are both anxious and on edge or feeling like they are walking on "egg shells," anticipating the next bad thing to happen. Even when the aggression doesn't happen.

When this happens, the problem can be difficult to work on. If this is happening to you, it's perfectly acceptable to take a break. Your dog will not wither away if he or she doesn't get their nightly walks for a while.

If your dog is being aggressive to you, then that's another matter. That's hard to deal with and you will want to have them at least sit for everything he or she wants. This will help encourage them to defer to you and provide both of you a predictable way to interact. Go to the *Sit, Wait and Attend* (**SAW**) section to see how this works. If your dog is only aggressive to you, and not others in the family, you could ask others to take over for you for a little while. But make sure that they can do it safely, and that they are using the SAW program to deal with them. It is okay to take a break from your dog if he or she is still being cared for.

EXERCISE FOR HUMANS

Ugh! Exercise! If you are not an exerciser, you have been dreading this one, haven't you? And besides, doesn't this just contradict what I just said before?

Sometimes we hate exercising because we push ourselves too hard or it's just plain boring. Try doing something you enjoy that is active and take it easy as you start. Take up squash if you have never tried it, or go roller-skating. Swim, or jump on a trampoline. Think of a tranquil place to go for a walk, such as the woods or the beach. Or, if you are urban-centered, think about a walk through an art gallery or a neighborhood you have never explored. And then, there is always shopping therapy. See what treasures you can find at a secondhand shop.

We don't just suggest exercise because it's "good for you" or because it helps you develop greater energy reserves (even though it is good for you and does help you develop greater energy reserves). We recommend it because there is so much compelling evidence that shows a decrease in chronic stress, an increase in the ability to learn and retain information, and even an increase in brain cell development. This is good stuff. Here are some additional human focused ways to manage stress:

PAY ATTENTION TO WHEN YOU ARE STRESSED

We can't expect to eliminate stress from our lives, nor would we want to, since it's part of what keeps us motivated and challenged, and as a result causes us to feel satisfied when we overcome challenges. But, some people thrive on the adrenaline they get from being stressed, and it becomes almost like a matter of pride. Some jobs and workplaces foster this attitude. Other people downplay stress and don't necessarily recognize it for what it is. Unrelieved, intense or chronic stress is bad for you. By recognizing when you are stressed, you can do something about it. You can…

- Practice deep breathing and get your heart rate down.
- Recognize what you *can* change to reduce stress.
- Remind yourself you can cope with this stress.

TAKE A BREAK AFTER A CONFLICT

It takes time to cool off. You don't necessarily need to resolve an argument with your spouse or your kids right away. Asking for time to cool off so that you can deal with it with a clear head is a better alternative.

RATE YOUR STRESS

The fact that your dog is behaving aggressively is always going to be a concern. But if you find you are getting upset in other areas of your life because you are under stress, the unfortunate result is that it causes more stress for you. In addition to de-stressing, rating your stress can help to put issues into perspective.

On a scale from 1-10, how important will an issue be to you in one month, in 6 months, and 1 year from now? Sometimes, you find you are getting worked up about something that in the long run won't be much of a big deal.

INTERRUPT WORRYING

This is particularly a good exercise for you, if you are the kind of person who ruminates or obsesses over things. When you know that you are over thinking something, it could be that part of your brain is getting stuck. This happens quite dramatically to obsessive-compulsive disordered people, but it can happen to the rest of us, sometimes, especially when we are under stress. The anxiety pushes you to try to problem solve, but when the problem is solved, the brain returns to the anxiety and the process starts up again.

The key for this is interrupting this process - acknowledge that it's a brain short circuit. Sometimes writing a list of the things that are troubling you helps, as sometimes people are afraid they will forget (for example, you know you need to do a number of things in the near future and can't stop running over it in your head). This gives you permission to have it, and let go at the same time. Then, find something to do that is wholesome and positive for at least 45 minutes.[20]

JOIN A SUPPORT GROUP

K9aggression.com has an online support group on Yahoo. Sometimes finding you are not alone in dealing with a problem like this can be beneficial because it removes isolation. Be careful, however, that you don't fall into the trap of being influenced by every suggestion that comes your way on the group. The group is meant to be about support, and not a training forum. Use your critical thinking skills before trying any advice out. But sometimes, it feels good to know that you are not the only one dealing with this problem.

MEDITATION

This might get a few "ugh!"s from some of you, too. If you are like I was, you might think meditation is frustrating and possibly boring. At best, you are never really sure if you are doing it right.

It's really not as difficult as it seems, and like anything, you improve with practice. But, the scientific research is now proving the benefits of meditation from coping with stress to having a happier life.[21] [22] [23] [24]

Some people resist meditation because they think they can't do it right. They find that their thoughts lead them to thinking about something, instead of concentrating on their breathing or some other focal point. But the thing is, that's ok. It doesn't have to be complicated. It is the *effort* towards the clearing of your mind that is the important thing.

It is not necessary for you to do it for very long either. You will find that even after five minutes of this, there are benefits. It can be as simple as concentrating on your breathing or simply trying to be without thinking anything. You can even do it while you are sitting in your office chair for a few minutes.

The simple way to meditate

1. Sit or lie down in a place that is comfortable, but not so comfortable you will fall asleep.
2. Close your eyes and breathe in slowly and deeply.

3. Hold your breath for a moment before slowly exhaling.
4. As you exhale count, repeat a calming word.

Variations on a theme

- Try simply listening, and not thinking at all. When you catch yourself thinking about something, just go back to listening.
- Imagine you can hear the ocean slowly edging up the beach and back.
- Try guided meditations if you find this too challenging. This does not help you with attention and focus as well, but it can be calming.

Meditation develops the ability to switch from one set of thoughts to another.

KEEP A JOURNAL OF WHAT IS IMPORTANT TO YOU.

This allows us to really understand what we value. All too often we spend too much time and energy on the things that are not really all that important.

- Write down the things that are important to you and review weekly.
- Write three things that you are grateful for every day.
- Write down one good thing that happened to you every day.

 # MY DOG IS UNABLE TO RELAX NO MATTER WHAT I DO!

As we mentioned, the brains of people who suffer from obsessive-compulsive disorders tend to get trapped in a sequence of worry and then try to fix the problem and are back to worrying again. This is the same for any of us who tend to worry about something that we should let go.

With people, it's possible to interrupt the sequence, label it as the brain getting stuck (opposed to worrying more about the worry), and then interrupt the process. Do something that feels good for long enough that the brain doesn't return to worrying, etc. This allows the brain to reconfigure its pathways and develop newer healthier pathways in the brain so that we don't fall into these old habits. But how do we do this for dogs?

As all animals have brains that are "plastic," meaning that they can adapt and change. Dogs are the same. In the case of a dog that is anxious, we need to help them by breaking the cycle and distracting them with an enjoyable activity. You may also want to take a peek at the relaxation work in Step 4 later in the book. But in some cases a dog doesn't seem to be able to relax no matter what you do. If your dog becomes anxious often and easily and seems to have difficulty in settling down and truly being relaxed, then it's possible your dog may have a generalized anxiety disorder.

GENERALIZED ANXIETY AS A DIAGNOSABLE PROBLEM

Generalized anxiety may be the result of a biological issue, and dogs can suffer from this. There may be signs that a veterinary behaviorist can recognize that indicate your dog may need some medical intervention. Here are a few things to look out for in the following list – any one of these things indicates that you should consider talking to a veterinary behaviorist about this (your vet should able to refer one or consult one on your behalf).

Possible signs of Generalized Anxiety:

- Hyperactive, always on the go
- Hyper-vigilant
- Resists moving at all
- Perpetually preoccupied with what is out the window or door
- He or she is rarely loosely sprawled out. Instead, they always seem to be holding their limbs and head close to the body.
- Overreacts to certain stimuli
- Stays worked up for some time after an aggressive episode
- Acts as if there is a threat when there isn't one

BLUEPRINT FOR TREATING DOG AGGRESSION

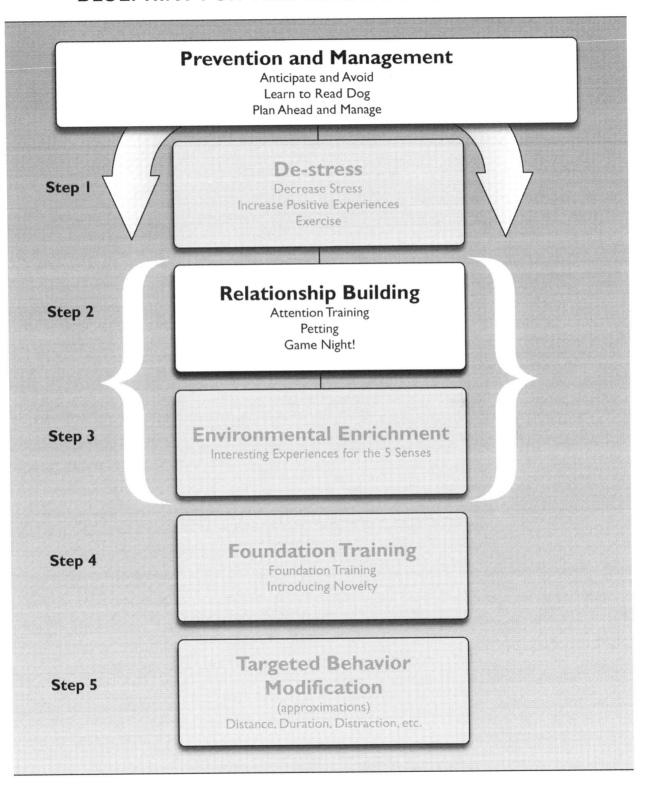

Prevention and Management
Anticipate and Avoid
Learn to Read Dog
Plan Ahead and Manage

Step 1

De-stress
Decrease Stress
Increase Positive Experiences
Exercise

Step 2

Relationship Building
Attention Training
Petting
Game Night!

Step 3

Environmental Enrichment
Interesting Experiences for the 5 Senses

Step 4

Foundation Training
Foundation Training
Introducing Novelty

Step 5

Targeted Behavior Modification
(approximations)
Distance, Duration, Distraction, etc.

STEP 2 – **Goals:**

Build on Step 1 by establishing a more trusting, secure and harmonious relationship between you and your dog so that your dog is more likely to take cues from you when uncertain, confused or anxious. This is key for Step 5, the *Targeted Behavior Modification Program.*

In addition, better communication ensures more positive regard and understanding for your dog, which results in less frustration, less stress and a better partnership.

This step can be done at the same time as Step 3, *Environmental Enrichment Program.*

HIS NAME IS A GOOD THING.

Why do we have names? *To get each other's attention.* "Hey You" gets a little confusing in a crowd at times. But, you wouldn't be the only one if you shouted your dog's name in frustration, especially when you are trying to get them to come to you and he or she is ignoring you. Your dog may actually want to ignore you when they hear their name because he or she knows they're going to get in trouble, or going to lose something they want – like freedom to run around like a hooligan in the neighborhood off leash, for example.

So throughout the day, call their name and when he or she looks at you, toss them a treat. Keep treats stashed around in different places in the house. Dogs know when you get the treat bag out they ought to pay attention. Many will ignore you when training is done and you put the bag away. We need to keep these clever pups guessing.

Practice saying their name in different ways – only varying a little each time in case he or she gets startled, or you immediately make them think they are in trouble (in other words, don't suddenly shout at them). Do this in a variety of situations, always starting from the easiest place, and working slowly up to the most challenging. Don't call their name twice if he or she doesn't listen. Just wait a moment and try again.

I did this with one dog of mine, and one day, I did shout at her because I was frustrated. Nevertheless, she immediately turned to look at me with such a hopeful look on her face that all my anger melted away.

You may also find that you have nothing else at your disposal except the ability to call your dog. When you think about the various things that could go wrong from a door and gate being left open to a collar breaking, great name response may be the critical thing to keep you and your dog out of trouble.

Once reliable inside, move outside, initially with few distractions. Put your dog on a long leash; call their name, wait until they look and dash away from them (not so far you end up pulling them). Reward them if he or she starts to chase you. If your dog gets too excited, don't run as fast, or ask them to sit before giving them the reward. The point is to make responding to you more rewarding and fun than watching a squirrel or a bicyclist. The more you practice this, the better the result will be.

Resist the inclination to shout at them when he or she is not doing what you want, and then scolding them when they respond to their name. Resist the inclination to repeat their name if they aren't looking! If they don't look, simply wait a moment and then try again when your dog is more likely to look. Don't practice too long. Dogs get bored, too.

 ## SIT, ATTEND, WAIT (SAW)

We go into a fair amount of explanation on the next section because the concept is so simple; most people over look how important it is because they just don't know why it is so effective.

> Sitting and lying down are naturally deferring behaviors for dogs.

The short form I created is: *SAW*, which is an

acronym for *Sit, Attend, Wait.* It is similar (but not identical to) the *NILIF* or *Learn to Earn* programs, if you are familiar with those (and if not, there is no need to know), and virtually identical to the Dr. Karen Overall *Protocol for Deference* that you can find and download from on the K9aggression.com website. The difference is really in the explanation that follows shortly where we place the focus on additional areas so that you understand what you need to do and why.

All you need to teach your dog to do is *sit quietly* and *pay attention* to you, and *wait* for your cue about what to do next, *consistently.* They should do this to get *anything* he or she wants (attention from you or other humans, food, to go for a walk, etc.). Easy, right?

But, that's the problem. It's so easy that people don't think it's all that important! The following passages tell you why, and this will help you get the best from your dog.

> **Consistency and predictability = stress reduction**

SITTING

Sitting itself is a naturally deferring behavior in dogs [25] and we want dogs to rely on us to make decisions since we know this human world best. Practicing this is a good idea. It should not be used as a management technique. In other words, if your dog has a hard time keeping calm on the leash when a person or other dog walks by, it is better to distract your dog while he or she is moving than it is to ask them to sit where your dog might feel trapped.

Don't trap them

It is key that your dog is not feeling trapped by being asked to sit. If you are close to something he or she is concerned with or anxious about and you can't move away, you are better off distracting them with something attractive, such as a toy or treat and moving them away.

If your dog is aggressive towards other dogs, the other dog that is all the way across the street knows something is up with *your* dog. Then, that dog becomes concerned and starts to behave in such a way that confirms to your dog that the other dog across the stress *was* something to worry about after all. The next thing you know, they are all barking and lunging at each other. Sitting has a remarkable way of communicating that everything is good. That same dog across the street might look over then, make a judgment call that there is nothing to worry about, and may show friendly interest or curiosity, but be happy to move on with its owner.

It also has this effect on people as well. Having been an owner of pit-bulls, I am often aware of how afraid people were of them walking down the street (when they recognized them as pit-bills). But the smiles I got when I stepped off to one side and my dog calmly sat were amazing. It makes people feel that you are respecting any possible concerns they have. Plus, they just love to see a dog that does what he or she is asked without you pushing on the dog's behind or shouting at them or jerking their collars so they'll sit.

But sitting as part of the *SAW* program is especially good for those dogs that show aggressive tendencies towards their owners in any context (i.e. petting, feeding, with toys, etc.).

Some dogs are literally anxious about interactions with people in general because they haven't learned how to read human appropriately, and really aren't sure what the intentions are. In some cases, behaving aggressively will provide the anxious dog with the information about the interaction – are you threatening or not, are you trying to "get in their face" and force them to respond with an aggressive display? Are you going to challenge them or not? Is this a test? Anxiety often produces the need to act so it's possible that your dog is provoked simply because he or she can't anticipate what you will do and can't handle the suspense in waiting for it. A confrontation will give them answers right away.

These are often the dogs that will drop a toy at your feet and then growl when you try to pick it up to throw it. These are the dogs that worry and tense up when you tell them to move off the bed or couch, or overreact when you are trying to step over them in the hall.

They are anxious dogs who are very much in need of information, and like many anxious people, these insecure dogs need to know exactly what the status of the relationship is regularly: is everything still ok or not, am I still safe or not? They need ongoing regular confirmation. When you incorporate *SAW* in your life for whatever the dog wants, *SAW* allows this information to flow in a very easy fluid way.

And while aggression is not about poor obedience training, having a predictable system tells your dog what they should be doing next in a way that reduces stress for your dog regardless of their issues. *SAW* becomes something your dog can default to whenever he or she is uncertain. It removes uncertainty about what he or she should be doing at any one time about anything. It also allows them to communicate to you when he or she wants something, in a pretty darn awesome way. Best of all, it's easy to incorporate into your life.

ATTENDING: PAYING ATTENTION

Paying attention to others is not only important for all social interaction, but the degree of attention, i.e. attention that involves active interest and focus, can also help facilitate learning.

Attention training is getting and keeping your dog's attention and working to increase your dog's abilities to *switch* their attention from something else, and then tune out distraction such as competing or conflicting information. This training will allow your dog to regulate their emotions better because it is part of the same neural system in the brain (See more on attention in the second part of the book). That's pretty exciting.

Participants trained to pay attention to non-threatening positive material showed significantly greater reductions in self-reported behavioral and physiological measures of anxiety than did participants that did attend to threatening material and those in the control conditions.[26]

If your dog is aggressive, your dog is likely making incorrect interpretations about whether something is actually a threat. So we want them to look to us for information on what they should be doing and how they need to act.

Unlike wolves, over the years dogs have been domesticated. Dogs now have an inborn readiness to look at (although not stare at) human faces, and will do so when they are unsure.[27] We want to nurture this so that whenever they are uncertain, they look to us for cues about how they should respond.

We want this skill to be *so* well learned, that it's pretty much automatic – so automatic that they can learn to do this even when faced with very big distractions (such as that threatening thing over there!) At that stage, we can direct their behavior.

We do not need the dog to *stare* at us in the face. The reason why many trainers suggest you train this is because they want the dogs to become comfortable with us looking at them. Some people also ask the dog to look at them so they aren't focusing on whatever is going to set them off.

But asking dogs to look at us in the face can be problematic for some aggressive dogs. You are better off when you are looking at your dog to not look too long in their eyes, but instead shift your gaze around the face – the ears, the mouth, etc.

At the same time, it is enough to know that your dog is *attending* and that includes listening and generally being aware of you. He or she does not need to stare at you. They *do* need to pay attention to you when you ask.

 WAITING

Asking your dog to wait is asking them to practice self-control. It doesn't need to be for long, as we will work on that in Step 4. But it should be you and not them that decides when he or she can have the thing they want. Asking them to wait a moment helps the both of you get into this habit.

Unless you have practiced a lot of obedience, your dog probably won't be that great at waiting. But that's okay. Self-control is like a muscle and it can be developed with practice. Your dog only needs to wait for you to give the next signals on what he or she should do. It's easy to deal with a dog that won't wait – they simply don't get what he or she is after until they sit calmly for a few moments. Don't worry – they'll eventually understand what they need to do if you are consistent.

Training long *sit-stays* can have the same kind of impact in terms of developing self-control and we will explore that in the Foundation Training in Step 4. The difference is, however, *SAW* is related to social interactions. It reduces anxiety for the dog because you have reduced uncertainty. Your dog starts to see you as a guide in life and it becomes an inherent part of your relationship. Best of all, you don't have to set time aside to practice this once your dog understands they need to sit, be calm and wait. Just incorporate it into your life.

Again, attention training will help your dog regulate their emotions because it is part of the same neural system in the brain.

PUTTING IT TOGETHER: SIT, ATTEND, AND WAIT (SAW)

Putting it all together, SAW is very similar to Dr. Karen Overall's Protocol for Deference with a bit more emphasis on my part on the paying attention and waiting because of the cognitive benefits. Also, the practice includes a name change (we will explain why in a moment).

Dr. Karen Overall's Protocol for Deference includes a clear set of instructions, and is in the public domain. You can find a copy of it in the Bonus section on the K9aggression.com website mentioned early on in this book. It is excellent.

It is important to understand that this training and these behaviors are part of a foundation of behaviors that lead to the final step: *Targeted Behavior Modification* (*behavior modification* that deals directly with your dog's responses to his or her *stressors* – detailed in Step 5).

This means that before you go ahead and start trying to work with your dog to improve their response to the things that trigger their aggression, you need your dog to learn a set of responses so well they become largely automatic. Having your dog sit on request, when you ask, and have them wait calmly until you let them know what they should be doing, is a big part of that. In other words, we can't get a university degree without going to grade school first.

The reason we are choosing not to call this program a deference protocol is that some people still confuse deferring with being submissive. If you look up the word *defer*, some definitions say it means to submit to another's wishes. This is not a submissive protocol and I am not encouraging you to teach your dog to be submissive. While this may

Why is this important?

We are training our dog to have improved self-control; and better regulation over their emotions. At the same time we are increasing their willingness to take social cues from us. This way they can look to us to for guidance instead of feeling the need to make their own decisions about whether or not something is a threat.

Attention training will develop your dog's ability to control him or herself because the ability to tune out distractions uses the same brain system as self-control.

Finally, the act of sitting is a naturally deferring activity for dogs. In situations where dogs are unclear about control, learning to sit and be calm will help them defer to you.

be splitting hairs to some, the very real situation is that some people are still treating their dogs in ways that is little more than bullying, and this can lead to disastrous results with dogs.

While it's true that dogs operate in social systems much the same as our own, we need to move away from loaded words such as dominance, submission, *alpha*, etc. Not only does it encourage people to behave threateningly, it causes people to assume that the wants and needs of the dog are not important. It does not encourage people to learn how to read their dog, and look for signs of stress, etc.

The idea is only concerned with power. If you are interested in learning more about *alpha* theories, you can find more in Part Two.

The general understanding at this point in time is that social systems in dogs are maintained and determined by those dogs that defer, not by those trying to overpower. If anything, we encourage you to think of your dog *allowing* you to lead the way. We know the human world better than they do. We make it worth their while, however; we encourage them, not scare them into it. See yourself, then, as a friendly adventure guide for your dog. Your job is to help your dog navigate our human world successfully, to translate the needs of our world to them, so he or she can live safely and comfortably within it, not to make them scared of you.

TIP

Sit, Attend and Wait
Make sure your head is facing your dog. If you turn your head away, research indicates your dog will become less responsive.[28]

Eye contact

While dogs are likely to look at a cluster of body language signals, the "ancient breeds" (as according to genetic patterns): Basenji, Saluki, Afghan, Tibetan Terrier, Lhasa Apso, Chow Chow, Pekingese, Shar Pei, Shi Tzu, Akita, Shiba Inu, Alaskan Malamute, Siberian Husky, and Samoyed, are more likely to find the human gaze unpleasant.[29] With these breeds, or any other dog that does not like being looked at too long, glance back and forth from the eyes to other parts of the dog's head. You don't need them to stare at you; you need them to simply make eye contact and be facing you, willing to pay attention when you communicate.

WHAT ABOUT NILIF OR LEARN TO EARN?

The principle behind *NILIF* (Nothing In Life Is Free) or *Learn-to-Earn*, as explained in various places on the Internet, is that the dog should perform a task at the request of the human for everything he or she wants. Some people go so far as to say if the dog anticipates what you want ahead of time (i.e. a sit), you ask the dog to do something different (i.e. shake a paw, do a spin, etc.) so that the dog will learn to be compliant and not manipulative. This practice is great when you want to teach dogs to be more obedient and pay attention to what you are specifically asking.

But, with the *SAW* program, we do actually want our aggressive dogs to anticipate what we want ahead of time. The worry that the dog is trying to manipulate is not a concern for us. It's a little like assuming that when a child used the word "please" is manipulative. It's not. It's polite.

Simply put, what could be better than a dog anticipating ahead of time that he or she can get what he or she wants by sitting calmly and waiting for your next signal? If we use the child saying "please" analogy, we want that child to be saying "please" on their own, unprompted whenever they ask for something because it's just the respectful way to interact. What we don't do is tell the child they must say a different word each time to get something so we can ensure they are not trying to wrap us around their little fingers and test to make sure they are obedient.

> ### Do dogs manipulate?
>
> Manipulation implies that someone has caused us to feel a certain way (usually badly) so they can get what they want. Like humans, dogs often have wants or needs. If they know the only way to get attention is by jumping on the counter, barking, or pawing at you, they will do what works. It's important for us to move away from projecting moral judgments on our dog.

NILIF vs. SAW

In the online world, Dr. Karen Overall's deference program often gets confused with other programs such as *NILIF* or *Learn-to-Earn*, among others, as this one potentially will. Many think they are one in the same and easily exchangeable. There is a critical difference, however. The act of sitting is a natural deferring behavior; the dog should be calm and look to you about what should happen next.

In addition to these principles, *SAW* focuses on the cognitive gains behind training our dogs to have more self-control and better regulation over their emotions. This is essential for *Targeted Behavior Modification.*

BONUS: YOUR GAME FACE

Research has indicated that dogs respond to facial expressions. Both adult dogs and puppies respond to facial expressions, especially anger and joy over neutral faces. Only, adult dogs react significantly to an angry face by avoiding it, and pay more attention to a fearful face, which suggests that they learn about us. [30] Keep this in mind when you grow frustrated or fearful. Keep your game face on!

 PETTING AND TOUCH

Dogs that don't like it

Not all dogs like petting, and not by all people. [31] And even in the case of the ones that do, not all dogs like the same kind of petting. Some dogs get very nervous when you reach over their head for example.[32] Other dogs may be being touched more than they like. So, pay attention to whether or not your dog actually likes it. One of my dogs didn't. One of my kids didn't. That's because she has some sensory integration issues (brushing her hair was a challenge!) My dog still preferred to sit very tightly against you (when cold) or just be near you. But, she merely tolerated petting.

Some people compulsively touch their dogs. In some cases, they are expressing their own anxiety about the relationship and aren't even aware of it and are compulsively seeking reassurance (or information about the status of the relationship – sound familiar?). Others are simply touchy-feely, never realizing that it could be an issue. If you are one of these people, see how much your dog actually relaxes and enjoys when you are petting them.

Do they move away when you pet them or after you stop petting, or do they nudge you for more? When lying down, do they rest their head? Do their eyes half close? Do they eventually flop out or roll over floppily for a belly rub? Then, you're good to go.

Otherwise, if your dog is ducking their head, or moving away, he or she may not like it, and you are just irritating them. If so, just imagine your dog has a perpetual sunburn and don't take it personally. It's possible that once you establish trust and safety – if that's the issue - your dog might enjoy it. But if not, that's ok, too. Some dogs don't like it and it has nothing to do with us.

Dogs that do! Do it!

Dogs that like petting make it obvious. If your dog enjoys petting, make use of it! Petting increases oxytocin in both humans and dogs. Oxytocin is generally thought of as the bonding chemical that is produced in both animals and humans. Research has recently indicated that oxytocin can reduce or trigger anxiety depends on whether they have a positive or negative social experience.[33] In positive social experiences, oxytocin can make animals and people more trusting and **less aggressive**.

In addition, petting may help lower the cortisol responses (i.e. stress responses) of dogs to other common aversive situations.[34] [35] So not only can petting make your dog less aggressive and more trusting, it can help alleviate some of the stress. If you have a good relationship with your dog and they enjoy petting, start a petting regime. Good for you; good for dog!

The reason why petting is not included in the section on stress is because of the risk that some dogs don't like it. You need to determine if your dog enjoys petting before figuring out if this can help.

Massage Or TTouch

Tellington Touch (TTouch) is a form of touch and massage which some believe reduces stress, increases a sense of well-being, and/or helps to release unfounded fear and anxiety. [36] Some dogs do not enjoy being petted, but might enjoy massages. But some dogs have developed a lot of anxiety around touch because they don't like petting and any kind of approach now just sets the anxiety off. Ensure that your dog does not become more anxious about being touched. If he or she does, discontinue.

 GAME NIGHT! BEGIN TO TEACH YOUR DOG NEW TRICKS

Clicker training is excellent for this and it's worth learning all you can about clicker training and timing. The more your dog learns, the more new cells develop, and the more ready for learning he or she will be. Best of all, he or she will associate fun with you, and let's face it – if your dog has been aggressive and you are feeling distressed, a bit of fun is what you both need!

Avoid frustration; keep expectations low. This should be all about fun. Don't get too caught up in this phase and try to train something really complicated, because at some point when we start *Targeted Behavior Modification*, we will discontinue this learning phase so that your dog can concentrate on the new learning phase he or she will be in for that part of the program.

Keep the sessions short and fun! Look in the Environmental Enrichment section for more information on play.

> **TIP** The engagement of owners in training, play activities, and/or time spent with their dogs is associated with fewer behavioral problems. [37]

CHANGE YOUR RESPONSIBILITIES FOR THE DOG

The length of time your dog will pay attention to you will depend on your relationship.[38] Dogs pay more attention to the members of the family that are responsible for them. Research indicates that dogs have favorite people in the family. Who are they most attached to? *The people who walk the dog.* [39] Walking the dog can be problematic for some of our aggressive dogs. We expand on playing and exercise in the next chapter.

If you share responsibilities for caring for your dog amongst other family members, but you are the one who will be doing the bulk of the training, temporarily shift all the responsibilities for looking after the dog to yourself. Alternatively, if your dog tends to be aggressive towards one of the family members, it might be a good idea to shift some or all responsibilities to them *provided* that family member is willing and will not provoke any more aggressive or anxious responses in the dog.

If you have two dogs (or more) that are fighting each other, you may wish to discontinue some of your responsibilities for the dog, except for when you are working with them, especially if one dog is *too* attached or the dogs tend to fight in proximity of you.[40] All people in the family should do this.

OTHER QUICK FIX DOG RELATIONSHIP TIPS

If you are like most people with aggressive dogs, you have experienced a variety of emotions when it comes to dealing with your dog. You have been on the roller coaster, ranging from fear and anger and even betrayal to elation when your dog doesn't react, only to plummet back down any time you have had a setback. Well, welcome to the club. Unfortunately, this can cause a rift in your relationship.

Here are a few quick tips that you can use to help you right now.

1. **Stop searching for perfection.**

    If you have ever done any kind of dog training and especially if you have consulted a trainer, you might be at risk for this (*might;* there are some supportive trainers around). We get into the habit of thinking our dogs should be walking perfectly on a leash, bark once at the door, etc. The reality is no dog is perfect. The reality is no person is perfect. Give yourself a break. You are going to have setbacks at first, as you learn. That is to be expected. It's not the end of the world as long as you are focusing on safety.

2. **Let your dog be a dog.**

    We like to over manage our dogs, sometimes. We assign human emotions and motivations to them, and wonder why on earth they would want to behave like that. This can make us upset on a number of levels. And like the point before, we sometimes have high expectations for them on what they should be able to do. Life is not perfect. Accept that their growls and their teeth are some of the few ways they have in driving others away. They are not evil beings. They are not vengeful and malicious (the way humans can be). Their aggression is rather pure compared to a person's.

    Once you can ensure everyone's safety, it's okay to let them just be dogs doing things that make them happy. Let them have a long sniffing walk instead of focusing on getting them exercised for a change. Set up a sand box for them to dig in. Know that they don't think about the past and future the way we do, and they learn differently than we do. They don't generalize as well. What they learn in one context doesn't transfer well to other contexts. And if you can't resist fussing with them when they want to be left alone, try picking up a camera and video them – it allows you to just observe them and gives you something to do while letting them be a dog.

3. **Accept that this dog has come into your life for a reason.**

If you are like the rest of us, we carry a vision of how we want our lives with our dogs to go. If you have had dogs before that were not aggressive, you may be yearning for that carefree life you had with your previous dog(s) – which is likely being remembered through rose-colored glasses in any case. If this is your first time owning a dog, you might have wished for that idyllic view of what dog ownership is supposed to be all about. This can be rudely interrupted by your dog's aggression! Let go of your illusions. Not only will this dog make you a far better dog owner, this dog has come into your life to teach you something about life. About yourself. Are you ready to learn it?

4. **Take a break.**

Yep. It's okay. For both of you.

5. **Remember that you have knowledge and are capable.**

You don't need credentials to help your dog. I get frustrated at the various "experts" in the field that act as if dog owners are hopeless at training. You're not. But, you may need to learn or you may need practice.

Some dog trainers forget what it's like for a dog owner to be learning a huge amount of information at once. Interestingly, some of them don't use the same techniques and patience with people as they do with dogs. I don't know why. But, dog trainers do know about how dogs learn and what people need to do to be effective at teaching them. And, they teach many different types of people who have many different kinds of dogs. Luckily, you don't need to. You only have to teach your dog(s), the dog(s) you have learned so much about simply by living with them. So hang in there.

You know things about your dog(s) that no one else does. You have an important role. You are more invested in your dog than anyone else.

Own that role – ask the tough questions, make sure you understand the answer, and never let an *expert* (self-identified or otherwise) bully you or make you feel like you are incompetent. You can learn what you need to learn. After all, they did.

6. Know what to be responsible for.

For those of you who are wallowing around in guilt, take a deep breath. If your dog is predisposed to aggression, it's not your fault. Sure, you can make the situation worse, but people often feel like they are bad owners who have caused the dogs to become that way. It's a common feeling, but if you've been trying your best, that's all you can expect of yourself at any one time. To assume you can do more is taking responsibility for things you shouldn't be taking responsibility for.

Instead of beating yourself up, be clear on what it is you *should* be responsible for:

- Take responsibility for the actions you can take to improve the situation.

- Take responsibility for keeping people and other animals safe.

- Take responsibility for the well-being of your dog(s).

- Task responsibility for your own well-being. Accept that if you made mistakes in the past, you were doing the best you could do with the resources and abilities you had at the time. Own it. Then let the guilt go. The reality is, unless you have been abusive, or used techniques that made your dog worse, you are probably less responsible for the fact your dog is aggressive than you think.

- Take responsibility for your own learning. Learn whom the best people are to consult, and consult them. Find the best books and read them. Take it one step at a time – don't overwhelm yourself. You are on a journey and there are rewards each step of the way. Own it. You'll find you will feel a lot more confident when you do.

BLUEPRINT FOR TREATING DOG AGGRESSION

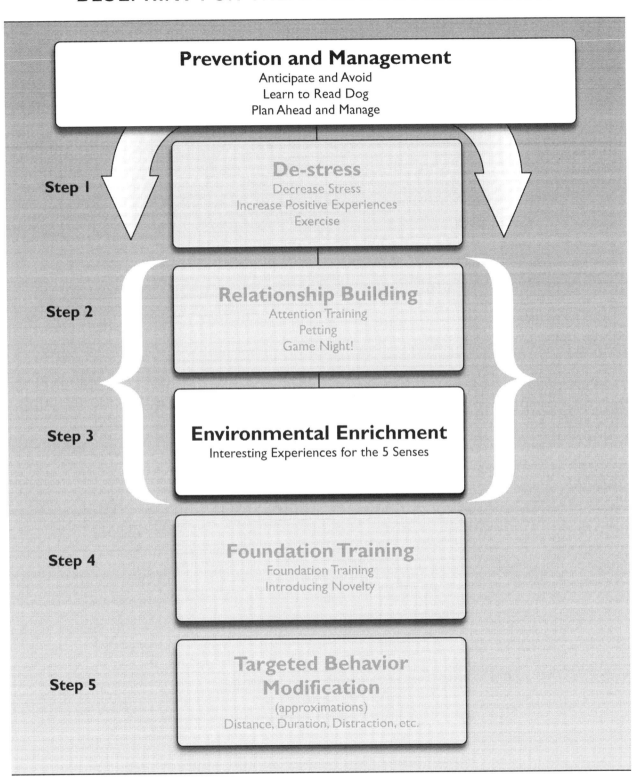

Prevention and Management
Anticipate and Avoid
Learn to Read Dog
Plan Ahead and Manage

Step 1

De-stress
Decrease Stress
Increase Positive Experiences
Exercise

Step 2

Relationship Building
Attention Training
Petting
Game Night!

Step 3

Environmental Enrichment
Interesting Experiences for the 5 Senses

Step 4

Foundation Training
Foundation Training
Introducing Novelty

Step 5

Targeted Behavior Modification
(approximations)
Distance, Duration, Distraction, etc.

STEP 3 – **Goals:**

By enabling your dog to have a greater sense of control over their environment through increasing the species-typical activities that your dog finds interesting (but not threatening), you can passively improve dog aggression, anxiety, fear and excitability; as well as improve learning and memory. This step sets you up for Step 4, *Foundation Training Program* and Step 5, *Targeted Behavior Modification Program.*

This step can be done at the same time as Step 2, *Relationship Building Program.*

ENVIRONMENTAL ENRICHMENT PROGRAM

 ## WHAT IS ENVIRONMENTAL ENRICHMENT?

Environmental enrichment is a big fancy word for making the dog's world more interesting in a way that satisfies their physical and psychological needs.

Why is it important to aggressive dogs? Research has shown that environmental enrichment has many benefits for animals from reducing stress, aggression, anxiety, fear and excitability to improving learning and memory.

 ## SPECIES TYPICAL ACTIVITIES

To start, think about what dogs typically do. Some of the areas that you can start to think about are:
- Introduce experiences that make use of the five senses.
- Novel objects
- Exploration of parts of your home they don't ordinarily get to, such as the basement or a closet or cupboard

- Positive training
- Social enrichment (provided the dog is comfortable with whomever he or she is socially interacting with)

Two points to remember:
- Nothing should frighten your dog or make them more anxious.
- It should be something they want to interact with on some level.[41]

Some examples

Many of these ideas involve food, since most dogs (although, not all) are food motivated. Those that aren't may be fed less at meal times to help. African wild dogs spend an average of 3.5 hours a day hunting for food, and resting the rest of the time[42] so we know that searching for food is a natural activity.

1. Let dogs try small amounts of new food – but check with your vet first.
2. For those dogs with no food or toy possession issues: use puzzle cubes and other toys that contain food such as:

- Kongs, (rubber play toys that can be stuffed with food a zillion different ways). Dogs can chew on these, and when they are thrown or rolled, they bounce unpredictably making them fun to chase.
- Buster cubes (deliver food as the dog rotates the cube)
- Boomer balls (hard plastic ball the size of a basketball or so that contains one or two holes at either end - used for zoo environmental enrichment - great for pit-bulls!)
- Home Alone toys (Aussie Dog Toy) balls (dog pulls rope/bungee cord to release a small amount of food in the ball from above – expensive, but popular)
- Inexpensive plastic bottles can be used - put some small amounts of food inside and see what they do!
- Make sure you supervise, especially when using plastic bottles - some dogs will crunch these too easily!

3. Introduce your dog to new smells (novel food, spices; second hand shops or garage sales can be good for finding items with different smells)
4. Teach them tricks (if they are not experiencing chronic stress)
5. Play <u>101 Things to do with a Box</u> – this is a fun clicker game.
6. Go for sniff walks – the aim here is not physical exercise, but the opportunity to explore the environment with their noses
7. Groom them with different brushes or even other things like sponges, towels, and clothes if they like it. Make sure that it is a pleasant experience.
8. Play different and unusual sounds (look for recordings of animal sounds, musical instruments, different human sounds!)
9. Give them ice cubes or other frozen things such as meat juice, fruit juice, frozen mini carrots, or marshmallows.
10. Scatter kibble or tiny food cubes in the back yard for them to hunt down. Try leaving scent trails with food.
11. Get your dog a plastic wading pool and throw toys or food into that.
12. Hide treats in different places (on shelves, under pillows, in pails, etc.)
13. Provide a sand pit for digging – hide food in it! Rake it too from time to time – dogs like "disturbed" soil to investigate – one reason they get into your garden!
14. Different kinds of bedding to lie on, nest, or dig.
15. Hang an old tire from a tree and hide some food in it. Make sure it's strong enough to hold your dog's weight and supervise to make sure he or she doesn't become tangled.

Use your imagination for more!

 EXERCISE

We talked about exercise in the de-stress section, and gave some examples on how to exercise your dog, but now we want to increase it. This will keep your dog less stressed, and will have some impact on improving both aggression and learning and memory, all of which is important in all *behavior modification*.

If your dog tends to get most of its exercise in the back yard simply because you were led to believe that was good enough, it's probably time to start walking your dog, *assuming* **that you can avoid the situations that cause your dog's aggression.**

But my dog is aggressive! I can't walk them outside!

Some dogs more than others get stressed out going for their walks because around every corner are other dogs and/or another scary person.

Despite how beneficial exercise is, dogs will not whither up and die if they miss a walk - even for a month. They don't necessarily *need* daily walking to live, although they will undoubtedly do better if they can have it (provided they are not becoming anxious in the meantime). You will need to weigh the mental and physical health benefits against the costs of risking the worsening of the aggression. There may be other ways to exercise your dog.

However, there is so much research on the positive impact exercise has in the treatment of mood disorders, mental health, stress, aggression and learning that you should figure out a way to increase your dog's exercise. It seems aerobic exercise tends to be best on improving well-being when it comes to stress.[43] Rhythmic exercise also appears to significantly reduce aggression in mistreated children.[44] In addition, taking the dog out for a walk creates a stronger bond with your dog and helps provide them with added enrichment.   All very good things.

Tips to remember:

- Avoid anything that might frighten your dog or make them more anxious
- It should be something they want to interact with on some level.
- Supervise for anything that could get damaged or tangled, etc.

    Talk to your veterinarian if your dog has generalized anxiety, and environmental enrichment results in an increase of stress or hyper-vigilance.

What to do if your dog gets aggressive on walks

It's challenging to walk a dog that gets aggressive during walks. Some of these suggestions have been repeated earlier, but here are some ideas on how to deal with it:

Walk your dog when others are not walking their dogs.

For those of you who have flexible schedules, this is easy. Walking your dog at 9 or 10 am on a weekday morning may be better than in the evening. If a dog walker is suitable, they might be able to deal with your dog during the day – but you need to fully disclose your dog's issues to them. If you have to, you might try at night or even when the sun comes up in the morning before the other dog walkers are out yet. Just keep in mind that your dog will be more reactive in the dark.

Walk your dog where you are less likely to run into other dogs/people

These might mean a factory parking lot, industrial park, a shopping mall parking lot or long country roads. You may have to drive there. We used to play ball with our dogs in outdoor tennis courts and made sure we took a lock with us so people couldn't just wander in. Be creative.

Remember, it's important to keep your dog moving.

Consider other ways to exercise your dog

- Teach your dog to target (touch with their nose) different objects and send them running around the house touching these things for the reward of treats.

- Use a flirt pole in a confined area to get your dog running around.

- Play fetch, throw toys, play hide and seek, toss kibble from one area of the yard or home to the other.

- Build a mini agility course in your back yard. A backyard set-up avoids the stress that a public agility set-up can cause.

- Invest in a treadmill, and teach your dog how to use it. Human-sized treadmills are good for smaller dogs. There are larger dog treadmills for larger, retriever-sized dogs.

- Play.

PLAY

We are only just starting to understand how important play is. Animals that play more often have longer and healthier lives. [45]

Play serves several purposes from relationship bonding to the development of physical skills. Mark Beckoff, professor of Biology and Ethology writes that play may be the basis of social morality in animals (although note, their morality is not the same as our own). When dogs play with others, it is generally considered a safe arena to try out things that might not be socially acceptable in other contexts, and mimics aggression or hunting, for example. It teaches dogs how hard to bite or how rough to play or when they need to stop because their partner needs a break. There are usually very clear communication signals that say, "what I am about to do next is play". When those signals are not clear or misinterpreted, **play can easily turn to conflict.**

Play between a human and dog has different functions, but generally humans that play with their dogs have better relationships. Play behavior and affiliative behavior (behavior designed to enhance relationships) between humans and dogs – with the absence of any behaviors associated with control or authority of the human part – helps to decrease stress. [46] Dogs that were more playful with their owners were less likely to show fear to an unfamiliar place. [47]

But, what we think of as play can make some dogs anxious when the dog is unsure of what is going on or they are not interpreting what we are doing as actual play. Dogs that have rarely played with humans may be suspicious or uncertain when we start to "act strange". Some people have the tendency to get very physical and wrestle, grab or tease the dog because they may have seen that behavior elsewhere. Play is only play when both parties agree that it's play.

Here are some suggestions on how to engage in play, but use caution, and make sure your dog is interested and not anxious.

How to establish play

Understand that if you haven't played with your dog before that you will need to teach them a little about how to play with you. So start small – don't act too wild. For example, he or she may be used to wrestling with their doggy friends, but you don't want them biting you on the neck. If he or she behaves too intensely, end the play session immediately for a while and walk away.
If your dog starts to get demanding about playing, and paws or barks at you to play, immediately leave the room if asking them to sit and wait does not calm them down. When you leave the room, make sure your dog is unable to follow you (for example, by closing a door to separate the two of you).

This first section describes play that is much more socially direct than other games, such as retrieve or tug-of-war that are in the section that follows. It has four parts:

- Attract (we get the dog's attention)
- Entice (we entice them to play by giving play signals)
- Engage (we engage in play)
- Ramp down (calm your dog down before they get over-excited).

1. Attract

Attract the attention of your dog by calling their name or by some other non-threatening attention-getting tactic.

2. Entice

Running away

> Dogs sometimes grab something enticing to display it to another dog, often shaking it, or tossing it to get another dog's attention, and then like a tease, run away. Dogs even try to get the attention of the other dog when there is no toy, such as barking, waiting until the other dog looks, and then running away. You can do the same: grab a toy if your dog does not show possession aggression, play with it in front of them, such as toss it into the air, and then run. If your dog is aggressive around objects, simply call his name, whisper, whistle, or some do other attention tactic that gets them to look at you; then run. Keep the run slow at first to see how they react.

Tapping your chest

> For whatever reason, tapping seems to capture the interest of dogs, but when you tap the floor, they might think you are trying to draw your attention to something on the floor, perhaps because it mimics hunting or digging behaviors. Research has shown that tapping your chest can motivate dogs to play.[48]

Play-bows

> Play markers often develop between dogs that basically communicate: "What I am about to do next is play." This takes the form of a play-bow.

> A play-bow is primarily recognized by the fact the dog has their rump up in the air, tail high and wagging, while their forelegs are bent down. Their mouth is often open. Humans can do similar actions that dogs seem to understand.

> Research indicates that play-bows occur around biting incidents between dogs and seem to be used to emphasize their playful intent as a way to avoid escalation to aggression.[49] They occur when the dog has made eye contact, which usually requires some kind of attention getting signal to be

used first. Not only do they surround questionable behaviors that are usually seen in other arenas (grabbling, biting, pawing, etc.) according to cognitive scientist, Alexandra Horowitz, they appear to start most sessions of play. They also occur after a pause in play where one of the dogs may have become distracted by something. This all suggests the play-bow is a social signal, rather than simply a playful behavior.[50]

Mark Beckoff has observed that the play-bow is pretty much a universal marker. If dogs tend to do it just before they do something that might not be acceptable otherwise, or do it just after, it is as if to say: this might get you going, but don't take it seriously.

Horowitz describes short panting, which is most likely the equivalent of what is been described as dog laughing. It is defined by breathy exhalations and is apparently exclusive to play and friendly greetings.[51] This may be part of it.

The play-bow may become truncated; in other words, it may be shortened between dogs that know each other into just stamping of the forepaws, or just a head bow. From personal experience, this may also become truncated with people, where the slightest jump and a slight hunching over or head bow indicates the signal to play.

But research also indicates that play between dogs, and play between dogs and human are structurally different and in conclusion, dogs have distinct reasons for engaging in play.[52] However, given that dogs know that we are different from dogs, dogs might use play as a way to learn about fairness, cooperation, etc. that takes place between dog and human relationships.

Dogs respond to our equivalent of play-bows, but also to lunges – a sudden quick movement toward the dog, which causes an increase in play bout frequency and duration.[53] **Caution**: be aware, especially if you have not played with a particular dog before that the dog may be unsure of what you are doing and may interpret your play bow as an aggressive lunge. It may be the combination of signals make it more clear to the dog that what you are doing is play including tapping chest, breathy exhalations, loose waggy limbs, etc.

Other effective ways to get a dog to play is to run towards or away from the dog (be careful that if you run towards the dog that he or she is not intimidated). Using play sound, such as a high-pitched voice in combination with play signals, may also help.

3. Engage

Activities you might try once he or she accepts your invitation are:

a. Chasing and being chased

b. Hide and seek (this can be behind walls, fences, trees and posts)

c. If your dog does not have possession or resource aggression, making a grab for a toy can work.

4. Ramp down

Ramp down frequently when first starting. This means only play for a short time before asking them to sit and be calm for a treat. If you think he or she is up for playing after this, go back to step one. You will find that ramping down will prevent dogs from getting too excited and unmanageable if you ramp them down before it gets out of hand.

Other playful activities

In some cases, social playing directly with a human is simply too anxiety provoking, or between the two of you, you just can't get to a play agreement. Here are some other activities you might try that are less socially challenging. Again, always use caution when playing with a dog that guards objects or may be aggressive towards others around food.

Tips for Social Playing

- The intensity of your play-bow should depend on the response you get. Start with a minimal version, and keep your head low. You don't want your dog to come charging at you with a full playful bite.

- Play should not include behaviors that are associated with control, authority or aggression, as these behaviors will increase the stress response. If the dog needs to calm down, always ask for a sit until he or she can be calm before resuming play. If they are unable to calm down, end the play session and leave the area.

- Keep treats nearby – if he or she is responding well, give them treats from time to time to signal that your dog is doing well.

- Try to incorporate your best version of a play-bow; from time to time, if you think you might have given an ambiguous signal. This play-bow signal is pretty universal among dogs that say what just happened or what is coming next is play. But also keep in mind that these behaviors seem to occur more frequently when there is biting involved so use caution. The human form of a lunge also has shown to increase play.[1]

- At a distance from your dog, you might try using higher pitched sounds, pouncing kind of movements, darting movements, and running away.

Other dogs like to chase and capture things, so try balls and objects that have unpredictable bounces to them, such as Kongs. Try rolling, tossing and bouncing them. Fill them with cheese spread or liver pâté or frozen broth (and/or fill the little end with something like peanut butter) to make them more interesting. By using clicker training, you can *chain link* or combine various behaviors to teach your dog to retrieve the object and return it to you. Some of the behaviors that are helpful to teach are picking up an object on cue, releasing an object on cue, holding onto the object, and coming while called.

- Tug-of-war: Dogs like to use their mouths and tug on things. **Caution**: dogs that have any kind of possession aggression, food aggression, or are resource guarders should not play tug-of-war. Children should not play tug-of-war with a dog because of the risk that the dog will get too excited.

  But for other dogs, tug-of-war may be a good outlet. A braided rope or a tug toy may be a good choice to play with. To catch the attention of your dog, try wiggling it around on the ground as if it were a small animal. Some dogs will tolerate you touching their feet with it, which will cause them to pay attention to it. Make sure you give some play signals so that your dog understands this is play. **Caution**: don't assume your dog will understand that it IS play - always observe how your dog responds to your play suggestion.

  Once your dog understands how to play, ask them to sit before any play session and use a cue word that signifies he or she should take the object. Teach the dog to release the object when you are done either by freezing or giving a cue word to release the object, and then provide a treat right under his nose to let go of the object. Anytime your dog may get too excited, ask the dog to sit for a moment with a treat. If he or she can't settle down, discontinue the play and walk away. If he or she continues to follow you grabbing or barking, go to a place where they cannot follow and ignore them for a length of time.

- The following may be less play based and more exercise based, but still good fun for your dog: If you sometimes feed your dog kibble, try feeding half their dinner one kibble at a time by tossing it to them for them to catch, or sliding it across the floor for them to chase. Dried liver or cooked chicken is another alternative. Then try tossing it elsewhere. Use a playful voice to encourage them to find it. If it is just bouncing off their head and he or she could care less about food flying through the air, that's okay, too. Some dogs might ignore that, but respond when you slide a piece of food across a floor. Experiment!

- Attach something to a string or twine that the dog can't break or chew and run around the house with it, the same way that cats like to chase string. A flirt pole is an extension of this by using a pole and attaching a string and object to then pole. Ensure from time to time that he or she gets a treat, so that the hunting "circuit" gets closed. Dogs are hardwired to chase for this very reason. They will need closure – let them catch it from time to time and reward with a treat!

- Some dogs enjoy chasing laser pen pointers, but not all. These pens can be problematic for dogs that have the potential to develop obsessive-compulsive disorder (OCD) or shadow chasing. If your dog has the potential for any of these issues, I would recommend against using it. If you think it will be okay and you decide to try it, **ensure that your dog gets an opportunity to actually "catch" it by landing the red dot onto a food-treat for them to catch and eat (the laser should go out once he or she has their paws on the treat)**. This is very important. This allows the hunting pattern to have closure. Otherwise, you can cause more stress and possibly other behavior problems. Don't use the laser for too long or too often, and don't let children use. Watch the eyes, too.

- Hide treats and then in a high pitch voice get them to find it by calling them and expressing a lot of interest in the hiding place. When he or she finds it, cheer for them and give them another treat.

- If he or she is not too good at catching on, try teaching them about the clicker and do **101 Things to do with a Box**. You can learn how by downloading the *Core Behaviors Training booklet*. The web address is in the Bonus section.

Dogs are unique

Okay, we know you know this, but it is worth saying. All dogs are different and respond to things differently. Certain breeds are more predisposed to certain activities than others. There is often great variation between individuals as well.

Some dogs are *play specialists;* in other words, they show a preference for one kind of game. Games might be defined as being cooperative or competitive or a mixture between the two. As mentioned earlier it might involve throwing an object, such as a ball for the dog to retrieve, playing tug-of-war, or chasing or playing "keep away". Dogs that play with other dogs might have learned only to wrestle or chase and nip and may not know how to play appropriately with people. It will be up to you to gently teach them. Don't allow the dog to get too intense.

I thought I was supposed to avoid Tug-of-war?

If your dog is a resource guarder (i.e. growls or snaps over valued objects), then it is a good idea to avoid playing Tug-of-war.

However, for many years, dog owners in general were cautioned against playing competitive games like tug-of-war because there was a concern that the game would make dogs more dominant and therefor harder to manage. This does not appear to be the case. In a study that looked at play between humans and aggressive dogs, there appeared to be no difference between the low aggression and high aggression dogs and the frequency of playing competitive games.[54] In a paper published in 2002 by Rooney & Bradshaw, they determined that tug-of-war does not cause aggression or dominance in dogs.

However, in another undated paper by the same authors, (that looks as if it might have been an earlier version); it indicated that aggression *might* correlate with dogs that tend to *initiate* the play.[55] So it's best that you, and not your dog, start the games to be on the safe side.

Caution: be alert to these conditions

Stop play and ask immediately for sits when:
- You start to become worried or scared that your dog's play is turning into aggression.
- The play just feels too intense – you don't know why.
- You know he or she is playing, but he or she is starting to jump on you, grab you, puts their teeth hard on you, or starts barking at you.
- You are feeling disrespected.
- You feel out of control.

Stop playing right away, and ask them to sit for a treat and then ask them to sit for a few moments longer for treats. Sitting helps calm them down. You DO NOT need to be sure that the play is meeting any of these conditions to interrupt the play and ask for a sit. In fact, interrupting this play for a sit and a treat is a great way to keep the dog from getting too worked up.

And as with any play, you need to be aware that it can escalate *out* of play. Always maintain play below threshold – that is to say, if the dog is getting too intense, you need to interrupt it and have them sit and calm down for a treat, whether you are playing tug-of-war or some other game.

Dogs who don't understand play

Play in aggressive dogs can sometimes be problematic. Dogs with poor impulse control, or who are unable to understand

- Make sure you introduce play. If your dog tries to start the play, just ignore them or ask them to sit and look to you first

- Ask your dog to sit frequently throughout the play to avoid them getting overly excited and out of control.

the play rules as they go along may actually become more anxious when they play. This is likely due to confusion in communication and confusion about what is needed to maintain fairness and cooperation in play. It may also be a result of an inability to figure out whether something is playful or not, and some dogs may never be able to figure this out.[56]

My dog doesn't get it or doesn't seem to like play.

If you don't normally play with your dog, your dog may be confused and concerned that you are not acting in a predictable manner. He or she may not understand your signals for enticement and shows avoidance, fear, or even frustration. If you have used punishment in the past, your dog may be unwilling to even experiment with you, as they know that when they don't understand something (and you think they are doing something wrong) is when he or she is most likely to get punished. Alternatively, if you do not tend to interact with your dog much, this may cause them to be more uncertain. Finally, if he or she is a rescued dog, they may be dealing with previous experiences that have caused them to be cautious.

If this is the case, dial down the amount of activity you do and increase the amount of play-bows, playful lunges from a distance, and increase the use of treats for appropriate behavior. Don't approach them head on, but curve towards them. Don't face them head on, but to the side. At any time if your dog appears to be anxious, let them know there is nothing to worry about. Simply turn your back to them, sit, or even lie down. If your dog is incapable of any kind of play, or becomes anxious despite what you do, discontinue. The entire reason for play is to reduce stress and strengthen your bond. If it's not working, don't continue.

Some dogs won't ever get it and this sometimes happens with adoptees. You toss a ball for them and they ignore it; you run around and they ignore you. They don't care about treats. It may be a result of a social deficit or perhaps they never learned as pups. But, you can still use the clicker training and **101 Things to do with a Box** as a way to interact with them in a positive way that still uses some of the similar skills like experimenting and investigation.

Tips and Cautions:

- Some forms of play are not appropriate for every dog.

- Be particularly cautious around food and resources guarders when using any food or objects.

- Dogs can get over excited and nip or bite. Never play roughly with dogs.

- If your dog has a tendency to get too "revved" up, then *before* they get revved up, bring them out of the fun to have them sit and relax for a reward before starting up again. If they are still unable to sit and relax, end the play session and leave the room.

- For dogs that need *more* enticement, use high pitch voices, fast darting movements, and lots of praise when they show some interest.

- A play-bow and running away may help them chase you – or jump you. Moderate according to your dog's responses and temperament.

- Make sure you use treats frequently, keeping the spirit of fun and good times alive.

- Make sure you know if your dog is actually enjoying him or herself. Play is good, but not if it's making them more anxious. Sometimes it can be challenging to tell. If unsure, it's ok to stop. **Video the play and analyze later. Are you seeing any stress related behaviors?**

- Ensure toys and objects are "bite worthy;" in other words, if they chew it, it won't break, or pieces won't easily get swallowed.

- Rotate toys on a daily basis for dogs that can have toys left around.

- Use objects that a dog might like to chase, fetch, pull or pounce on, or anything that will encourage them to hunt, stalk, or perform other species-typical behaviors.

 DIET

Before making any changes to the diet, your veterinarian should always be consulted and when possible, a veterinary behaviorist should also be consulted in the case of behavior issues. But it's worth having a look at some of the considerations to address with your vet. Your vet (or veterinary behaviorist) may have other suggestions as well.

Unfortunately, determining if a change of diet is necessary or whether a change has helped is challenging. Veterinary behaviorist Dr. Lore I. Haug recommends trying a particular diet for at least four weeks before deciding whether it has helped.

Diet is obviously an important concern for any being. If dogs are not getting what they need – and this may be individual to the dog – their systems might be thrown out of whack. Just like people, this can cause health problems, and in turn, when a dog is not feeling well, he or she is more likely to be aggressive than they would be if they were feeling fine.

Neurotransmitters and hormones act as chemical messengers in the brain and modulate behavior. Therefore, the chemicals that create neurotransmitters, such as amino acids like tryptophan, will have an impact on behavior if there is a greater need for them or a deficiency, or if there is some other problem in the mechanism that processes them.

There are a lot of factors that influence the availability of different amino acids that are the precursors to neurotransmitters, from the amount and timing of food intake, to how the body is able to digest, as well as the combination of other foods at the time overall.

Before adding any supplement or making any changes to the diet, your veterinarian should always be consulted and when possible, a veterinary behaviorist should also be consulted in the case of behavior issues.

Natural Diets

There is a lot of controversy around feeding raw diets, which we won't get into here, but feeding a diet that is low in additives and preservatives may be a first start at trying to improve a behavior problem through diet. You might also look into a home cooked diet, although it can be challenging to make sure that your dog is getting the nutrients he or she needs. You might also look into products such as *Go! Now!*, *California Natural*, or *Nature's Variety* for example (there may be other ones). Your local health food shop may also carry natural dog diets.

Tryptophan, alpha-casozepine and low protein diets

Tryptophan, which is an essential amino acid for dogs, is considered to be a precursor to serotonin, which is one of the main neurotransmitters that has been implicated in aggression across species, including dogs. While tryptophan is carried in most foods that contain protein, ironically, other amino acids, which are also in proteins in greater concentrations, compete against tryptophan in getting into the brain. This means a high protein meal may actually lower serotonin in the brain because there is less tryptophan available to make it.

Diets low in protein are thought to make more tryptophan available in the brain. Experiments have also suggested that supplementation of tryptophan appears to decrease aggression in humans, dogs, pigs, poultry, and fish, and it may reduce fearfulness and stress in calves and poultry.[57]

Aggression in dogs that displayed *dominance aggression* (the old and misnamed term for those dogs who behave aggressively towards their owners) was reduced in dogs that were either fed a low protein diet, or a high protein diet supplemented with tryptophan.[58]

Supplementing diets with tryptophan does not appear to have a positive effect in all cases. Another study looking at protein in diet alone found no effect on dominance aggression, although it did have an effect on those dogs that displayed territorial aggression and were fed the diet over a period of two weeks (provided they were not being fed a high protein diet).[59] Its possible supplementation over a longer period of time would have allowed for the diet to have a greater impact. It's also possible that the tryptophan may treat those dogs that would have been formally diagnosed with dominance aggression, but now would currently fall into impulse aggression, as serotonin has been associated with impulsive behavior. It's difficult to know what the criteria were in diagnosing these dogs at that time.

In dogs that displayed mild anxiousness, tryptophan does *not* seem to affect behavioral scores. The reason for this may be due to whether or not serotonin plays a part in the anxiety. The research conclusion was that tryptophan does not appear to have any effect on dogs that do not obviously display *clear signs* of abnormal behavior. [60] This makes sense, just as anti-anxiety medications do not work in people who biochemically don't need them. It's likely that mildly anxious dogs are not actually abnormal or pathologically anxious.

Whether or not tryptophan can help problem behavior on pathologically (i.e. disease) anxious or chronically stressed dogs has not yet been established to my knowledge.

Tryptophan combined with alpha-casozepine (found in nature in milk) has some significant effects in dogs in response to stress.[61] Although it's difficult to know if the effects of this diet were a result of the tryptophan, the proportion of protein, or the supplementation of the casozepine, Alpha-casozepine has reduced anxiety in rats and humans. Compared with Diazepam (which is like Valium), alpha-casozepine was similar in reducing anxiety, but doesn't appear to impair memory, is not addictive, and does not lose its effect over time, (unlike Diazepam). It also does not appear to increase risk-taking and aggression either – an important consideration for the use in aggressive dogs. [62]

However, so far it needs to be determined how long-term supplementation of tryptophan affects behavior and health.

A study with men using alpha-casozepine demonstrated that they experience less stress than the control group who were given a placebo.

Ask your vet if this is an option for you. Your vet should be monitoring any supplements and diet changes and may need to do tests to establish a baseline to measure change against.

Theanine

Theanine is an amino acid that has been used in people for treating anxiety and high blood pressure and can be found in Green tea. Research has indicated that Theanine may be useful in treating anxiety-related behaviors both in cats[63] and in dogs in the form of Anxitane tablets, as well. [64]

Omega fatty Acids - Fish Oil

A certain amount of fat in the diet is essential for the maintenance and growth of certain tissues. Of particular interest are the essential fatty acids, which are essential to the brain. Deficiencies are common especially because they break down so easily during processing and storage. The most common signs of a mild deficiency according to Dr. Richard Picturn, are:

- Dull, dry coat
- Excessive loss of hair
- Greasy skin
- Accompanying itching and scratching

There is a fair amount of research in the area of omega-3 fatty acids in relation to mood disorders, impulse control, etc. in children and adults.[65] From this standpoint, it seems peculiar there has been very little research to see if fish oil could improve aggression in dogs.

Lower omega-3 fatty acids – common in fish oil – appears to be linked with aggression with dogs,[66] although whether there is a direct cause appears to be unknown at the time of writing this. This link appears to be echoed in mice as well.[67]

There is some conflicting research on whether polyunsaturated fatty acids can impact learning ability (i.e. deficiency caused a *decrease* in learning ability, supplementation caused an *increase* in learning ability).[68] But supplementation may be something to talk to your vet about.

Before making any changes to the diet, your veterinarian should always be consulted and when possible, in the case of behavior issues, a veterinary behaviorist should also be consulted.

Try a particular diet for at least four weeks before deciding whether or not it has helped.

 ## ALLERGIES

Some dogs may have allergies and this may add to their issues because they are irritated or uncomfortable. It's not easy to tell if the allergies are a result of food allergies, although one tip-off is whether the allergy appears to be seasonal or all year around. Other health issues might look like allergies so these should be ruled out with your vet.

Signs of allergies in dogs

- Itchy skin around face, feet, ears, forelegs, armpits
- Chronic ear inflammation or ear yeast infections
- Hair loss, or excessive scratching
- More than 3 bowel movements a day
- Gastrointestinal problems
- Chronic diarrhea
- Chronic gas
- Licking their feet
- An itchy rear end

Common Food Allergens

- Beef
- Dairy products
- Wheat
- Egg
- Chicken
- Chicken eggs
- Corn
- Lamb
- Soy
- Pork
- Rabbit
- Fish

Always talk to your vet if your dog shows signs of any kind of discomfort. Even chronic conditions can be alleviated to make your dog feel better.

BLUEPRINT FOR TREATING DOG AGGRESSION

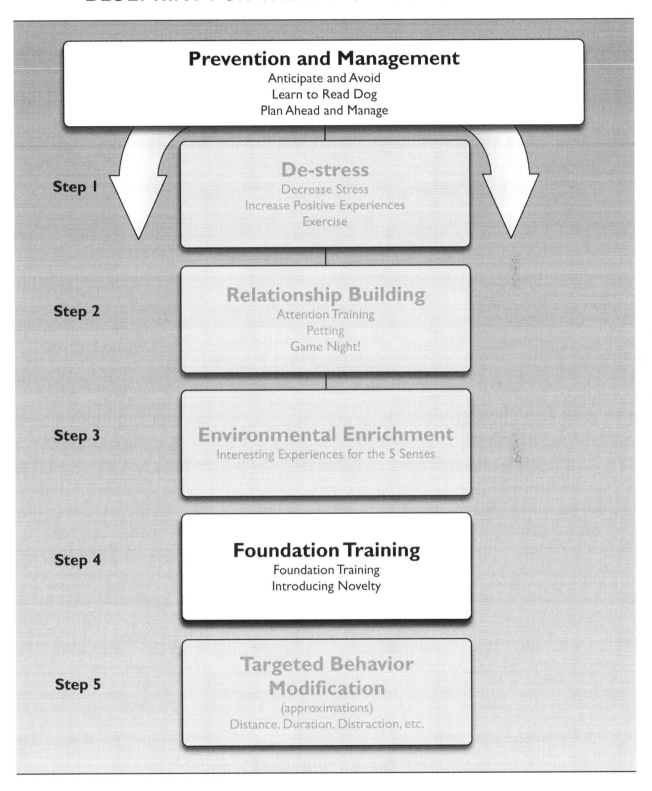

Prevention and Management
Anticipate and Avoid
Learn to Read Dog
Plan Ahead and Manage

Step 1

De-stress
Decrease Stress
Increase Positive Experiences
Exercise

Step 2

Relationship Building
Attention Training
Petting
Game Night!

Step 3

Environmental Enrichment
Interesting Experiences for the 5 Senses

Step 4

Foundation Training
Foundation Training
Introducing Novelty

Step 5

Targeted Behavior Modification
(approximations)
Distance, Duration, Distraction, etc.

STEP 4 – **Goals:**

Prepare your dog for Step 5, *Targeted Behavior Modification Program* by increasing your dog's ability to regulate emotions by developing better self-control, and teaching your dog to relax on cue in non-threatening environments. This is the most important step to ensure success in the final step.

Don't skip ahead!

Ok, you keeners, pay attention! This is one of the areas where people consistently go wrong – yet it is so simple to deal with: people don't practice the foundation training long enough (if they do it at all). This foundation work is the simple process of teaching your dog to relax in a variety of situations, as well as developing greater self-control. It is like the *SAW* program – so easy it's deceptive, and in fact, builds on the *SAW* program.

 ## FOUNDATION TRAINING OVERVIEW

Here we teach the dog a set of behavioral tools, which is absolutely critical for success when it comes time to actually deal with the situation that is stimulating your dog's aggression (*Targeted Behavior Modification* in Step 5). It includes two key components: the further development of your dog's self-control and teaching your dog to relax on your cue.

Stay or Wait training, which helps to develop your dog's self-control, can also be called a *sit stay* or a *down stay*, (note: he or she might feel trapped lying down if they are worried about anything).

In addition, there are a couple of other tricks up our sleeve that involves teaching your dog to control their urges. These are little more than standard obedience exercises. But we will explain why it can help in a moment.

Relaxation training is a little trickier because it involves teaching the dog to pay attention to their inner state, and it involves you recognizing the transition when it happens. But not only can you do it, this process will give you a greater sense of confidence when you are working on the next step.

Without the foundation training, not only will your dog's ability to overcome their aggressive response be largely compromised, you actually risk making the dog worse if you move ahead with *Targeted Behavior Modification* in Step 5 and your dog can't relax or have some control over their emotions.

If it is so important to do, why don't people do it? Much of the time it is because people want their dog's aggression problem to be solved *now*. An aggression problem causes a sense of urgency. But if you have been preventing and managing your dog's aggression well, that sense of urgency should be diminished.

There are other reasons why people skip the foundation training. Sometimes it is because they think their dog can sit and stay *good enough* and that is enough to move to the next step. Other times it's because people just don't know that they should do it, or what they should be doing or why. It is easy to pick up incomplete info.

Some people who *know* they should do it don't take it seriously enough. They don't take it seriously enough for three reasons:
- It seems too easy.
- It doesn't feel like they are actually doing anything to treat the problem *directly*, so there is no immediate gratification for them.
- They don't understand just how important it is and why, so it feels like it's something they could skip after trying it out for a few days.

There are people who start it, but don't continue. They might give up for any number of these reasons:

- They are trying to do too much training at once and/or get bored.
- They aren't being rewarded by seeing any huge changes, so the incentive to continue decreases.

- They focus only on the end result and get impatient with the process.
- They are only looking at the big picture and get overwhelmed.

But without a good foundation, you're setting you and your dog up to fail. If a dog is unable to sit and relax and look to you for signals on what to do next in non-threatening distracting situations, how can he or she possibly be expected to do it when there is something around to worry about? Simple answer: they can't.

Overlearning foundation training

When we learn something, there are a number of processes that happen to make experiences and behaviors strong and permanent. The human brain has limited amounts of resources, which is one of the things that make it so amazing. It operates on about 40 watts of power (the equivalent of a light bulb).[69] The bandwidth of the optic nerve is about the same as a cable modem – 1MB per second. If you think about the amount of video that a cable modem can stream, you know that it in no way resembles our subjective experiences of seeing the world. The brain only processes what is changing.[70] In addition, it updates, prunes back, and strengthens those pathways based on what we tell the brain is important. We tell the brain certain things are important either with our emotions or through practice.

> The brain is going to choose the most well used neural pathway in response to a given situation.

This process of pruning back or strengthening neural pathways in the brain is why we forget and make room for new memories. It is why we get better, faster, and more efficient with practice, and why we get rusty when we don't practice.

More critically, the neural networks in the brain are highly *competitive*. We go into this in more detail later on in this section, and then into more detail in the neuroplasticity section, but for now, imagine that you are trying to find your way through a field with very long grass. Each time you go through it, you get better and better at it. But you also wear down some of the grass to create a pathway making it easier and faster to get through the field.

In time, you will choose these well-used paths rather than start a new path through the long grass, because it is *the path of least resistance*. Even if someone were to suggest that there is a more direct way to go through the field, we might be reluctant to explore it, because finding a new way would take time and more of our energy. It also would take awhile before that path was clear enough that it was just as easy as the old path.

The brain is just like this. It's going to choose the most well used neural pathway in response to a given situation. The neural pathways that are part of the anxiety/aggression sequence are usually well learned and have been laid down to memory with the help of some strong emotions. To behave this way, despite the risks, is often a result of a path of least resistance for some dogs.

Once learning becomes so ingrained, it becomes automatic. We don't really need to think about how to do it – it just happens, like tying a shoe or driving a car. This learning and memory process is called *overlearning*.

Our foundation training needs to be so well practiced and the skills *overlearned* so that when we ask our dog to do this, they do it without conscious thought. This frees up the brain to learn and puts them in a state ready for new learning which is necessary to change attitudes and responses. Reporting your progress with someone or a group is a good way to stick with the practice. And practicing for shorter periods may also help.

> Self-control operates like a muscle. It gets easier to practice self-control long-term.

STAY TRAINING OVERVIEW

Why is Stay training necessary?

In people, the lack of self-control is an important component in aggression as well as the inability to inhibit other inappropriate behaviors. Those that score high in self-control are less likely to behave inappropriately. But, do dogs actually try to inhibit their aggression? There are indications that they do.

Given that many dogs show bite inhibition, whether it's through avoiding making direct contact with the target or in the case of contact, not biting as hard as they could, definitely indicates that dogs have some measure of self-control.

Evolutionarily speaking, aggression is risky. It uses up valuable resources in the body and you could get hurt either by your opponent, or even by others who may decide to join in. So it's important to understand that dogs become aggressive because the threat is overwhelming, and they can no longer contain themselves in the face of a perceived threat, or they have a pathological problem (i.e. physical or mental disease).

> **Good news:** You have already been doing some of the foundation training with *SAW (Sit, Attend and Wait)*.

Asking people to use their will power seems to temporarily deplete the resources necessary for self-control, making them vulnerable to lose self-control in an event that follows. This is why people tend to give into urges of over eating or alcoholism after a mentally challenging day.

However, self-control has been shown to operate somewhat like a muscle. Initially there is fatigue, but it gets more and more easy to practice self-control over the long term with regular practice. In people, there were effects in little more than two weeks (although, we don't know how long lasting these effects were).

More exciting, it didn't seem to matter which self-control exercises were practiced; the mere fact that people were exercising their will power was enough.[71] So this is why these exercises are important. When your dog is challenged later, greater self-control will give them a much better chance to succeed.

How to apply

Teach your dog to do down-stays and sit-stays. *Slowly* increase the amount of time the dog is required to stay.

In this case, your dog does not need to attend to anything. If they choose, he or she can lie down. What they shouldn't do is stand up. Use a timer and record your progress. Again sharing your progress with others will help your motivation to continue.

TEACHING THE LONG WAIT

Goal: Your dog can do a sit-stay or down-stay for a period of time despite a number of distractions.

Your dog should already be able to sit when you ask to start this. Practice in the most boring room (to them) in your home to start with (step 1 below). When your dog can master the exercises in one room, be sure to try it other places. If he or she already does reasonably long sit-stays, you can move to step 4 of this exercise.

1. At first, work in the most boring area for your dog that you can find. A bedroom or a quiet place would be good and work during a time of day where he or she is most likely to relax, such as before nap time, after meal times, or after exercise. As they learn, you will start to change elements in small ways one at a time.

2. Ask your dog to sit. If you haven't taught this to your dog yet, you can use the training guide to help you. See the Bonus section in the book for the web address to download the basic training guide for core behaviors.

3. Extend the length of time he or she must stay before you give them a treat (and you should use a *release* word to let them know it is ok to go). Extend the wait in baby steps, as they may just get frustrated if you wait too long before giving them a treat). If they lie down, that is ok. A timer will help.

4. Once your dog can stay for a reasonable length of time, we increasingly provide greater and greater distractions to develop their self-control. It will help to make a plan of what you will do next.

Starting with the least difficult challenge, make a plan on how you will teach them to wait despite distractions. Some things you might consider are:

- Acting as if you are not paying attention to them.
- Walking to one side of them and then the other.
- Doing jumping jacks, or other active physical actions.
- Making different sounds, such as clapping, singing (don't use any of your cue or command words, however)
- Walking behind them.
- Leaving the room

Dr. Karen Overall has a relaxation protocol that is in the public domain that breaks down a series of steps that you might find useful for Stay Training. You can download a copy from Bonus section of the K9aggression.com website. See the Bonus section in the book for the web address.

Caution: As important as it is to practice, don't let it get tedious. If you start to get bored, you will start to avoid practicing it.

TEACHING YOUR DOG TO DELAY GRATIFICATION

It is hard for dogs to contain themselves at certain times like meal times or when they want to go out. They are prefect opportunities to help your dog develop self-control.

When it is time to let your dog through any door, or have their dinner, your dog should wait until you tell him or her that it's ok to go through the door, or eat. This will take a little patience, but it is very easy to teach.

AT THE DOOR

Goal: The dog does not go through the door until you tell him or her to go through.

1. At the door, ask your dog to sit and wait.

2. Open the door a tiny crack. The moment your dog moves to get up, gently close the door.

3. If your dog remains sitting slowly open the door a little further, but the moment your dog moves to go toward or through the door, gently close it again.

4. Repeat this until you are able to open the door the full way and your dog remains sitting.

5. Let your dog out with a *release* word, ("Let's go" might work).

6. Going through the door is their natural reward. No treat necessary.

If your dog is food aggressive, skip the next training with dinner, as you might just want to put the food down in a separate room first before letting them in to eat. However, you can still practice waiting at the door or any other situations where you can teach them to wait or stay and delay their gratification.

WITH DINNER

Goal: The dog is able to remain seated with the dog bowl down in front of them until you say they can have it.

1. When feeding your dog's dinner, ask them to sit.

2. With the dog's dish in your hand, slowly start to put the dish down

3. The moment they get up from their sit, raise the bowl

4. If your dog remains in a sit, continue to put the dog bowl on the ground. Wait a moment before letting them have it.

WITH A TREAT

Goal: Your dog waits to be told they can have a treat in front of them.

1. Hold a treat in the palm of your hand.

2. The moment your dog goes for the treat, close your hand.

3. When your dog no longer tries to take the treat without you saying so, give them a cue to take it.

> **CAUTION**: Do not work with your dog doing *Targeted Behavior Modification* on a day when you are doing this training. He or she should absolutely not be provoked in any way with their triggers. They are more likely to behave aggressively after this work because working with self-control is very hard work and will temporarily deplete the resources needed to control their behavior. But remember, it's like exercising a muscle. Practice will improve their ability to control their behavior. This will translate in the ability to control their emotions and their attention to you when you ask.

Tips for your dog

- Expect your dog will become frustrated at times. This is natural. They may bark, paw at you, or get up and move around. If it is not too bothersome, let them do these things. If it is really bothersome, simply end the session and go into another room.

- Keep quiet outside except for the cues you give them.

- Let your dog have some physical free-time after this training.

- Practice this every opportunity you get, except for the days that you are doing *Targeted Behavior Modification*.

Tips for you

- Develop a schedule you will stick to for training. It will make it easier for you to commit to the training. It will also prevent you from over doing it with your dog.

- Make a plan so you know what to do in each session.

- Set a timer. Short frequent practice is better than less frequent longer sessions.

- Keep a journal – recording how your dog responds will not only prove to you that progress is happening, but it motivates you to pay attention to their behaviors. This added requirement helps make the work more interesting – and more like you are actually working on improving their behavior.

- Update interested people about your daily progress. Not only will this motivate others, but also the social aspect will help keep you motivated. Join a support group, or even write a blog!

- Reward yourself! You deserve it!

RELAXATION TRAINING OVERVIEW

Why is relaxation training necessary?

Unfortunately when people start to try *desensitization* or *counter conditioning*, they often don't recognize the signs of stress in their dog and have no idea their dogs are not relaxed at all. This leads to frustrating setbacks.

Relaxation is considered to be incompatible with aggression. If your dog can be cued to relax, he or she can't also be aggressive. If your dog can't relax, you risk further sensitizing your dog, rather than *desensitizing* your dog to the things that make him or her aggressive. This is one of the most common situations where people go wrong.

In people, *desensitization/counter conditioning* works by approaching the tiniest approximation of the thing that is threatening, and then using relaxation strategies to relax in the presence of that thing. Then, with dogs, we reward them usually with a small good treat (because it can be delivered easily and doesn't get them over-excited).

Dogs really don't know how to relax unless we create a situation where they can pay attention to this inner state. The best way to do this is through a form of clicker training and you may wish to have a trainer help you. There is a basic clicker training guide in the Bonus section of the website (see the Bonus section of the book for the web address). The click/reward process motivates them to pay attention to patterns so they can guess what is causing you to click/reward. But you can also do this without a click if you are right beside your dog, your treats are handy and your timing is good.

The good thing about relaxing is that it's actually self-rewarding; so combined with the treat, we got something going for us.

People often have trouble with knowing when their dog is actually relaxed unless they know what to look for and have train themselves to pay attention to it. Even experienced dog professionals are not always in agreement about how stressed a dog is or how he or she feels. It's even harder to the average dog owner. What does it mean for *your* dog to relax?

Working on training your dog how to relax has the added benefit of teaching you how to recognize when your dog is relaxed. Get this part right, train it well, and you set up your dog for success when it comes time for *Targeted Behavior Modification*.

How to apply

One of the best ways to teach your dog to relax is through *shaping*. Shaping is a process where you work towards an end result through a series of baby steps. It is best explained with an example that we will describe shortly. You can use clicker training if you are already familiar with it, but we would not advise to use it if you are new to it, only because it's a lot to be thinking about. You can read more about shaping in the section on *Behavior Modification Terms and Techniques* in Part 2 of the book.

The focus of this work is identifying any *transition* that indicates your dog is becoming further relaxed and rewards that transition.

During this work, it is not so much being able to *stay* relaxed, as it is *how* to relax. This process begins to make them aware of the relaxation process, and in time, how to make that happen at will. Through this work they will learn the following:

- **What it is specifically that you want them to repeat.** They will initially be more confused about exactly what they are doing that earns them a treat. That is because dogs can be action oriented. Even though they display outward signs, it may take a while for them to identify that what you are rewarding is the *transition* to a more relaxed state. Persist. If you are really having a tough time, wait until he or she is very tired, and start with a down stay instead of a sit.

- **What relaxation is.** Many people don't know what it feels like to be relaxed until someone helps them through it. I used to find I'd keep my shoulders just slightly raised, or my face tense – I wasn't even aware of it. When you learn to tense and relax your body, it helps you understand. But we can't do these exercises with our dogs; we need to set up an environment where it's most likely to happen and simply have to wait until they do it on their own. But once your dog understands what you want and how it *feels*, he or she will start to repeat it. It takes time, so you should relax too, and then watch and be patient.

FIRST - TEACHING YOUR DOG WHAT IT MEANS TO RELAX

Making them aware of the transition to a more relaxed state.

1. This step requires a LOT of patience, but it's super important so get comfortable. Work in a quiet area with no distractions.

   Have your dog sit-stay. Watch for, mark and reward any signs that indicate a *transition* to a more relaxed state. To mark use a clicker or a word – a quiet word might be better – just train this as you train them to respond to a clicker. If they become more alert at the mark/reward, that's ok. Just wait for them to settle again. Ideally you have been working on the stay training earlier, so this should not be too much of a problem. Don't do any other training besides the *SAW* program at this time to avoid any confusion.

   They will be confused at first. They will become alert to each treat they get, but they won't know what they are doing to get it at first. They may grow frustrated, so it's important you work when the dog is most likely to relax on their own, and that you catch each signal that they are growing more relaxed (examples to follow). Video record to analyze later.

   With good timing, enough consistency and exposure, they will start to see the patterns. In time, you will find they will start to lie down and relax on their own. But make sure you are rewarding for each *transition* to a more relaxed state. There will be times when you don't want them lying down, you only want them more relaxed than he or she is at the moment.

Examples of transitions:

1. Sitting

2. Cessation of whining, pawing, or any other activity designed to get your attention

3. Relaxing their ears – they may be shifted forward to pay attention to your next move, but eventually he or she will lose interest and their ears may relax – reward this. You might recognize this as boredom. But don't reward them for simply getting interested in something else.

4. Relaxing their face – look at their forehead and the way they hold their mouths and lips.

5. Shifting from a squat like sit position to sitting more relaxed on one hip or moving from a sit to lying down.

6. Shifting from a squat like lie-down position, to lying on their haunches or putting their head on the floor.

7. Loosening or un-tucking their legs or tail so they are farther out from the body from where they were tucked in.

8. Sighs.

9. Breathing slower. Look at their body to determine this.

10. Closing eyes.

11. Moving from lying down to flopping out on their side.

12. Un-tucking or loosening tail, paws or head away from their body while on their side lying down.

2. **Introduce the cue word:** When they seem to get it and understand what you want them to do and they are going through the transitions of relaxing fairly quickly, start using a cue word just prior to them transitioning. More than anything else you need to keep this exercise very consistent – always work in the same place and do the same thing at first, before you attach the cue word. Don't do any other new training. You want them to think every time you start this, he or she needs to relax.

Say your new cue word before you start the exercise, and if you can, before each transition to the next stage of relaxation. This is tricky; if all you can manage is to say it before the exercise starts, then you are one step ahead of the game. Again, remember, there will be times when you don't want them lying down; you only want them more relaxed than he or she is at the moment, so use the cue word before each transition and remember to continue to reward each transition to a more relaxed state.

Don't use the word "sit" or "down", or anything you have already established for these behaviors. Use something that you will think of easily, such as "relax", "calm", "easy", etc.

3. **Helping them generalize:** Once your dog is doing this reliably, you can create a plan to vary things so that they learn they should relax in a variety of situations. These include slightly changing one of the variables below, one at a time in small increments:

- How you say the cue word
- Location – move from different places in the room to different places in the home; work from the least challenging to the most challenging
- Your posture: hunch, squat, sit, stand, arms out, arms up, etc.
- While your dog is wearing a head halter, leash, and/or muzzle
- Different times of day; Start when he or she is at their most sleepy, and then try working when they are a little less ready to rest
- Different distances between you and your dog
- While you are doing different actions, such as moving your arms, moving from sitting to standing, or standing to sitting, walking around, talking, and so on
- Distractions: Try this when someone else (they trust) is in the room; when the TV is on; the curtains are open, etc.

4. **Moving it outside:** You eventually want to try this outside if your dog is likely to get aggressive outside of your home for any reason. This is going to be challenging. When you first try it, make sure your dog has had plenty of time to sniff around, absorb all the sounds of the area, is well exercised and tired out. Start the exercise inside near the door at first, and then while still in your home with the door open (on a secured leash of course!). If you live in an apartment building, you can start with your hallway. Lower your expectations about how much you want them to relax – having your dog lie down while outside may be impractical because they will feel unsafe if they are approached.

You will have a tougher time with wind. Wind has the result of blocking and confusing sound and smell, as well as causing a variety of things to move around.

Tips for your dog

- Initially start this work during a time when your dog is mostly likely to relax – this could be in the evening, after exercise, or before a nap. If necessary, keep notes of their rest patterns for a few days.
- Always make sure your dog is given the chance to succeed at this by being aware of any distractions in the environment.
- Be patient – this exercise is incredibly valuable, but also challenging. If you stay calm, this will help them.
- Once your dog is repeating this behavior reliably, only change one thing up – *slightly*. If your dog can't manage it, return to the previous step; wait until he or she is 80 – 90% successful before trying again. This time don't make the change so great.

Tips for you

- Don't get overwhelmed! Create a plan, but then only focus on what you can do today, one step at a time.
- Ensure your dog knows how to do long down-stays.
- Practice your own relaxation exercise when you do this – might as well, right? But there is a good reason for this – it will help you understand what your dog has to go through. But also, when it comes time for you to work with your dog's threats – you too will probably be a little stressed. In order to keep a clear mind and keep focused on your task, being able to relax when you choose will really help. Your dog is also sensitive to your body behavior – your relaxation can help them relax easier
- Use a video camera. Sometimes during the exercises the dog will get up or do something else unexpected. Let's see if you can predict when by reviewing the video footage and identifying what the dog is doing before that.
- Get comfortable when you are first teaching your dog this because it will take them some time to learn how to relax. Exercise balls are handy to sit on and move around. But as you practice this, you will eventually want to practice it sitting in various chairs, standing, and eventually when you are walking around.

SECOND – STAYING RELAXED

Dr. Karen Overall also has a useful relaxation protocol that your dog should be able to complete before doing *Targeted Behavior Modification* that you can not only use for the stay training, but for relaxation training as well. While the protocol does not specifically teach dogs what it means to self-relax, it does ask dogs to stay relaxed while sitting (or lying down if he or she wants) under different and changing conditions.

As these protocols are laid out in a step-by-step fashion, it is recommended you download these and complete this exercise. Because it can't be guaranteed that where these protocols are now on the web will still be there by the time you read this book, you can find a copy of these protocols on the K9aggression.com website for you to download. See the Bonus section in the book for the web address.

Benefits

Relaxation work is the magic ingredient that is key to reducing your dog's reactivity towards the things that have made them aggressive in the past. If your dog is unable to relax during *Targeted Behavior Modification*, then you will be unable to *desensitize* and *counter condition* your dog effectively.

> If your dog is unable to relax during *Targeted Behavior Modification*, then you will be unable to *desensitize* and *counter condition* your dog effectively.

But one of the most useful aspects about this work is that it will teach you to recognize *when* your dog is relaxed. This will go a LONG way towards helping you when you are doing *behavior modification*. You will know when your dog is relaxed and when they are not. If not you can get your dog out of the situation before the situation makes them worse or before they become aggressive.

This foundation work also operates on the principal that the relaxed state is part of the parasympathetic nervous system response. The *parasympathetic nervous system* response is the part of our system that is associated with stabilizing the mind and body and achieving a balanced condition.

This state is opposite to, and more or less incompatible with, the *sympathetic nervous system* (fight or flight) response, which is designed to be temporary and helps prepare us for the kind of emergencies that are threatening. This fight or flight state prepares our body to freeze, flee, or fight, both emotionally and physically, and is activated when we feel threatened.

When they can relax on cue, we can use this cue to communicate whether or not there is something to worry about when they are on the threshold of becoming concerned. However, it will also benefit them to look forward to something positive when they used to feel anxiety as well! If your dog is feeling dread or anxiety, he or she is in no mind to enjoy themselves which makes it virtually impossible to change their attitudes about the things that they are becoming aggressive about.

Practice might be boring, but essential

It is the practice that you will be challenged by more than anything else; so figure out a way you can stay in the game long term. *Overlearning* takes newly learned skills and masters them to the extent that the skill level is higher than the challenge level. *Overlearning* **helps improve performance in state of high arousal.** [72] This is exactly what we are looking for.

 INTRODUCING NOVELTY

At this stage in the system your dog has developed a stronger bond with you. Oxytocin has been produced, making them trust you more and reducing their aggression somewhat. You have been avoiding the things that have triggered them in the past so your dog is a calmer animal. You have created a system of communication that allows your dog to predict their environment better and understand what he or she needs to be doing at any one time. And, they have learned to respond to you better than ever now that you have changed their brain so that paying attention to you is important to them. They have learned what it means to relax, and will relax when you ask them to, in a variety of non-threatening situations. It's time to move to the next phase: introducing novelty.

Stress resistance

We need some novelty in our lives, but novelty can also be a *stressor*. Any new situation your dog encounters can set the stress response in action. So why do we want to stress our dogs out when we have spent all that effort in trying to reduce stress earlier?

Because, repeated exposure to *planned* and *expected stressors* may create resistance to stress.[73] Therefore, we want to develop a level of protection against stress before dealing with the dog's triggers directly. Offset the stress using these suggestions:

- Start off with the lowest intensity of novelty and eventually work up based on your dog's ability to adapt.
- Make the experience predictable.
- Give your dog as much control as you safely can to help them cope with the stress better (i.e. a long leash if possible; failing that, a loose leash).
- Use the relaxation exercises, but keep expectations low for how long he or she should be able relax to begin with.

Strengthening self-control: Reminder

Research indicates that maintaining self-control is mentally taxing. If we are mentally taxed, then we are less likely to be able to keep our cool. This is why parents tend to blow up at their kids at the end of a mentally demanding day. Studies have shown that when people have to prevent themselves from eating a delicious treat, they are more likely to give up on solving a puzzle, than they are if the treat is not there to have to resist. The ability to inhibit inappropriate behaviors in response to frustration or anxiety becomes compromised even when we know better.

However, as mentioned earlier, the ability to control ourselves acts like a muscle: the more we practice at it, the better we get at it. This is absolutely what we want to do for our dogs. We want our dog's abilities to be strengthened as much as possible *before* we start to work with their *stressors*. In time, when a behavior, practice, or habit is *overlearned*, it requires much less self-control.

Novelty: Breaking habits of thinking

The human brain comprises only 3% of the body, and yet consumes 20% of its energy. All brains require so many resources that it only adapts when it has to. If it's easier to follow the same neural pathways to send messages, it will. For this reason, it can be incredibly difficult to change perception and habits. That is where novelty comes in, too. Novelty causes new neurons to form in the brain. Novelty will kick start the brain's process to re-think and learn which is helpful to us at this stage. This is also a good way to challenge your dog's ability to relax without it being overly threatening to your dog. We need the ability to relax in different scenarios to be practiced again and again so that by the time we start *Targeted Behavior Modification*, the practice to calm on your cue will have become a habit for your dog.

TIP: Novelty, as a tool can be used in other ways. Should you find yourself in a situation where your dog becomes aggressive – do everything you can to interfere with the consolidation of the memory after the event happens by introducing them to a completely new situation as soon as you can. Memory consolidation occurs within minutes of an experience and can last several hours. Novelty and learning can help interfere with the memory formation of what just happened.

How to apply

On a schedule you can maintain, introduce your dog to a novel environment. Develop a predictable schedule so it will be planned and expected for your dog; this minimizes unneeded stress and helps them cope with the stress of novelty better. It will help to write a plan for this next phase, so it's easier for you to be consistent about it.

Communicate to your dog that a novel experience is going to occur.

Learn how to give your dog a series of predictable cues that a novel experience is about to happen. This could be anything that the dog is likely to notice, but it should not be the same as anything else. It can also be a combination of things.

Some suggestions

- A certain kind of treat you give them only used for this occasion
- A special smell you introduce to them
- A toy you bring with you in the car
- A sound you use (don't make this sound jarring)
- A behavior, such as walking around your car five times. OK, that might be excessive, but you get the picture!

Take your dog to a place he or she has never been before.

Start with something that is not too stimulating at first - you can even drive there if you wish and open the window for them at first for short period of times (always keeping in mind your first priorities: safety and avoiding triggers). All it needs to be is new. As you progress, there will be new sights, sounds, and smells for your dog to learn about.

Increase their time in the novel environment and try to allow as much freedom as safely possible to explore the environment. Try to reduce the effects of restraint if it's possible to do this safely. This is not always possible in an environment where a dog must be restrained; however, the restraint may undo the positive effects of the novel experience.

In rats, agonistic behavior (i.e. any social behavior that relates to fighting, including threats, retreats, etc.) increased in response to threat, but decreased in response to novelty with no restraint.[74]

Relaxation exercises

Ask your dog to sit, relax, and wait for your cue to go explore again. Anytime he or she is getting concerned or stressed about anything in the environment, call them and do the relaxation exercises. Release them to explore. Reminder: where possible and you can be sure your dog will not be a threat to anyone, allow freedom. If they are unable to relax, remove them from the situation and try again later in a less stimulating environment.

Recovery

There needs to be downtime to allow your dog to recover from the stress and absorb what they have learned. A return home to a quiet space may help.

Suggestions on locations to try:

- Agility training when there are no classes - let your dog explore the equipment if he or she is unfamiliar with agility.

- Rivers, lakes, and beaches
- Parking Lots
- School Yards
- Forests
- Fields
- Other people's homes, garages, and sheds
- Warehouses
- Abandoned buildings
- Garbage dumps, provided there is no food or toxic waste dumping, and be careful that there is no rotten food to get into
- Different areas of town or city

Suggestions on activities to try:

- Bring home different smells
- Play different sounds
- Train new behaviors, or play the clicker game, *101 things to do with a box*, except use different objects

TIP: Continue to use a camera if you can at all – either set up a camera on a tripod, or better yet, have a family member or friend help you out. This work will support your learning about your dog's ability to relax in a new environment. It will be very valuable when it comes time to working with your dog in the presence of their trigger.

TIP: Continue to work with the relaxation exercises. By the time you start introducing novelty, the relaxation exercises should be well learned and almost automatic. But if not, keep in mind that novelty will interfere with the memory formation of learning that may have just occurred prior to the novel experience. If you have recently taught your dog to do something just before the novel experience, he or she might not remember it as well as they would if they were in a familiar situation.

BLUEPRINT FOR TREATING DOG AGGRESSION

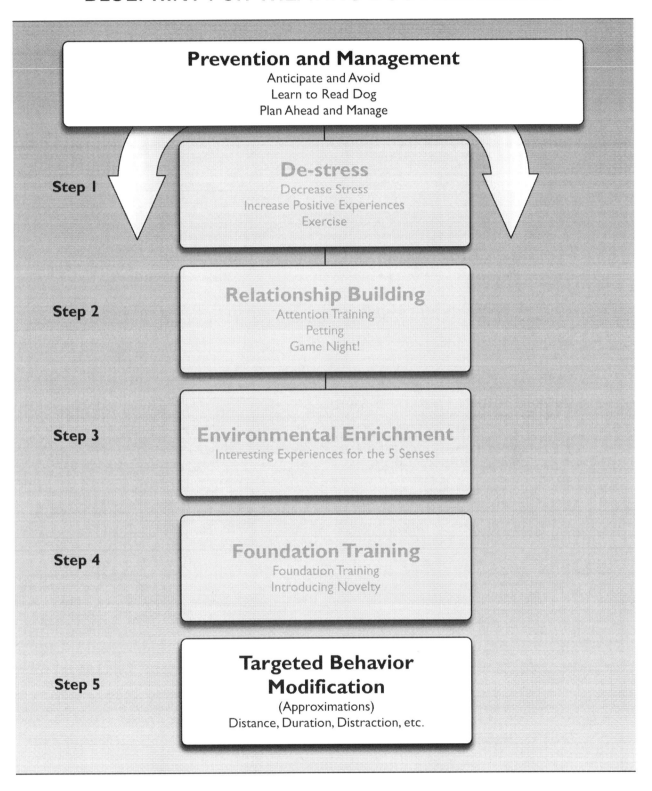

Prevention and Management
Anticipate and Avoid
Learn to Read Dog
Plan Ahead and Manage

Step 1

De-stress
Decrease Stress
Increase Positive Experiences
Exercise

Step 2

Relationship Building
Attention Training
Petting
Game Night!

Step 3

Environmental Enrichment
Interesting Experiences for the 5 Senses

Step 4

Foundation Training
Foundation Training
Introducing Novelty

Step 5

Targeted Behavior Modification
(Approximations)
Distance, Duration, Distraction, etc.

STEP 5 – **Goals:**

Change your dog's attitude and responses to the situations and circumstances that caused the aggression to occur through systematic *Targeted Behavior Modification.* This step depends on your ability to read and interpret dog behavior (see management and prevention) as well as the completion of Steps 1, 2 and 4.

Behavior modification is a big scary phrase for changing or altering problematic behavior using a systematic approach, which we have been doing the whole way along. But essentially the tactics that involve dealing with a direct target – as in any likeness of the actual situation (*stressor*) that causes the aggression to happen, we will call *Targeted Behavior Modification*.

Blinded by science?

There are several techniques and phrases people like to use when referring to *behavior modification*, which we explain in detail in Part Two of the book. Unfortunately complicated and unfamiliar words can have a way of both confusing you and making material difficult to remember. Some professionals take advantage of jargon to help convince dog owners that the professional is an authority on the subject. Jargon can also cause dog owners to feel insecure about their own knowledge. This can cause dog owners to be less clear-headed.

It helps to be familiar with these terms, so you can be more knowledgeable whenever you are talking to other people, such as other dog owners or professionals you might want to consult. It also will help you understand how these techniques work. We explain some of the terms in this section, but consult the second part of the book where we demystify the common terms for you. It's not too hard to understand.

There are two main approaches to behavior modification that may help your dog: *Classical conditioning* and *desensitization/counter conditioning*. Most lay people who haven't learned the difference attempt to use *classical conditioning* with the idea that what they are actually doing is *desensitization/counter conditioning*. It is important to understand the difference and when to use.

CLASSICAL CONDITIONING

The most common understanding of *Classical conditioning* is that it links something neutral with something else that causes a reflex. A classic example is how the sound of a can opener, or the sound of a kibble bag causes a dog to salivate because the sound predicts that food will come. The first time a dog hears a can opener, it means nothing to him or her. The salivating is a reflex in that it is an **automatic unlearned reaction to a stimulus**. People sometimes think that classical conditioning can be used to make a dog "like" strangers or other dogs. It usually doesn't work like this when a dog has aggressive tendencies towards them.

Classical conditioning may help to lower arousal IF used properly. It may help avoid the onset or escalation of the fight or flight response, which as mentioned earlier, is part of the nervous system that gets activated when we perceive a threat. The technique makes use of the body's physiology and does *not* provide the dog with a way to cope. However, it may lower arousal enough that it becomes possible to then *desensitize* and *counter condition*.

Classical Conditioning: How to apply

The essential concept is to give a treat immediately after an occurrence enough times that the occurrence comes to predict the treat in the mind of the dog. If the dog is actually salivating, their *parasympathetic nervous system* is engaged. This system is thought to be incompatible with the *sympathetic nervous system* response (the response that gets engaged when a dog becomes aggressive).

Unfortunately, many people complain that when their dog sees the threatening dog or person, they won't take a treat. Of course they won't: they are too stressed. By the time that dog is that stressed it's too late. Even if they do take the treat, it doesn't mean that they are comfortable with the target of their aggression. Dogs can be undecided or uncertain even when accepting treats.

However, the technique can be used when something consistently occurs just before the threatening thing happens; the way a doorbell always signifies that there is someone at the door. The doorbell is neutral. It is not threatening to a dog that is aggressive towards people who enter the home. Instead, the doorbell signals that the threat is coming and this sets off the dog's nervous system response

> A dog can be ambivalent about the person he or she takes a treat from.

to threat. Therefor the technique is to give the treat at the sound of the doorbell repeatedly *without* having anyone come in.

This way it may be possible to lower the dog's arousal and engage the *parasympathetic nervous system* response. If a dog is given a treat too late when anxiety is in full-force, it will have virtually no effect. The dog either eats it mindlessly, doesn't appear to enjoy it, or he or she simply won't take (or notice) the treat.

In this scenario, the best way to handle this is simply have someone ring the bell, and someone gives the dog the high value treat *regardless* of how the dog is behaving. Several repetitions of this technique are necessary to make the change, upwards to several times a day for a month. In this case, you may have only reduced reactivity, but not eliminated it, nor have you changed his attitudes towards the actual threatening thing. But at least the dog is not going ballistic at the door, and you may be able to try *desensitizing* and *counter conditioning*.

Challenges

The most difficult part for people is to realize that in *Classical conditioning* the dog does not need to do *anything*. *Classical conditioning* is largely subconscious learning. Many of us get stuck into the idea that the dog needs to be *good* to get the treat, but this is known as *operant conditioning*, and the circumstances must be

> *Classical conditioning* is primarily subconscious learning. The dog does not do anything to earn the treat.

different for this to work. *Counter conditioning* which we will explain in a moment relies on *operant conditioning*. If you get stuck on the idea that your dog must behave in a certain way to earn his or her treat, then you may lose the advantages *Classical conditioning* has to offer.

If you are one of those people who struggle with this concept, have a quick look at the definitions between the different types of conditioning (training). There is *Classical* (or *Pavlovian*), *operant* (or *instrumental*), and *counter conditioning*. Reading the definitions may help you understand the difference and why trying to force a sit, or get the dog to do something will defeat your purpose, and how you will not make any headway because the treat comes too late for the wrong reason. Once the reactivity is lowered, then you might start asking for a behavior to earn the treat.

Classical conditioning can only go so far. The fact that your dog can take a treat does not mean your dog is associating good things with the target of his or her aggression. This is another common area where people get it wrong which is why I am repeating it. Your dog can be in conflict: want the treat but still not like the person or dog. The treat may just be serving as a distracter. But the illusion that the dog must like the person or dog because they are taking treats from them, causes some people to think their dog is safer than they actually are.

Nor does *Classical conditioning* teach a dog to do something that is incompatible with aggression. This is why we need to do *desensitization* and *counter conditioning*.

But in some cases, even when you have done all your homework in the foundation *behavior modification* exercises, you can't make any headway with *counter conditioning*. This may be because you can't achieve the distance you need, or find some way to reduce the intensity of either the threat or the things signally the threat is on its way. In this case, *classical conditioning may* be the only technique that will make *desensitization/counter conditioning* possible.

Regardless, at some point we need to provide the dogs with a new way to cope. *Classical conditioning* can't do that for us; it can only be part of it. But in order to *counter condition* – that is, train the dog to do a set of incompatible behaviors such as relax, he or she must learn the set of behavior patterns that is incompatible with aggression in the previous step (Step 4) *before* we get to the *desensitization/counter condi*tioning part. Because if your dog can't relax in non-threatening situations, how can they learn to relax and learn do something – *want* to do something - other than behave aggressively?

Ensure you have done the previous steps before moving to *desensitization/counter condi*tioning in order to give your dog every opportunity to succeed.

DESENSITIZATION AND COUNTER CONDITIONING

Desensitization is the process where your dog becomes less sensitive, and therefore less anxious about the target of his or her aggression, which means they are less likely to behave aggressively. *Counter conditioning* teaches him or her an alterative way to behave in a way that is incompatible with aggression. *Desensitization* and *Counter conditioning* often occur at the same time.

The essential practice is that the dog is rewarded for sitting and remaining calm and relaxed when in the presence of or a likeness of his or her *stressor* by starting with the least threatening scenarios, and gradually increasing the challenge.

Challenges

It is essential the dog remains relaxed. If your dog becomes anxious you risk further *sensitizing* your dog to the threat. There are a number of things that can cause people to make mistakes that you should be aware of

- Dog handler does not anticipate or consider other circumstances or occurrences that have either added or will add to the dog's stress load.

- People don't always recognize their dog is anxious because
  o They are distracted from paying attention to the situation
  o They are thinking about too many things (i.e. leash, treats, emergency response plan, approach of target. etc.)
  o Have not done the foundation work adequately.

Avoid the anxiety

It is critical that you do not expose your dog to their *stressors* in a way that makes them anxious or aggressive. You will need to be practiced in recognizing when your dog is relaxed and when they are experiencing stress.

Neurons that fire together wire together, neurons that fail to sync, fail to link

Neurons that fire together wire together means that when a dog is feeling anxious and they are around their *stressor* (the thing that causes the aggression), these two things will become completely linked. It's like a coalition in the brain that forms. This coalition becomes very effective and fast and more or less, bullies out other neuron coalitions.

There is another saying by neuroscientists that is *neurons that fail to sync fail to link.* We don't want our dogs to link the site and circumstances of the trigger with their anxiety/aggression process any further.

That means every time your dog experiences that trigger and he or she gets anxious, we must *interrupt* the anxiety, and then ensure that we don't cause them to be anxious next time.

> *Neurons that fire together wire together, neurons that fail to sync, fail to link.*

While dogs will never forget their fears, we can weaken the link between the *stressor* and the anxiety/aggressive sequence to allow different processes, better coping skills, and better responses to develop. While we know it can be hard to break an old bad habit, we don't realize how much harder it is to replace the bad habit with a good one. The good habit would be far easier to develop if the bad habit had never been established to compete.

On the other hand, when we don't use those old neural pathways, other neural networks get stronger and will dominate.

RISKS

Unfortunately in times of stress and strong emotions, the amygdala in the brain will hijack our rational cognitive processes. So we have to accept that while our dog may appear to be cured, we will always live with the risk that under times of duress, our dog might resort to old habits.

Others cannot be put at risk during *Targeted Behavior Modification.*

You should use more than one safety measure, including gates, head halters or muzzles, unbreakable leashes, and/or reliable collars that are checked every time they are put on and properly fitted. You must also safeguard the wellbeing of any subject that is helping you, people or other animals. Ensure you have an *Emergency Response Plan* in place and any tools you need. If any aggression or emergency occurs, you may not be able to think of what to do because your fight or flight response kicks in. So prepare now.

Without the foundation training, not only will your dog's ability to overcome their aggressive response largely be compromised, you actually risking making the dog worse.

Desensitization and Counter Conditioning: how to apply

It is highly recommended you consult a qualified expert in dog behavior for this part of the program, because if not done properly, you can lead your dog into an aggressive situation or make the anxiety/aggression worse. The reason for this is often because dog owners are not trained enough to stay in tune with how relaxed or anxious their dog is.

Not only will they be able to help determine what are truly the issues, a qualified expert will also know exactly what to look out for, what to avoid, how fast or slow you should progress through this part, or what you may need to adapt for more success. They can offer you advice on how to plan the program and how to conduct it, as well as what you can improve on. This is important, because there may be several things to be thinking about at once. However, if you have done your homework, this should be a smoother process for you.

SET-UP

1. **Reserve the day.** We advise that you do not do any other training besides your regular *SAW* or deference program on the day. We want to use all your dog's brain resources for dealing with this part.

2. **Plan approximations of the situation the dog becomes aggressive about to start with.** Your professional will help you find the least threatening likeness of their *stressor*. Some examples:

   a. If your dog is toy aggressive, work with an object he or she doesn't care much about.
   b. If your dog is afraid of strangers, work with a family member he or she is not afraid of.
   c. If your dog is worried about you when you raise your hand, only move your hand a little.
   d. If it's a door knock or door bell ring, try using a recording of the door knocking or bell and play at the quietest level.

3. **Find the right distance or duration.** While paying attention to any other distracters in the area, your professional can help you to find the *distance* between the place where you dog is not concerned about their *stressor* (the thing that causes the anxiety or aggression), and the spot where he or she starts to pay attention. It might be 10 feet, it might be less or it might be more. If you can remember some of the situations from your history, use that as your guide. Keep in mind, this distance may vary from day to day depending on:
   a. Brain resources available. If your dog has been holding him or herself together, is performing a behavior consciously (opposed to performing a behavior automatically), or is using any kind of self-control, he or she will have fewer resources available to control their emotions and behaviors.

b. Your dog's overall stress load.

c. Other distracters in the area (this can be other people, animals, sounds, smells, movement, etc.)

At this distance your dog should not be getting upset. Even if you think that they are not making any progress because they are not reacting – that's what we want. Any practice at all will *always* be helpful. If your dog is unable to keep him or herself together, immediately break their focus, use your body in a bouncy, quick way to lead them farther away, and play, or if he or she can manage, sit for a treat. Immediately interrupting the anxiety is critical.

OR

If you can't find a distance either because your dog is reactive from any distance or there is no space, then your professional will help you to find a way to minimize the *duration*. An example for a dog who is aggressive towards strangers: Put you and your dog in a room, have someone quickly walk by the door so your dog only sees that person briefly.

You should know how to read your dog's subtle signs of anxiety and your professional can help you with this. Review the section on reading your dog's cues, and consider investing in a video camera in order to help you learn faster and have someone record for you.

You MUST be able to read these signs, otherwise allowing your dog to become and stay anxious you risk making the problem worse. Get fluent with these signs, so that you can read them without spending much conscious thought interpreting – because you mind is going to be on other things.

PRACTICE

1. Get your dog's attention and your dog to sit, wait and give them the cue to relax if needed. Reward them for staying calm!   If your dog does not respond to treats in general, your professional will help you find the right treats, change how you feed the treats (typically the treats should be raisin-sized, but can depend on the size/type of the dog) or find different rewards, but food is generally recommended.

2. Wait until your dog notices the target. As soon as he or she looks at it, reward them!   Your dog should be still relaxed: you are looking for openness, relaxed gaze and absence of stress signals. If not, and your dog doesn't respond to your cue word to relax, then the intensity of the trigger you are using is too strong.   In that case, use a less threatening likeness of the trigger, increase the distance between your dog and the trigger, or reduce the duration. If your dog still cannot manage this, return to the foundation training and work with more distractions until he or she is ready.

3. After your dog has had their treat, wait until they look over at their trigger again, and reward. Repeat several times.

4. Release them from a sit, *increasing* the distance slightly and if your dog likes and he or she doesn't get revved up or hyper - play for a short period of time if your professional recommends this. You may find this tends to be distracting. But you or they may also want to ease any tension that your dog may be feeling and continue the positive feelings.

5. Change *one* element *slightly*. Your professional will help you to determine how and when to do this. Here are some examples:

    a. Make the trigger object just slightly more like the real thing, **or**

b. Decrease the distance slightly, **or**
c. Increase the duration slightly, **or**
d. Change the location slightly, **or**
e. Change your voice or body positioning **or**
f. Increase or add a distraction (this is probably the last thing should work on in your program)

6. Make the situation just slightly more challenging and repeat. Your professional can help you determine how to do this. If your dog cannot tolerate the change, you may be making too big of a change, or perhaps have worked too long. Go back to the previous step where he or she can be successful and minimize the change. If they become reactive, then stop the session. Use the *Emergency Response Plan* detailed in the management section.

7. Don't work too long, but work frequently. Over-learning is critical! Make sure you give yourself and your dog every opportunity to establish some good habits. You want the experience to be fun and rewarding for you. You don't want to be burned out. If you are experiencing problems or feeling overwhelmed, contact your professional for help. You will want to respect your professional's time, but if you need help, reach out. If they are unable to help you directly, they may be able to recommend someone who can. A support group can also help if you are feeling overwhelmed.

8. You can also ask your dog to perform the tricks you taught them in Step 2 between exercises to keep both of you from getting bored. End each session on a success! Repeat, repeat, repeat!

Dogs need more breaks than we realize. Learning and practicing is tiring. Don't work until your dog makes a mistake. It is always better to work for too short of a time, than too long. Creating a plan on paper can help you to avoid pushing for more than you should.

Trouble shooting

If your dog overreacts, you may have done too much too soon.

If you are stuck at the foundation stage, you've put in the time and effort and he or she is still unable to relax even around non-threatening distractions after more than a couple of months (or at least the equivalent of training 30 to 60 consecutive training days approximately 20 – 30 minutes a day), then your dog may have a biochemical reason for staying hyper-vigilant. In this case, consult a veterinary behaviorist to determine if your dog needs medication to deal with this issue first.

Contact your professional if you need help or encounter a snag. They may be able to help you directly, or recommend someone who can work with you.

Your professional may recommend using something other than food treats. If so, find out why. Treats are the most commonly used rewards for this kind of work. Food treats are quick to give and rewarding. But if food is just not powerful enough, there may a reason for it.

For example, your dog may actually be too anxious and no one is recognizing it. If so, move to a greater distance or work with a less threatening target. It's also possible the dog is not interested in the food choice itself (so if they don't like freeze-dried liver, try cooked chicken or cheese for example). The dog may also not be that hungry. Try feeding the dog less food in general.

Be aware of the trainer who resists the use of food. They may feel the dog should work for praise, petting, play, or other rewards. That is okay for behaviors that have been well learned and are now being practiced, or in addition to food rewards. Make sure you understand exactly why, and do your due diligence to make sure your professional really knows what they are doing.

Generally with this work, food is always more desirable because it capitalizes on the *parasympathetic nervous system* response that is associated with appetite. Again, this system is more or less in opposition to the *sympathetic nervous system*, which is concerned with the freeze, fight, or flight response.

As mentioned earlier, the fight or flight system prepares the body to be ready to handle conflict. The heart rate increases, blood pressure goes up, the immune system is activated, and different chemicals are released to produce emotions that encourage the person or dog to take action. We have less appetite at this time.

How long should this take?

The brain can change very quickly, but these changes are vulnerable, and it takes regular practice and time for certain changes to become solid.

Assuming your dog does not need medication, or is on medication that is the right kind and dose, you should see change within 30 days if you are doing everything correctly by:

- Avoiding the circumstances causes the aggression except during Targeted Behavior Modification
- Ensuring the foundation behaviors have become habit, and can be performed in a variety of situations with a number of distractions. Remember the cliché: we need to learn how to crawl before we can walk.
- Working with your dog regularly – several times a week if possible for short periods
- Not pushing your dog too far or too fast in the program where he or she is allowed to become anxious.

In a study that got people to cut off their sight completely through the use of blindfolds, changes in the brain occurred in as little as two days. Their abilities to sense through sound and touch became highly sensitive. The visual areas of the brain became used for touch and sound since there was an increased need to get the same kind of information (such as judging space) normally received from the visual system. However, this change did not occur if there was *any* kind of light because the visual areas in the brain are so strong, they would rather process visual information than sound or touch.

After the blindfolds were removed, the participants had a difficult time seeing and judging space. Nevertheless, after 5 days of being blind folded it only took 12 to 24 hours for their brains to return to their previous states.

So change can happen relatively quickly provided there is the incentive to change and consistency with the practice and the incentives. However, it takes much longer before that learned behavior no longer requires self-control and becomes habit. The speed with which this occurs is hugely variable. One study in humans indicates between 18 and 254 days. Habits that replace old ones are much harder to establish because the brain wants to rely on what is already automatic and any opportunity to revert to the old habit, it will.

However, if you are not seeing any change within 30 consecutive training days for about 20 to 30 minutes each day, *and* you are managing to avoid the circumstances that cause the aggression every time except when you are out working with them, *and* within that time, you have not pushed your dog to the point where he or she is becoming stressed and anxious, then it's time to visit a veterinary behaviorist.

Many dogs can't manage 20 to 30 minutes of non-stop training. You are better off working for shorter sessions a few times a day and vary it up during sessions if possible. If your dog is starting to seem less responsive or attentive during a session then it is time to stop because your dog may have had enough. Make note of the time and aim to work for a shorter period next time.

Skipping a day is fine, too. However the above guideline about not seeing change is to discourage people from working months without making progress. To work for so long without seeing any improvement can be very frustrating and needlessly puts stress on the both of you. If you are not seeing improvement, you need help.

TIPS

- **Make sure you are practiced at looking for clues of anxiety.** One of the main reasons why *behavior modification* is not successful is because the dog handler is missing clues that the dog is anxious. Always remember that a dog can be feeling ambivalent even when he or she is taking treats.

- **Use high value rewards for each baby-step that has just been accomplished.** Once the dog has acquired the skill, then you can use lower value rewards to maintain it. In time when the behavior is well learned, you can make the rewards intermittent without patterns.

- **The dog should be rewarded immediately.** The clicker-training model can help with this, but timing is important. If not using clicker training, make sure you reward the dog immediately for them to connect the target, the relaxed state and the reward.

- *Overlearn*: Because we never lose our fear memories, it's possible these memories can come up any time especially when the prefrontal cortex in the brain is occupied with other tasks. However, *overlearning* means that we are learning something to the extent that it becomes largely unconscious and automatic.

  This means that despite the fact our dog may be doing well under certain circumstances, we should continue to develop those positive associations over and over again. Even more importantly, develop these associations in a variety of situations.

- **Work at a greater distance than usual, and for shorter periods of time in new situations.** Be aware that novel situations will cause your dog to be thinking about the novel environment. Your dog will not perform as well in new situations.

- **Make sure your foundation training is strong.** Most times when *desensitization* and *counter conditioning* fails, it's because the foundation training is simply not strong enough. Resist moving to the next step before your dog is really ready.

- **Make sure your *Emergency Cues* are regularly practiced**. If you are ambushed, you will be able to quickly redirect your dog from focusing on their *stressor* with anxiety.

- **When in doubt of a situation, get out of it.** Too many times, we ignore our instincts. You won't do any harm by misreading a situation and removing your dog from it. But all too often, people keep working with their dog when the dog is too stressed, and this actually causes your dog to feel more anxious and furthermore, practices all the things we are trying to change.

- **If you or your dog is bored, change things up or just stop.** If we want to establish new habits, we are in this for the long haul. That means we have to keep the experience fun and pleasurable for both the dog and us.

- **Don't overdo it.** Your dog will become bored and unresponsive under the best of circumstances if it goes on too long. Removing your dog from a situation before it becomes a problem is never a problem.

- **Don't train just before a *Targeted Behavior Modification* session.** When you are ready to work with a dog's triggers, don't tax their mental abilities beforehand. A study that looked at drug detection dogs showed an increase in shyness with a stranger after training in all of the dogs. [75] Nearly any task that involves some form of holding back or self-control will make aggression much more likely to happen immediately after. [76]

  The reason for this is the resources that fuel cognition can be temporarily depleted when involved in mentally taxing activities. When this happens, it becomes much harder to control emotions and behavior.

- **Let your dog rest after a successful session.** Encoding learning to memory (consolidation) happens over time. The more you do after learning, the more likely you will forget it, because the new experiences interfere with the previous ones, especially when the situations are similar or the experiences that come after are novel or emotional.

- **Keep your game face on.** As said earlier in the book: dogs can read our facial expressions, and respond most significantly to joy and anger. Adult dogs in particular avoid anger and pay attention to fear. They can also interpret our tone of voice[77]. If dogs can understand these subtle cues, they probably have learned to read us in other ways too – such as how fast we are breathing and what we are doing to the leash. So keep your mind space positive. Relax! Stay jolly!

- **Head-halters** are very similar to what horses wear. The Gentle Leader is one of the most well known head-halters on the market and was invented by a veterinary behaviorist. When used properly, they can be a super valuable tool to have for many dogs, especially those large and powerful breeds. It does not prevent biting like the muzzle does, but it can give a relatively small person a great deal of control to manage pulling or lunging, and manage where the head and mouth is going (where the teeth happen to be!). In many cases, simply wearing the head halter helps calm the dog.

  To use them properly, the neck strap (and not nose strap) should be quite tight above their throat and the handler should aim to walk them on a loose leash and avoid having the dog pulling on the leash ahead of the handler. There are several different ways to teach dogs to walk on a loose leash. Seek help from a force-free trainer if you are having troubles.

  While dogs should be *desensitized* to head-halters, they may rub to get them off: this may be more a tickling or sensitivity response to the halter. You can download a step-by-step guide written by a veterinary behaviorist on how to both desensitize and train your dog to wear a head halter or muzzle from the K9aggression.com website. Again, you can find the link to the web page to download the files in the Bonus section of this book. This step-by-step process helps desensitize your dog to the halter and has them wanting to put it on. It is amazing to see your dog actually poke his or her nose into it all on their own!

Research indicates that dogs are not physiologically stressed wearing them despite nose pawing, and dogs will gradually adjust.[78] In fact, as mentioned earlier, may have a calming effect on dogs at times. Don't use them when running with your dog in high heat however; although the dogs can open their mouths (and bite, too), they may not be able to open them wide enough to pant when really hot.

- **Hands-off t-shirt for dogs.** Often dog owners report frustration that people refuse to listen when they ask them to stay away from their dog. It is particularly difficult when your dog is acting well behaved to keep people from touching your dog. So we had a t-shirt for dogs to wear that has a "hands off" sign on it to help communicate to people that they should not approach your dog. It can be purchased through the K9aggression.com website.

- **Find support.** We can keep these sessions short and fun, and keep a log of progress to remind ourselves we are making progress, but we often need outside help or support to keep us motivated.

  Sometimes we feel like no one else understands or we get discouraged because of setbacks. If you can find a friend or family member to help with the sessions, this can really help you in the long run. Otherwise, perhaps your professional can help you with support, or can recommend someone who can.

  We also set up a Yahoo group almost a decade ago for just this – a place people to share their experiences, both good and bad. Some of them have formed groups with others to help with training in the real world. An extra pair of hands and eyes can help.

The following diagrams demonstrate how any action might be broken down into small steps as a way to allow a dog to gradually adjust and accept a situation. The amount that an action is broken down depends on your dog. But you don't lose anything by breaking them down in the smallest amount possible.

HELPING A DOG GET COMFORTABLE WITH BEING TOUCHED ON THE HEAD

Many dogs do not like being petted on the top of the head, (especially smaller dogs who have to worry about being stepped on or run into by humans). Some learn how to enjoy it, but many just tolerate it. It's amazing how many dogs will move their head just before contact, move off to something else, or put up with, but show their stress by licking their lips or yawning. Regardless petting on the head is something most people simply cannot resist doing to dogs.

This can lead to irritation or anxiousness the moment someone reaches for them whether it is to pet them or simply to attach a leash to a collar and this can add to the dog's stress load. Therefor it's a good idea to get your dog comfortable with being touched and petted on the head.

Here is an example of getting a dog used to someone touching him or her on the head. In this case, the person can reach just a little toward the dog, and then toss them a treat and return to their regular standing position with their arm by their side. Repeat this until the dog gets comfortable before moving to the next step. Change up a little. In this case we have broken the process down into 4 steps.

In some cases, you might find that a dog tolerates things to a certain point, but you just can't seem to make it to the next step. When this happens go back to the place where the dog was comfortable and try again. The next time you change anything try make the change much smaller. You might find that you need many more steps as illustrated in the next example. That's ok. You need to find what works for your dog.

HELPING A DOG GET COMFORTABLE WITH A HUMAN RAISING HIS HAND UP

Dogs don't naturally raise their limbs over their hands the way people do. So it is not uncommon for dogs to flinch when someone raise a hand. It is not always because the dog has been abused; it just makes some dogs nervous.

In this situation, the person gets the dog's attention and raises his arm just a little. When the dog remains relaxed, you can reward the dog with a treat.

Note that there are more "steps" in this shaping illustration than the previous one. The number of steps needed depends on your dog. Some dogs generalize more than others.

Question: Is it necessary to start off with such a tiny movement? It depends on your dog's comfort level. But starting off easy will certainly not do any harm. When the dog is comfortable with each movement, you can move to the next step.

 ## MOTIVATION

Although, different types of dog aggression have been categorized on K9aggression.com, the reality is that there is no real agreement about categories of aggression. Classifications by four different veterinary behaviorists were shown to be different from each other.

The most difficult aspect is in determining why the dog is behaving aggressively. While it is not always essential to understand exactly why the dog is behaving the way they are, (if you can teach the dog how to relax, and provide them with a better, healthier way to cope and behave), understanding motivation can be essential understanding in where else the dangers lie, how to manage around that, and understanding what course of action to take.

For example, here are some varying motivations for a dog that growls at their owners while in their crate.

Impulse control aggression or owner directed aggression

This is a dog that growls at their owners or a specific person in the family in situations where there is ambiguity about control. It's possible the dog feels more secure when they are in their crate, causing them to growl when ordinarily he or she would not be confident enough to challenge. In this case, the work is between the dog and the owner and the crate may be incidental to the extent that a communication system has been set up to reduce confusion and anxiety. In this case the dog needs understands what they need to be doing in response to cues, and learns how to relax.

Alternatively, he or she actually feels anxious about being trapped in a confined space and this makes the problem worse. In this case, it's best to confine the dog when necessary in a manner that does not cause the dog to feel trapped and anxious. More below.

Concern: A dog who has this kind of aggression may develop aggression or react in other situations where control is an issue, such as when the dog is reached for, collared and leashed, stepped over, scolded, pushed or shoved or forced somewhere, etc.

★ *Has territorial aggression*

This is a dog that is defending their space because he or she sees a threat where there is none. After following through with the foundation protocols, it may be possible to teach the dog to react differently the cues that had previously set off the aggression. Removing the crate may or may not influence whether or not he or she chooses to defend an area. However to minimize anxiety and aggression, they should be kept in areas that are considered of low value (i.e. a spare bedroom opposed to the bedrooms where the family member sleeps.

Concern: A dog that displays territorial aggression may develop territorial aggression or even possession aggression in other circumstances. A dog that is territorial towards their owners is likely to be more territorial when it comes to strangers. Territorial aggression can develop even further when the dog is left out in the back yard or behind fences.

★ *Has anxiety about being in the crate*

This dog may have negative associations with being in the crate. Having the dog sleep elsewhere may be preferable. Or, he or she may be claustrophobic in the crate or suffered from deprivation on the past. Either way, the use of the crate should be discontinued.

Concern: This dog may have issues in any situation where they are confined or perceived as being trapped. Cars may be an issue, as being leashed might.

★ *Fear aggression*

This dog is behaving aggressively as a way to keep people or animals away. There are usually related postures that go along with fear aggression, such as their ears being pulled back, a lowered *slinking* overall body posture, and the tail might be tucked in. The fear is likely related to the target of their aggression. As with impulse control the crate may give the dog a little more confidence, *or* more anxiety. This dog might startle easily, and this may occur more often when he or she is resting specially when they are in the crate.

Concern: Fearful dogs are more likely to behave aggressively if they feel cornered. Crates can make this worse, as being under a table, chair, or blanket; in a car; on a leash where the owner has used leash corrections or has not let the dog back away when fearful; or literally cornered.

So these are some examples how motivation can be different for a given situation. Context and history is important. In addition dogs often show more than one type of aggression.

In the case of aggression towards other dogs, the situation can be even more challenging because the social interaction is often quite mysterious to humans. Most certainly, we are not nearly as skilled at being present in the moment and tuned into the physical aspects of dog behavior as dogs are.

What we are good at is *theory of mind*, which allows us to imagine what is going on for people. We instinctively know that relying on words alone will only get us so far. We are attuned to recognizing the subtleties of sarcasm and humor, when people are protecting themselves with lies and half-truths, or who is assigned higher status and who actually earns it. We spend a lot of mental energy in assessing this on a continual basis and it is very fluid and entirely depends on context. While some of us are more skilled at it than others, the reality is most of us are highly skilled – we have to be, it's part of being socially comfortable and socially accepted. Any deviations from social norms causes us to feel threatened because we can no longer trust the person will behave in acceptable, and therefore safe, ways. Our social rules and manners foster trust.

But one of the biggest challenges in aggression towards strange dogs is that not only can we not control the trigger dog – the dog that is stressing them out – but also we are not very capable of reading the behavior of those dogs ourselves. On top of which, we can't expect to have a clue about any olfactory clues (clues involving scent and smell) that may be involved.

That said, while your dog may never fit in at the dog park, he or she also might not want to be at the dog park. Removing that burden may be a relief for them. While your dog may never really figure other dogs out, they can learn how to take their cues from you about how they should be behaving.

One of my dogs used to only react to certain dogs. She seemed to be able to tell something about certain dogs from a large distance away and would start to become concerned. It wasn't with all dogs, but dogs that were particularly rambunctious she seemed to have problems with. To my eyes, when my dog started to get concerned, the other dog seemed to be walking quite calmly on their leash. But by the time the dog got closer, it would start to react to mine: pulling, jumping around, barking, etc. at the end of the leash. I always wondered – how does she know? And what was I missing?

In the case of aggression towards people, how much is a result of confusion around social status, frustration, anxiety or fear? If your dog experiences anxiety or fear; is it a result of confusion about what is expected from the social interaction; fear of being hurt; fear of being rejected (if dogs feel that) or left alone, or is it a result of generalized anxiety? It can be complicated.

Other elements can be chained to an anxiety/aggression sequence

It's important to remember that the stress-anxiety-aggression sequence usually requires very little *practice* to get encoded into memory. It simply does not serve us well to have the same kind of dangerous situation happen again and again before we learn how to predict it will happen. The fact that we learn very quickly under fearful or traumatic situations would have helped to keep us alive.

Anything that may serve to predict that danger is around the corner will get encoded. Have you ever been in a car that has hit a car in front of you, where someone applied breaks just before you hit? If so, you will find that in any situation where there is a car in front of you and the breaks are being applied a little more quickly than usual, it will cause the same kind of fear response that ordinarily would not have fazed you before the accident.

This means that our very presence and behaviors can be linked to an aggressive sequence for dogs – before the aggression occurs. Unfortunately we don't always recognize that our dog is anxious, or when. Instead, we pull up on the leash, or leash pop (short sharp yank), or perhaps scold, push etc. In time, these things can trigger the sequence starting if there are enough other cues (i.e. you are in the park, there is a strange dog near, etc.).

 # REDIRECTED AGGRESSION

Other complications are that sometimes dogs will redirect their aggression. Think of the days when you have had a hard day at work because your boss chewed you out for something, or perhaps your kids have been pushing your buttons all day, or someone was rude to you. Sometimes you end up being a little snappy towards your family or friend when they had nothing to do with what caused you to feel that way. Dogs can be the same way. When a dog is getting frustrated because of another dog behind a fence, for example, he or she may turn around and snap or bite at the person trying to grab them by the collar. This is a very obvious cause of redirection, but it can happen in other ways too. When the cause is not identified, the aggression can seem out of context or sudden.

This can complicate determining what the aggression is truly caused by. Review your dog's history for clues to figure out how it started and progressed. It can be helpful to break down the anxiety/aggression sequence in small pieces, and treat each element on its own through behavior modification. In the crate example, desensitize/counter condition with the person, the crate, the space, etc.

Figuring it out

A qualified behavior consultant can help you sort these out for your particular situation. But pay attention to where the aggression started and how it evolved. Look at the range of behaviors and situations you are seeing it in. Try not to ascribe human motivations and responses to your dog. Dogs have a smaller frontal cortex, and do not rationalize the way we do.

There may be clues in the history and this will help you with applying *Targeted Behavior Modification* in just the right way. It does not cause further harm if you get the motivation wrong provided you don't put your dog into a situation that makes him or her unduly anxious. You just may fool yourself and think your dog's problem is resolved when it's not. Additionally, you may not accurately predict when the aggression is likely to occur, making management and prevention a greater challenge.

Note as well, dogs generalize less than we do and discriminate much more than we do. This means what they learn in one situation may not

> **TIP**: Your dog does not generalize well. What he learns, he may not apply to other situations. Aggression may occur in new scenarios that you did not anticipate. Always be on your guard in new situations or when any circumstances change.

transfer, or *generalize* well to similar situation. This means you need to practice in enough scenarios that they learn to generalize, but also keep in mind that it may be the one thing you didn't think to *counter condition* for that will cause an unexpected resurgence of aggression to occur again.

DOG-ON-DOG AGGRESSION IN THE HOME

While owner-directed aggression has been reported as one of the most common forms of aggression seen by veterinary behavior clinics, more people appear to be searching online for information on treating dog aggression towards other dogs.

The biggest challenges in treating dog-to-dog aggression can partly be explained by the fact that aggression between dogs in the home is largely a social problem, opposed to fear of strangers or intruders, for example.

Unfortunately, as typical dog owners, we interpret things through our human viewpoint. Most of us have not been trained to understand the social workings between dogs or how to interpret their behavior. We know how we want our dogs to behave, but we don't know what our dogs desire of each other.

This is a challenging problem to resolve, because this is often a social problem where the personalities and dynamics are unique to each situation. It can be made even more complicated with those dogs who may have other issues such as generalized anxiety disorders, or who seem to be incapable of reading signals from other dogs accurately.

> Warning: aggression between females in domestic dogs, feral dogs, and wolves is potentially the most dangerous, which means it is considered to be the most difficult to treat in domestic dogs.

The information on how to handle this particular problem is varied and conflicting and few, if any, provide sources, which make it difficult to muddle through which approach is best.

Many veterinary behaviorists such as Dr. Karen Overall, Dr. Gary Landsberg, Dr. Andrew U. Luesher, to name a few refer to treating dogs by taking into account dominance theories or social hierarchy theories. Others such as high respected trainer Brenda Aloff and Jean Donaldson downplay this approach. Aloff states that supporting the dominant dog as being a highly dangerous strategy. Jean Donaldson in her book basically discounts the entire lot of various social hierarchy theories by stating that while one of the models may be true there is very little research on social organization in domestic dogs therefore none of the theories have yet to be established.

The challenge is that dominance theories have recently come under scrutiny, despite the huge number of real and would-be trainers still talking pack theory and showing your dog who's boss. The concept of *alpha* has unfortunately caused people to treat their dogs in ways that are ultimately dangerous for the humans and harmful for the dogs. Even the very phrase *dominance aggression* has come to be called other things such as impulse control aggression or owner directed aggression, etc.

However, in a study that looked at 38 pairs of dogs with inter-dog household aggression, owners reported a 69% overall improvement following treatment which included implementing a nothing-in-life-is-free program (similar to the *SAW* program), giving one dog priority access to resources and administering psychotropic medication.[79]

Although two dogs can fight with each other in the home, the more dogs you have in the home, the more likely you will have problems.

Our tendency to anthropomorphize dogs means we sometimes ascribe human characteristics to them that they don't actually have. We may look for motivations that don't actually exist. The issue of social rank is particularly complicated, as many owners would rather not see one of their dogs as *weak* or as a bully. In addition, just like the majority of parents with kids, we play favorites, protect, or blame based on how we feel, often without knowing it. Sometimes, we get so used to a particular quirk in our dog that we don't realize it may be an indication of a larger problem.

Normal vs. abnormal behavior

This must be addressed first if one or both dogs are not behaving normally, because if one or both has a greater problem, the aggression will be difficult to resolve. But occasionally aggression towards another animal of the same species

Here are the important elements to consider of any in-home dog-to-dog situation:

- Normal vs. abnormal behavior.
- Stress and anxiety in the home, reactivity.
- Exposure to other dogs (some dogs may have not learned the social behaviors required for settling conflicts).
- History of the relationship between the two.
- Territoriality: Who was there first?
- Age, illness – younger dogs tend to follow older, more experienced dogs, but this changes as a dog ages and grows weaker, or adolescents mature.
- Size – while size does not necessarily impact who influences whom, dogs are aware of size discrepancies.
- Motivation: who values what resource the most?
- Allegiance with the other dogs and/or people in the house: who is on whose side? If it comes down to it, who will gang up on who?
- Breed: Some dogs are more predisposed to fight than others.

within the group is considered to be normal, especially when the younger one is maturing into an adult, or the older one is aging. It is also common towards newcomers in a group. However, it is important to understand that the aggression is largely restricted to posturing and vocal signals, to keep fighting to a minimum.

The question for the owner, who will likely need professional help in assessing this, is whether or not the dog(s) are behaving normally. Supporting one dog over the other may backfire if you are encouraging a bully *to bully* even more. In addition, we might be supporting the dog that really should be backing down – and this prevents the conflict from resolving.

Unfortunately, this is very difficult for an owner to assess accurately on their own because they usually do not have the background to determine it. They are also too close to the problem to be able to see it, and often project their own anthropomorphized viewpoints of what is happening onto the situation. That is not to say that you don't have valuable information that can help a professional – you do. You know your dogs best because you live with them. But, we shouldn't expect you to be someone who is an expert at diagnosing behavior problems if you are not.

> **TIP**: The closeness of our relationships, along with our tendency to attribute a human characteristic, motivation, or personality may blind us from seeing our dogs' situation accurately.

Things to watch out for

Anxious dogs are more likely to respond defensively, but more importantly, are unable to assess the situation accurately. On the other hand, what may look impulsive to us may be a matter of us missing or ignoring or not recognizing the cues that indicated developing tension.

Consider these points that may indicate your dog is not behaving normally:

- The dog is reacting as if there is a challenge for status when there is no challenge. Learn to read behaviors that indicate challenges before jumping to this conclusion.

- Your dog's reaction is too intense for the context (but the history needs to be taken into account here, because the aggression changes over time).
- The other dogs in the house are actively avoiding the problem dog.
- Your dog refuses to let go of the other dog, even when the other dog is showing appeasement behaviors such as whimpering, rolling over on its back, etc.
- Your dog is difficult to calm after an aggressive episode has happened.
- Your dog has separation anxiety.
- There is aggression towards others (people or dogs) in the home.
- There is aggression towards or fear of strangers.
- There is some form of obsessive-compulsive disorder.
- Your dog has difficulty settling down: practicing the relaxation exercises will give you some idea of how he or she can relax.
- Your dog is often rigid and uncomfortable.
- Your dog is hyper-vigilant, always on the lookout for something happening through the windows, door, on walks, etc.
- One dog constantly seems to be testing the other even when the other dog is backing down. This may occur in play so keep note of how intense the play is and who seems to be constantly initiating it and who attempts to end it.

If you think there is a possibility that one or more dogs are not behaving normally, then you should consult a professional and consider keeping the dogs separated until you can.

Now let's look at some of the important elements in more detail:

Stress and anxiety in the home, reactivity

If your dog(s) is stressed out for whatever reason, it will be difficult for the relationship to improve.

History

If the fighting has continued for some time, it will be difficult to resolve because the aggression and resentment are so well practiced. The history of resentment or fear will make it difficult for the dogs to tolerate one another and each dog is a constant reminder to the other of this. You may get the dogs so that they are reluctantly getting along, but the potential exists for conflict to occur in the future.

Territoriality: Who was there first?

The dog that was there first will want to protect their territory. There are evolutionary reasons for this. Serious aggression in wolf packs where aggression is relatively low often occurs with strangers in the groups, or territorial issues. While dogs are not wolves, and don't need to actually hunt, domestic dogs are still not in control of their resources. The problem might then be greater if the second dog that is introduced is naturally more interested in and motivated to gain access to the things the other dog cares about. This may lead to allegiance or territorial aggression where the aggression occurs within proximity of the owner as well.

Age, Health

Socially immature dogs (usually under the age of 1 ½ to 2 years old, but can vary) usually do not aggressively challenge older dogs. But, it is common for socially maturing dogs to want to test the adult dogs, it's also not uncommon for the older dog to recognize this and become concerned about the maturing dog challenging them. However, even in wolf packs, aggression is rarely used to resolve hierarchy disputes. In wolf packs, as well as feral dog situations, the young adults always have the option to disburse – i.e. leave the group and go out on their own, either as a lone dog or wolf, or to form their own pack. In some cases these dogs will remain close to the pack, but live on the outskirts. Domestic dogs in the home don't have this option.

When dogs' health starts to fail, and they grow weaker, it can be an opportunity for younger dogs to start challenging the older dog. Physical play can provide the dogs will a lot of information about stamina and strength, as well as the attitude of the older dog. An aging dog may be less tolerant or less willing to engage. Other dogs in the group will be aware of this.

Size

Dogs may be aware of the size of the other dog when they assess a risk of going after a valued item or resource, although there is no direct evidence of this that I could find. If the dogs have played together, they will likely have a good idea of how fast, strong, and tough the other is.

Personalities

Some dogs are naturally more intense. Some need clear unambiguous communication, while others are more laid back. Some need more attention, while others do not. Some are pushy or anxious; some aren't. Some dogs are highly fluent in *dog* and others are socially inept. It's more than possible that pushy, socially inept dogs may irritate dogs that are more fluent, and may get into more conflict than those that are more socially tuned in. Like people, dogs may be more attracted to certain personality types than others. Breed types may factor in here as well.

Motivation: who values what resource the most?

Dogs will value certain resources more highly than others. Again, breed and personalities will factor in here. We learn to yield when another's motivation is strong or places high value on something, and dogs respond similarly. Dogs that can't do this for each other when a resource is highly valued for both (and not necessarily for the same reasons) may continue to fight. Removing the resources should be done as a matter of management. If the "resource" is the owner's attention, you may have to ignore both dogs when together until you can work with each through *Targeted Behavior Modification.*

Allegiance: who is on whose side? If it comes down to it, who will gang up on whom?

Allegiance in social groups has a strong protective and survival value. When we come to the aid of a more subordinate dog, our action may encourage the subordinate dog not to defer to the other. This is problematic when deference is the primary way of maintaining pack cohesion.

A dog might gain confidence if the owners appear to favor them more than the others. Because dogs can feel simple envy,[80] we know that they weigh the exchanges, not just in themselves but between others as well. Therefore, the actions of the humans are very important. Research also indicates that in feral dogs, the number of dogs in the other group influences the likelihood of becoming aggressive toward another pack. In addition, if there are more than two dogs in the group, the actions of the relationships of each will be measured. Aggression often occurs when a dog becomes sick or dies because the dynamics change.

Group cohesion

Advice may be to support the most dominant dog; however, in many cases, there are simply no clear-cut signals to determine which is actually dominant in a given relationship. In addition, it is not the dog itself that is dominant, as dominance is not a trait (despite the many trainers and lay people who think it is), so much as it describes and *predicts* an outcome of a given situation – i.e. which dog is most likely to yield in a particular situation.

The dilemma: equality is doomed to fail

As much as certain practitioners insist you should not attempt to create a hierarchy, inevitably the dogs will perceive an alliance based on your actions, as it will still be difficult to aim for complete equality and fairness in the eyes of the dogs. And if we are to look at sibling rivalry in children, we learn that equality is doomed to fail, as it presses the children to constantly measure and compare if each situation is fair.

Instead, in the case of normal dogs, we should look at the needs of the dog. They should always be asked to sit, wait and look to you (SAW), the owner or handler, but we can't let two dogs go through a door at the same time usually. If it's vital to one dog that they get out the door before the others, we can allow that dog to do this, as long as the other dog defers. Barging through first may not actually be an issue of dominance; we simply may be reading it as dominance. The dog may be highly motivated to go out first because of the high level of excitement he or she has for being outside. One dog may be highly motivated to chase the ball inside, but will let the other dogs chase outside. This could be because the dog understands that other dog wants something much more than they do, therefore, they are willing to give in to the other dog. But deference is what we want to concentrate on and encourage.

Who goes first?

But what do you do when you cannot tell? After all, if things were so clear-cut, they probably would not be fighting in the first place.

Do you support the dog that is most likely to assert themselves in a given situation by siding with them and rewarding them? Or, do you reward the dog that is showing deference, since it's the deferring dog that is the peacekeeper?

Well, the answer is you do both when both are communicating appropriately. Dr. Karen Overall writes, if one dog stares at the other dog, *and the other looks away*, this is normal, reward both with food treats.[81] However, if the dog growls, interrupt the growling and follow the *Emergency Response Plan.*

Giving a dog attention, food, and access to prized places and resources first appears to give dogs more confidence, which is why you want to be very careful about selecting the right dog to do this. The dog that has more confidence, and is more motivated will be boosted; the one who is not will then be more likely to acquiesce. In this case, it appears that it's better to support the dog that is more motivated to go after a resource.

Don't put the abnormal dog in charge

However, choose the bully, or the abnormal dog that constantly needs to test the other because of anxiety regardless of the response, and you are supporting an unhealthy situation for both. You will need a qualified expert to determine whether your dog is abnormal or not.

The greater the difference in status between the two, the more likely there will be peace as the roles and positions are clear cut and each is satisfied. The problem for us humans is in feeling comfortable that this is the way it should be. Humans are notorious for feeling like things should be *fair* and we want the subordinate dog to feel loved. The notion of dominance and submission is troubling to us. In actuality, the illusion of dominance and submission in people is often a state of mind.

Ritualized behaviors

Allowing others to go first or get the bigger piece *could* be about being too fearful to assert yourself. Or, allowing others to go first or get the bigger piece could really be a signal of confidence, generosity, and politeness. But regardless, our rituals have been established to minimize conflict.

Think of the ritual of a man opening a door for a woman. Clearly, this is an unnecessary gesture as women are more than capable of opening doors themselves. However, it is worth asking who is the most dominant in this exchange? The answer is that both defer to the other.

The woman does not assert leadership by opening the door, but instead waits (in fact, often times, the man is walking behind her). The man does not assert leadership by going in first, but instead waits for the woman to go in first. If this was an issue of dominance, both are more than capable of opening and going through the door first and would. Instead, it is perceived as a measure of politeness: one appears to be doing a service, the other allows for this to occur. Deeper down, this is a ritualized social behavior that prevents confusion and conserves resources needed for the brain to figure out how to resolve what happens each time.

The presence of dominant or submissive displays may be an indication that one or more of the dogs is feeling anxious about the social dynamics. However, the presence of these ritualized behaviors is meant to resolve conflicts so that aggression between dogs does not occur. When aggression occurs, the ritualized behaviors have not worked. On the other hand, if the intent is to cause harm, rather than resolve conflict, then there is a problem.

Play follow-the-human-leader

One way to minimize the importance of rank is by clearly establishing the leader/follower dynamic between humans and dogs. In wolf packs, the top wolves do not always eat first, but they do decide who does. Both (or all) dogs must learn to depend on the human. This removes the necessity for the dogs to have to make all the decisions about resources. Dogs should be taught *SAW*, as well as a release cue. They should be released one at a time.

Keep in mind that, as mentioned before, practicing self-control depletes the ability to maintain self-control. So consider how well your dog(s) can do this and what situation might follow the request for self-control. At the same time, practicing self-control will develop their ability to control themselves in the future and this will help in future exchanges.

Practice grows the ability to control themselves, so exercises in self-control should be ongoing and their abilities should be challenged.

Emotion control

Aggression is driven by emotion and arousal regardless of why it happens. Like people dogs can vary in their intensity and abilities to control themselves. By having the dogs relax on cue and respond to the cues about what they should be doing next, you go a long way at keeping the peace where the dogs are in proximity to the owners.

Classical conditioning where the dog does nothing to earn a reward, but only comes to associate some kind of *stimulus* with a reward may help to lower aggressive arousal. A lowering of arousal may allow greater success for *operant conditioning* (where the dog needs to do something to earn the reward) to change both the emotional activity and the behavior pattern.

Warning: treating aggression between dogs in the home is difficult. Even after the aggression appears to have resolved, you will have to always be vigilant. The dogs may simply not like each other and be stuck living together in a continually strained situation for the rest of their lives. You will have to determine whether this is in the best interests of the dogs.

If you consider re-homing one dog out of two, you should re-home the one most likely to succeed in another home, as re-homing can be stressful. It's possible that a one-dog home (your home) will be just right for the aggressive dog. You may find he or she relaxes and becomes a generally easier dog despite the removal of your other dog.

DOG AGGRESSION TOWARDS FAMILY MEMBERS

Dog aggression towards specific family members can occur for many reasons. Your dog may be anxious about the behavior of a particular member of the family (either unpredictable behavior or the dog perceives threats), or he or she may be concerned about protecting their space or their things – essentially whatever is important and valuable to them. Your dog may be unable to adequately read and interpret behaviors of people. In this case, it's important to work hard on the *SAW (Sit, Attend, and Wait)* and the relaxation work. Review page 51 for tips on dealing with a dog who is aggressive towards you.

In addition, teaching the dog a variety of *obedience* behaviors can go a long way to reducing your dog's anxiety, because he or she will understand specifically what you are asking and what they should do. The most valuable behaviors to teach besides the *Sit, Attend and Wait (SAW)* include coming when called, coming to touch (or follow) a hand, and going to a target or a space when asked.

It's important to understand that dogs behaving aggressively are not acting dominantly. At most, dogs may be concerned about their social status, but this is probably less about trying to get on top of you or a family member, and more about what might happen if he or she loses status so far that their mental health or even survival is at risk.

This will be a far greater concern for those households where the dog may have been punished, yelled at, or otherwise threatened. But, it can also happen in households where the dog simply can't read the behavior. And although I have not personally seen any evidence of this, I would theorize that dogs that are lonely – those ones set out in the yard on a chain, left at home hours at a time, or otherwise isolated – are also at risk for aggression.

As with people, we need to feel part of the group – the function of the feeling of loneliness is to encourage us to bond with a group. We need this to ensure our survival. Mothers need the group to help her when she is looking after babies and cannot fend for herself; hunters need the size of the group to track down prey.

At the same time, it is equally possible to irritate our dogs with too much affection – especially when they are unable to interpret our behavior correctly. In this case, every moment of our suffocating affection causes irritation and stress, and stress, as we learned early in the chapter, will increase aggression.

Finding the right balance of attention is important, and having that attention and interaction being structured enough to allow the dog to feel secure is important, too.

In other situations where the dog is a hoarder or aggressive around toys, their crate, etc., often removing free access to these things - while not eliminating the aggression – prevents the aggression from becoming more firmly entrenched, and makes it a more safe environment and reduces the stress load for all.

For example, some dogs seem to be particularly aggressive in their crate. There may be many reasons for this, from associating something fearful with the crate, to feeling trapped, to wanting to defend it, etc. But it's always worth asking yourself – do you need to have your dog in a crate? Can he or she be put into a room or even given free access instead? If your dog sleeps in a crate in your room, perhaps you can move the crate to some other less desirable place (another room perhaps).

Food aggression

When a dog is aggressive in the presence of food, this may be more challenging to deal with because protecting food is a natural part of a dog's survival skills. But food guarding may also be linked to other events that make the food higher value – such as all the excitement and your interaction at dinnertime.

First thing to do in this case is give the dog free access to a full bowl of food for at least 24 hours before starting the program. This conveys that food is not scarce and makes sure the dog is satiated (but watch for bloat).

Approach the food bowl as closely as you can *without* having the dog stiffen up, show the whites of their eyes, hard stare, or show any signs of aggression or anxiety. Then toss in small bits of dog food that is a little tastier than the free food your dog has. Repeat this several times. What this does is have him associate your approach with getting something even better than what he or she already has. If your dog is continuing to behave aggressively, wait until they are safely away from his bowl before filling it, and try again.

When they are starting to lift their head out of the bowl reliably when you approach, then you can start the shaping. Eventually move closer. When your dog is comfortable bend down just slightly as if you were about to put more food in the bowl or pick the bowl up, but instead drop the treat in. Ensure your dog is not becoming anxious. Repeat this a few times. Increase the amount of bending.

By the time you can bend right down, and your dog is still behaving comfortably, take the bowl and exchange it with something even better. At this point, start asking him to sit when you approach the bowl. Generalize: practice this in different areas and with different people. Here are two dogs that displayed food aggression at a shelter and were helped with *behavior modification*:
http://www.aspcapro.org/behavior-modification-in-action.php

When appropriate *desensitization* and *counter conditioning* can be done – ALWAYS start with the least important object, resource or location and always start with the least threatening circumstances, minimal distraction, minimal duration, etc.

YOU: Aggression in the home is a sure fire way to cause conflict among humans. One person decides they want to get rid of the dog or you can't agree on how the dog should be treated. You may come to feel betrayed and resentful of the dog, if not outright fear. Outsiders secretly – or not so secretly – may think you are a weak leader, or that you abused the dog.

It's time to put those thoughts away. You might try finding a sympathetic and qualified trainer or consult a vet behaviorist who has seen many cases like yours. And, consider joining the K9aggression-support e-group on Yahoo, where there are people dealing with all kind of different aggressive dogs. There at least you know you are not the only one who wants to make a difference.

DOGS AND KIDS

Dogs and kids can be a disaster together unfortunately. One big reason is because of a child's desire to have some influence or control over their environment. They want to do stuff to dogs, and have them react as a result. Often, this is quite well meaning and loving. Other times, the dog simply serves as the subject for experiment. Children learn to empathize with others at different rates, boys slightly behind girls. They also learn self-control at different speeds. It's important to remember that children are still learning about the world in general and simply will not always do what is expected.

> **WARNING**: If there has been a history of a lot of physical contact with your child and your dogs, it is possible that anxiety is or has been building up. Your dog may react aggressively without your child doing much at all to provoke them – like simply reaching for the dog.

The first thing to teach your children is that most dogs don't like hugs. And the younger your child is, the more you will have to remind them. Not hugging a dog is difficult; in fact, even talking about not hugging makes them want to do it. Most dogs tolerate it, but most don't enjoy it. If a dog enjoys a hug, he or she will lean into you, relax and close their eyes, and ask for more if you stop.

Trainer Karen Pryor identified these behaviors during Dog Prevention Week in 2012 on her blog as indications that your dog is not enjoying the contact. This should be taught to all kids: dogs that like petting usually make it quite obvious.

If your dog is not enjoying a hug, he or she may do one or more of the following:

- Turn their head away from you
- Lick your face repeatedly
- Lick their lips or flick their tongue out
- Yawn
- Lick or chew at him or herself

- Sneeze
- Wriggle to get away
- Hold their body tense
- Shake off vigorously when you let go
- Show a half of moon of white in their eye
- Wag their tail stiffly

Another reason dogs and kids are not a good mix is that children's behavior is far more different and unpredictable than an adult's is and this can cause a dog to feel anxious. This can especially be a problem with toddlers. Children are smaller, they dart around or don't move like adults, they have high-pitched voices, and often are unpredictably loud. Children even smell different. Many dogs are simply unsure of what is going to happen, and this can be made worse when a child grabs, pinches or hits a dog, or if there are conflicts between children in the home.

Parents' behavior in relation to children is also different, and can indicate to the dog that the child, especially a toddler, is a concern. While parents may be simply preventing a child from damaging anything or getting hurt, dogs understand that the adult has some need to pay extra attention to the child. While many parents attribute jealousy to the dog and may respond by giving more attention to the dog, it's just as possible the dog, especially an anxious one or one who has difficulty interpreting human behaviors, is interpreting the adult's behavior as if there is a reason to be concerned by this strange creature, and therefor they too, should also be watching them carefully.

WARNING: If your child is young (under the age of 6 or 7 depending on the maturity and compliance of the child) and your dog has actually bitten, the risks are far greater. Re-homing could be considered if a responsible and willing owner can be found and the dog is not too aggressive. The unfortunate situation is that kids are kids and sometimes won't follow instructions.

If a dog growls, get in between the dog and child immediately. Children should respect the growl and move away or be moved away immediately. Yes, this will teach a dog that growling works; on the other hand, it is better than teaching them that growling does not work, and therefore, they have to escalate the aggression to get space away between them and the child.

If your dog has never bitten, has not shown a lot of tension, or perhaps has only growled a little, depending on how well your children can take instruction, you might be able to do an adult-supervised *desensitization* and *counter conditioning* program. An example of this is while having the dog on a head halter, the child asks the dog to sit. If the dog is sits and shows signs of being relaxed, both are rewarded. The rest of the time the children shouldn't interact with the dog.

Make sure you are using rewards for both the dog *and* the child when the child is young and needs motivation. The child could be allowed to win some sort of reward for showing self-control. A spoonful of ice cream, individual *rockets candies*, pennies, and minutes earned on a computer, television, etc. may all help as a reward. The sessions should be short and fun for all.

If your dog is nervous about children in general, taking your dog to a schoolyard or park at a good distance away where he or she can relax and observe (ensuring that your dog is well secured) may help your dog become accustomed to children's behaviors while playing, but safety measures need to be taken and you need to know when your dog is relaxed in a stimulating environment.

Always follow the *desensitization* and *counter conditioning* rules of not progressing too quickly and ensuring the foundation training is solid. Set your dog up for success!

Ensure your *Emergency Cues* are well practiced. Everyone in the house, (even including babysitters and guests but excluding young children), should practice these with the dog.

Note that as children grow, their compliance and behavior around adults gets better. This can lead you into thinking a situation is safer than it is. Children are children; they are immature. They might know something is wrong, and still make bad choices when alone or be influenced by others. It's not that your child is bad; it is simply the role of a child to behave this way.

Why is my dog aggressive towards adults and not children?

Despite that some dogs may think children are entirely different creatures from adults; some dogs are less threatened by children because children's voices are higher and they are smaller. Unfortunately, this doesn't mean that a risk doesn't exist.

DOG AGGRESSION TOWARDS STRANGERS

Trying to understand what kind of stranger your dog is afraid of is natural. However, it can be unsafe because you might predict incorrectly. If your dog is reactive, err on the side of safety and assume he or she can be reactive towards anyone.

Aggression towards strangers is often due to the fact the dog does not actually know if the stranger is a threat or not. In some cases, a dog might act in a certain way to *test the waters*. Depending on what the stranger does, determines whether the stranger is an actual threat or not for your dog. This is one reason it is a bad idea to growl or bark back at a dog, or behave in some other way that is threatening to them.

In other cases, it may be a matter of territory. A dog bred to guard against strangers may not view the stranger a threat to himself or herself so much instinctively react as through the stranger is a threat to his or her resources.

Other breeds, such as herding types that were bred not to commit to the kill with livestock, may be more likely to develop fear aggression (should they develop aggression at all) than other kinds of aggression. Keep in mind that the *majority* of any kind of breed is not aggressive.

> **YOU**: There is nothing worse than having your dog go off on a stranger, particularly if it's a neighbor. People are more tolerant when your dog doesn't like their dog, but feel personally threatened when your dog targets them. Using a Gentle Leader can really help with this because it will allow you much more control.

Is my dog protecting me?

It's more likely they are protecting themselves and are braver about it because you are nearby.[82]

Be ready to monitor their behavior and redirect as necessary, and remove them from situations that will cause them to be nervous.

Desensitization and *counter conditioning* can be done anywhere you can control the situation and control the length of time the stranger *appears*. For example, using corners of a building outside can help. Dr. Karen Overall suggests using a T-shaped hallway, or a room with a doorway out to a hall, where the person can pass by and the dog only sees them briefly. [83]

People and even trainers have often used the environment as it is, and find strangers wherever they are. But keep in mind that:

- You can't control strangers you just happen to come across very well and they may behave unpredictably.
- Any stress and even distraction reduces the chance of success in the beginning. You are always better off with the most neutral, quiet boring environments, and most boring neutral subjects to start with if you can at all help it.

If you can, find people who can help. Trainers or owners of other aggressive dogs may be more than willing in exchange for similar favors.

Remember to take things one tiny baby step at a time, adjusting the factors that are outlined earlier in the *Targeted Behavior Modification* section.

Obedience

It's really important to emphasis how important practice is. While it's possible to *desensitize/counter condition* to strangers, you can never be entirely confident in assuming your dog will not react to the next new person or situation. Obedience training can go a long way towards giving you more control to navigate unpredictable situations.

As boring as it can be to practice something that your dog already knows, strengthening those neural pathways in the brain ensure that competing behaviors have less chance of dominating. Turning *SAW (Sit, Attend, Wait)* into a habit, or following the hand, coming when called, going to a mat or bed when asked, etc. can get you and your dog out of some tough spots and give you more control to navigate unpredictable situations. Plus, it allows your dog a structure of interacting whenever he or she becomes uncertain. Incorporate this training into your life.

Regular practice tells the brain the behaviors that are being practiced are important. So strengthen those neural pathways, make them become more efficient, and your dog will become even quicker to respond when you ask. Once a behavior has become well learned, continue to vary the reasons for them to be motivated to respond, such as intermittently rewarding them with treats, play, etc., although rewarding every single time becomes less essential.

Avoiding approaches from other strangers

There is something about some people and dogs – I'm one of them: they have a compulsive need to approach the dog and say hello (luckily, I've learned). Dog owner after dog owner complain about these people, because you want to keep your dog from becoming aggressive and these people seem to just ignore you.

Or sometimes, you might feel embarrassed about telling the person to stay away; other times, you really don't want to admit there is an aggression problem in case of a negative response (especially around neighbors).

Keeping people away from your dog

The K9aggression.com "Hands-off" t-shirt for dogs (i.e. your dog wears this, not you) was designed to be a solution for this. They are designed to communicate quickly that your dog should not be approached. The fact that your dog is wearing anything at all will draw attention, and it uses a symbol that even children understand pretty quickly. This can be even more effective than you calling out to the stranger to not touch your dog. The shirt indicates you mean business without communicating that your dog is aggressive.

In addition, if you are wearing a shirt or hat that says Dog Trainer (there are different variations on the K9aggression.com website), people will understand you are working with your dog. This goes a long way towards conveying the impression that you are a responsible person – and not someone who abuses their dog. You can order Dog Trainer or Dog Rescuer, or Dog Trainer in Training, etc. clothing through the K9aggression.com site if you think it will help you feel less judged. The proceeds from the profits go towards spreading the word.

If someone still approaches, simply put up your hand in the stop position, and explain that your dog is highly anxious and may not respond well. In most cases, people are happy to comply and happy you have warned them (if you can get their attention!).

The following diagrams demonstrate a possible scenario to work with your dog and strangers. You will need helpers to do this in some cases. You can also use these same kinds of set-ups when working with aggression towards strange dogs.

It involves the dog being relaxed, and then seeing the stranger for a very short period of time initially. After they notice the stranger, they get a treat. This is repeated several times until you can be sure that your dog is able to remain calm. Then you can extend the length of time the dog sees the person. As the dog learns to remain calm, you might have the person stop, and even enter the room.

Make sure the dog does not feel trapped during this work.

You can use a hallway, or a room for this kind of set up. They have pros and cons to them both (i.e. a room might make the dog feel trapped, or a hallway might make the dog concerned about what may come up behind them). Just be aware of this and make sure that your dog is relaxed.

TARGETED BEHAVIOR MODIFICATION FOR DEALING WITH STRANGERS SET-UP

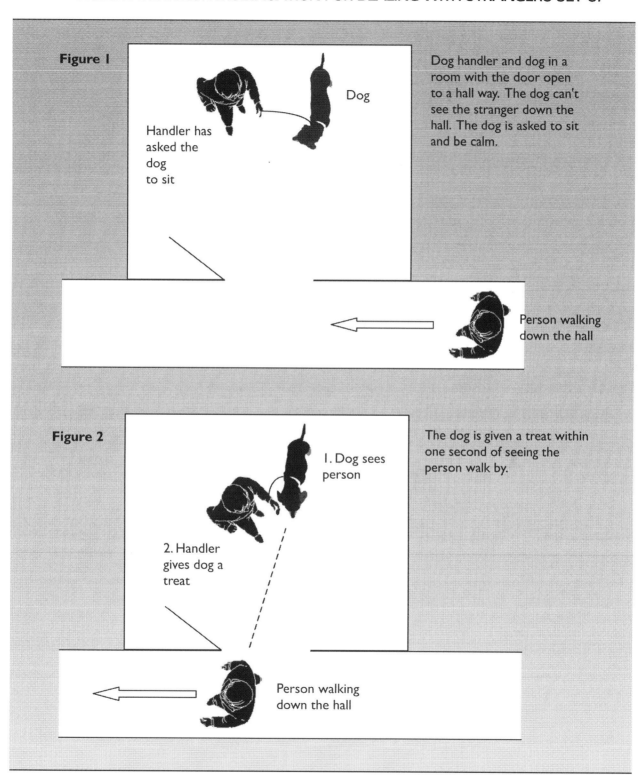

Figure 1

Handler has asked the dog to sit

Dog

Dog handler and dog in a room with the door open to a hall way. The dog can't see the stranger down the hall. The dog is asked to sit and be calm.

Person walking down the hall

Figure 2

1. Dog sees person

2. Handler gives dog a treat

The dog is given a treat within one second of seeing the person walk by.

Person walking down the hall

TARGETED BEHAVIOR MODIFICATION FOR DEALING WITH STRANGERS SET-UP

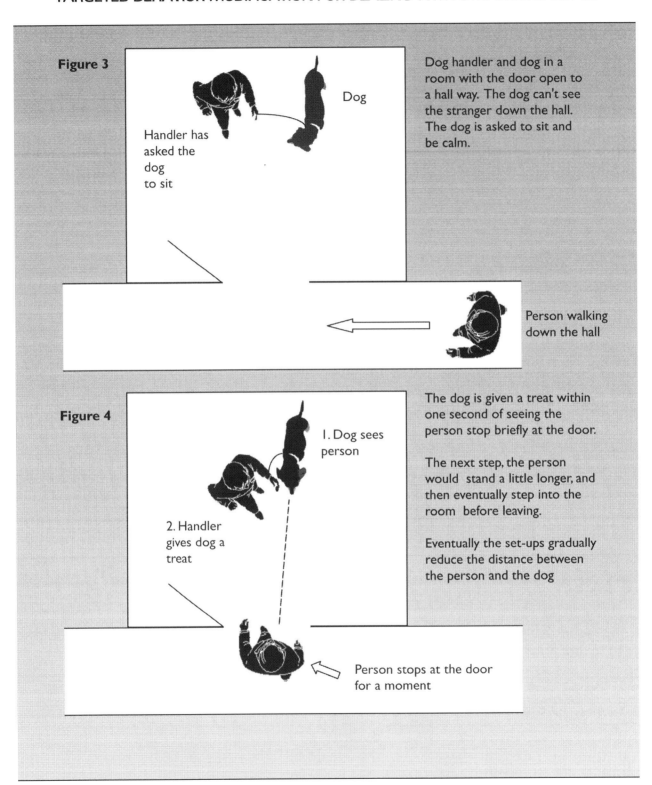

Figure 3

Handler has asked the dog to sit

Dog

Dog handler and dog in a room with the door open to a hall way. The dog can't see the stranger down the hall. The dog is asked to sit and be calm.

Person walking down the hall

Figure 4

1. Dog sees person

2. Handler gives dog a treat

The dog is given a treat within one second of seeing the person stop briefly at the door.

The next step, the person would stand a little longer, and then eventually step into the room before leaving.

Eventually the set-ups gradually reduce the distance between the person and the dog

Person stops at the door for a moment

DOG-ON-DOG AGGRESSION OUTSIDE OF THE HOME

If your dog is aggressive towards other dogs, you might be feeling a little sorry for yourself when you look at all those other dogs at the dog park, or running or hiking with their owners that you see. But remember, those that have dogs that are aggressive are probably not taking them out as much. You are by no means the only dog owner whose dogs don't like other dogs.

Some dogs are perfectly fine meeting new dogs; others are not. But we think that dogs *should* like other dogs, because dogs are social animals. In the wild, wolves are often incredibly aggressive towards wolves outside of their packs. And while dogs have evolved to be very different from wolves, it still helps to keep in mind that they are not necessarily meant to be continually meeting strange dogs.

> Review the sections on how to exercise or walk your dog when your dog is aggressive to others in the De-stress and Environmental Enrichment section of the book.

Dogs that are aggressive towards strange dogs might behave aggressively for the same reasons that dogs are aggressive towards human strangers too, so ensure you read that passage.

Dogs are naturally more socially tuned into each other in that they understand *dog* better than we do. Variances in breeds mean some dogs have different motivations than others, making them a little more confusing to read for some dogs. Differences in their bodies can obscure signaling such as shortened tails or floppy ears. Some breeds play and socialize differently. For example, I had a greyhound that used to bump and nip when she chased other dogs during play. My pit-bulls hated it and did not interpret this as play at all, but instead were threatened by it. They only liked chasing that involved pawing and open mouth jaw sparring. They also loved wrestling, which the greyhound never did. This difference in play and interacting between the breeds was identified by one veterinary behaviorist as being a potential issue in their relationship.

One thing that dogs don't have a good sense of is time because of the way their brains are. This means that any time another dog meets another dog, he or she has no way of knowing whether or not this dog is going to be in their life forever. The same social processes start and – just like people – will include assessing each other's perceived social status.

Dogs are three times more likely to threaten a dog of the same gender than the opposite, and five times more likely to bite a dog of the same gender as they are of the opposite gender.[84]

While threats and bites still occur regardless of gender, it may be helpful to initially choose dogs of opposite gender to work with as dogs are less likely to threaten or bite dogs of opposite gender than they are of the same gender.

Check out the diagrams of possible targeted behavior modification set-ups you might try with your dog. You will likely need a helper. Sometimes finding someone else who owns a dog with similar problems may be willing to help.

Keeping people and their dogs away from your dog

Again, as mentioned earlier, K9aggression.com's "Hands-off" or "Do Not Pet" t-shirts for dogs (i.e. your dog wears this, not you) is a solution for this. They are designed to communicate quickly that your dog should not be approached. The fact your dog is wearing anything at all will draw attention, and it uses a symbol that even children understand pretty quickly.

In addition if you are wearing a shirt or hat that says Dog Trainer (or Dog Rescuer, or Trainer in Training, etc.), people will understand you are working with your dog. This goes a long way towards conveying the impression that you are a responsible person – and not someone who abused their dog. You can get these too, if you like, via the K9aggression.com site. The proceeds from the profits go towards spreading the word.

If someone still approaches, simply put up your hand in the stop position, and explain that your dog is highly anxious and may not respond well. In most cases, people are happy to comply and appreciate being warned, but be aware that dog owners are often preoccupied with their own dog. Don't give up.

Off-leash dogs

Well, we know that dogs don't read, or if they do, they are keeping it under their hat, so what do you do about off-leash dogs? In many cases, these dogs are very friendly, so friendly that the owner never thinks to put them on a leash. Curiosity and a desire to socialize may bring them over. You can ask the owner to call their dog off, but often the desire of the dog to interact with your dog overrides their compliance, and if your dog is already starting to react, he or she may even be too afraid to turn their back on your dog.

Carrying citronella spray or opening an umbrella (although this may get a little unwieldy) may be one way to deal with this problem. Another that has worked for me in one case was to shout at the other dog and wave them away. I must have seemed crazier than my dog and the dog literally stopped in the middle of the street and turned around. My dog was unconcerned because she was *conditioned* to this behavior of mine. We can get boisterous in my house. When you do your exercises you might want to think about desensitizing them to these kinds of things.

If this is a neighbor's dog, the neighbor may feel perfectly justified in allowing their dogs off leash even though they are wrong and may feel they have perfect control over their dog. Worst of all, if their dog does come over, and your dog attacks them, you are the one that will be blamed, as unfair as it is. In areas that have dangerous dog legislation, this can be a real problem.

Again, we recommend using the t-shirts as a way of communicating to people to stay away, but it conveys nothing to the off leash dog. Explain ahead of time that your dog is highly anxious about other dogs, but you are working with them to improve the situation. So ask if they see you and your dog to avoid you or give you space.

About leashes

Quick note, the extendable, retractable, *flexi* leashes, or spring-loaded leashes – the kinds of leashes that allow your dog to move different distances away from you and keep no slack in the leash- should be not be used with an aggressive dog. Not only do you have little control, but also it's not good for the dog to be constantly pulling against the tension of the leash.

LEASH AGGRESSION

Another common situation is the development of leash aggression, which occurs when a dog becomes frustrated – in other words, actually prevented from getting what he or she wants. This often occurs in interactions between dogs. And while we complain about dogs pulling, it is just as frustrating to dogs. Leashes are so common in our interactions with dogs that we don't tend to consider how annoying they can be to dogs. Owners are puzzled when their dog lunges and carries on at another dog across the road, and yet when given the opportunity to interact, all aggression seems to disappear and they play instead.

In fact, restraint is actually a *stressor* they use on animals such as rats to induce stress. After 30 minutes of restraint, there was an increase in antagonistic behavior in rats up to 24 hours later. Interestingly, research suggests that the detection of such chemical signaling of stress may play a role in triggering intense aggression in rats.[85] Could it be the same for dogs?

> **CAUTION**: Leashes and collars can break. Make sure your leashes are good and strong, and check the clasps and buckles of any product you are using every time you use it. Ensure that your dog cannot slip out of any collar or harness as well.

Dogs are twice as likely to threaten another dog when they are on leash, than when they are off leash.[86] The owner's presence may give them confidence to threaten. Another theory involves the owners tightening up on the leash, or perhaps responding in other ways (change of voice, change in perspiration, heart rate, breathing, etc.) communicating tension to the dog and signaling there is something to worry about. In some cases, the dog on the leash may feel more vulnerable because it is unable to run away. However, the use of a leash appears to have no influence on the occurrence of biting.

A dog that really wants to meet dogs, but is so excited that he or she can't contain him or herself, might start to feel frustrated at being prevented from greeting and this causes them stress. When they start barking and lunging, the owner is confused because it seemed like they really want to meet the other dog. Also, dog owners regularly interfere with the natural greeting behaviors by holding the leash so tight so there is no opportunity for normal sniffing or posturing or other signaling that dogs naturally do. Sniffing is likely the most important interaction between dogs while on walks.[87]

Should you let them go over to meet the dog if that is what he or she really wants?

No, because they will learn that all that pulling and lunging will get them what he or she wants. In addition, your dog is actually starting to get stressed and this makes this situation risky, especially if they are showing any kind of aggression-related behaviors. And finally, other dogs don't like to be ambushed. If your dog is not behaving calmly, or using the normal social rules dogs use, this will alarm other dogs, increasing the chances of those dogs responding negatively to yours.

The good news is that this does not confirm your dog has a serious aggression problem. The challenge will be in overcoming your dog's excitability, and you should determine whether there is a degree of anxiety related to this. Remember, dogs can be ambivalent about situations. What may seem like an exciting situation may also be anxiety provoking.

Teaching your dog to pay attention to you and to be calm in the presence of dogs is the key here, although you will need to work hard on getting your dog to relax. Your dog may have other issues related to over-excitability or anxiety, which should be addressed with your vet/vet-behaviorist.

Should you get your dog to sit?

If your dog can sit when a person or dog passes by, and your dog is RELAXED, then this is wonderful. It will have a positive effect on the dog that is passing by. BUT the insistence that your dog remains stationary may make them feel trapped. Using some kind of lure, whether it is a highly desirable toy, or treat to distract them and redirect them while moving may be the best way of managing the behavior.[88]

REMINDER: PREVENT ANXIETY AND AGGRESSION

We have already talked about this at the beginning of the book, but unless you can prevent the aggression from happening, there is virtually no need to try *Targeted Behavior Modification*.

Essentially, if your dog is still being placed in a situation where he or she can get anxious and even act aggressively, then that neural network that handles that behavior process is not getting pruned back.

In other words, that process leading from anxiety through to aggression is not getting less efficient or being replaced with other behavior sequences. It's just getting faster and more effective because it's being used. That the behavior sequence (starting with anxiety) is getting used at all, tells the brain that this behavior sequence is important. The brain needs to be faster, better, and more efficient at it.

Because the neural networks are actually competitive, it will actually push out alternate behavioral choices (and this is why if your dog *needs* medication, you should not delay). There are all sorts of evidence that proves that the brain is highly adaptive in this way. It's why we get better with practice and why we forget things that are not so important.

That means we really need to strengthen and practice other behavioral alternatives or coping strategies. You can ask yourself – is the behavioral alternative of *SAW* and relaxation so well practiced, it's become automatic? Is that neural process strong enough that it can compete with the beginning of the old aggressive behavior sequence? It has to be habit because evidence shows that we don't forget our fear memories.

When the amygdala in the brain starts processing our fear, the prefrontal cortex can actually over ride it under certain conditions. It's the prefrontal cortex where your dog has learned to Sit, Attend, and Wait, and where he or she has learned what it means to relax and how to relax.

Research: Why we look at other animals as a way to understand dogs

There is a trend now to insist that dogs are not wolves – they are different. And, they are. So what is the value of looking at research done on mice or even humans for that matter, when we look to understand dogs better?

Other animal models – yes, even wolves, are good models for certain kinds of research because there are so many similarities in the brains of mammals. Jaak Panksepp, who wrote "Affective Neuroscience: The Foundations of Human and Animal Emotions" (Oxford University Press, New York, 1998), stated, "Fortunately, if one learns the subcortical neuroanatomy of one mammalian species, one has learned the ground plan for all other mammals. Indeed, by mastering the brain of one mammal, one immediately enjoys a good understanding of the subcortical neuroanatomy of most other vertebrate species." (p.60)

He goes on to write, "the evidence now clearly indicates that certain intrinsic aspirations of all mammalian minds, those of mice as well as men, are driven by the same ancient neurochemistries." (p. 145)

The same neurons in both dogs and humans control basic bodily functions such as the regulations of breathing and heart rate. These systems are directly related to our freeze, fight, or flight responses (*sympathetic nervous system* response). Nerve cells that regulate sleep and wakefulness are identical. Some of the neurotransmitters involved, such as the much talked about serotonin, are not only involved in sleep regulation, but in aggression, impulse control, and anxiety across species, including people and dogs.

We may all look differently, but we are remarkably similar from a physiological and anatomical level.

However, when we look at social systems, we can't necessarily assume that our systems all work the same. For example, research among domestic dogs and wolves show that dogs respond to us differently. Dogs appear to be more willing to look directly into our faces for clues or hints when confused than wolves do. Dogs have evolved with humans differently, and they have also been artificially selected for qualities that made them more desirable as working partners or pets. These qualities may have meant that we also selected them to communicate differently to us than wolves naturally evolved to do.

Research is not fixed or without limitations. And you will find you will learn so much more from living and working with your dog than can come from any book. But research provides verifiable and repeatable evidence. It provides us with indications and possibilities for further exploration. It's the best we have and it's ultimately far more preferable to the unfounded assertions humans make when there are other motivations at play, beyond getting to the truth.

ALPHA DOGS AND DOMINANCE

There is so much in the pet dog literature and information that says you have to dominate the dog to avoid behavior problems. This often involves the use of force as a way to ensure that you are *top dog* or the *alpha* in the pack.

There is now a growing movement away from these concepts, because it leads to inhumane training practices, and in many cases, causes more problems than it solves, particularly where aggression is concerned. Further, much of dominance theory as it applies to dogs has arisen from early studies on captive wolves. This was influential because the domestic dog is thought to have descended from the wolf.

Dominance in Wolves

David Mech, one of the leaders in the science of wolf behavior, feels responsible for the introduction of the word *alpha* in the dog training industry because of his influential book that was written about captive wolves in the 1970's.

He has since said the use of the concept *alpha* is not appropriate, because in the wild, aggression is generally not used to maintain pack cohesion. The wolf pack in the wild is actually based on family structure with the leaders of the pack actually being the parents and the remainder of the pack primarily made up of offspring.

Today, there is a trend amongst the more educated to dismiss dominance theory and consider it dated because of its association with forceful methods.

But in trying to get a handle on all this to understand what my own thoughts were on the situation, I wondered why packs in the wild were necessarily a better model to study than wolves in captivity. After all, domestic dogs are not usually siblings (although they can be), nor did they have a choice to join the *pack*. They are also not in the position to disburse, which is what male wolves will often do when they reach a certain age.

Dogs are not wolves.

I decided to keep an open mind. One thing should be stated again though. Dogs are not wolves. They have changed with the process of evolution. They look different, their behavior is different, and even their cognition might be different. Dogs bark more and tend to have retained more puppy traits as adults, such as playful behavior that occurs far less frequently in wolves.

Dogs' sensitivity to human signaling differs from wolves.[89] Research that compares sensitivity to human communication in dogs, human-reared socialized wolves, and 10-month-old human infants showed that dogs and infants responded similarly, whereas the wolves did not.

Other research has indicated that dogs responded to pointing, even without intensive socialization, where wolves cannot.[90] Attachment behavior towards humans also differs between wolves and dogs with dogs being more responsive to their owner than to an unfamiliar person, where extensively socialized wolves were not.[91] Dog puppies tended to display more communicative signals that could potentially cause social interactions, whereas wolf pups showed more aggression and more avoidance in testing situations.[92]

It may be that the difference is a result of how we have co-evolved, socially evolved together, and that communicative behavior in wolves may have been the basis for selection. It may also be a result of genetic mutation that caused certain wolves to start to bond to us.

Genetically, wolves and dogs are different. *Gene expression* is the process that takes inherited information in your genes to make a specific functional product such as proteins. While there is a close genetic relationship between dogs and wolves,[93] their gene expression in the brain is different.[94] This suggests that dogs have developed to relate to us differently than their ancestors related to each other.

Dogs know that we are people and not dogs.

In addition, evidence suggests that dogs know that we are not dogs. It is not a stretch to assume that dogs do not treat us like dogs either. They don't respond to our touching or our smiling the way they respond to other dogs' similar actions. In fact, where a dog may react negatively to a paw on the head, shoulder or back, many dogs pursue a similar kind of contact with their owners: petting. Research also indicates that they look at our faces differently, reading it from left to right just as people read faces.[95] The right side of the face shows nuanced emotion more than the left. It appears that dogs are sensitive to this. Interestingly, dogs don't read other dogs' faces (or monkey faces or other animate objects for that matter) like this.

Research also indicates that play between dogs and play between dogs and humans are structurally different and therefore there may be distinct reasons why dogs play with people.[96] So it is not a complete stretch to assume that dogs do not need us to adapt their social system in order for us to live peacefully together since they know we are different.

But! Dogs *are* similar to wolves.

It seems to be the trend amongst the more educated people in this field to look at the differences between dogs and wolves at the time of writing this. This is in part because the differences tell us about ourselves, how our social systems evolved, and so on.

But in the information online, the concept that dogs are not wolves is usually used to promote the position around force-free training. And while there are clear differences, dogs probably *are* more similar to wolves than any other animal.

Not only have they descended from wolves, dogs and wolves continue to interbreed. Dogs, like wolves, tend to live in groups. It is generally agreed that dogs have inherited many of the signaling behaviors from the wolves they have descended from. Infant dogs, wolves, and coyotes, for example, use the play-bow.[97] As the play-bow appears to be used for communicating that an ambiguous action is play, it seems that many forms of signaling and communication, as well as conflict resolution, might be shared between wolves and dogs.

Other research suggests that possibly the difference in sensitivity to signaling in dogs compared to wolves might be a result of the testing environment, and not a result of domestication.[98]

Can we learn anything to help resolve aggression from other wolves?

By refusing to acknowledge the link between wolves and dogs, are we ignoring possible opportunities to understand dogs better? Domestic dogs live in such a managed and artificial environment that we are not always clear on what they might naturally do to resolve conflicts. Is there anything we can learn from wolves that could help improve aggression between domestic dogs that live together, for example?

With that in mind, I looked at research from wolves in the wild. I looked at research from captive wolves, and I've watched hours of captive wolf footage from the International Wolf Centre. I have also looked at free-ranging and feral dog research, (although there are indications that these dogs are also different from domestic dogs).

Throughout this, I also kept in mind that the researchers might be seeing a social hierarchy where there is none. And where I could, I tracked down research that addresses real cases of inter-dog aggression in the home.

Wolves

In wolf packs, hierarchies are established and maintained by ritualized behaviors.[99] Dominance contests with other wolves within a pack are rare, if they exist at all, as the parents are the pack leaders, and *alpha* status is considered fluid. Attacks that result in deaths in wild wolves are usually between different packs (opposed to between pack members) and involve territory.[100] The only consistent demonstration of rank (as the researchers defined it to be) in natural packs is the animals' postures during social interaction.[101] Most rank issues were simply resolved according to the age of the wolves and were maintained by deferring behavior, rather than the top dog enforcing their status.

In captive packs, the unacquainted wolves apparently form dominance hierarchies featuring *alpha*, *beta*, *omega* animals, etc. and the aggression appears to be higher as compared to packs in the wild. But we need to ask ourselves, how much of the posturing is a result of dominance and a desire for status, and how much of it is a result of anxiety? It's possible then, that the wolves that back down may have more fear or anxiety reflecting the natural variances within a species with respect to social avoidance, boldness, etc.

What it does not necessarily indicate is whether a pecking order is a natural way to resolve conflicts. The increase of aggression or anxiety may be a result of the stress of living in captivity. That stress might interfere with more natural, less confrontational ways to resolve conflicts. Does this mean that the captive wolf is a better model in which to understand dogs? After all, they are more or less living in captivity. Or are they? Dogs have co-evolved with humans. Studies of feral dogs indicate that feral dogs are unable to sustain themselves without human involvement.

Free-ranging, Feral or Stray dogs

Looking at feral dogs or stray dogs might be a good option to determine just how domestic dogs conduct themselves. Some research argues that feral dogs do not in fact form wolf-type packs at all. [102] Some research suggests that they do.[103]

Other research indicates that in some cases there is a relatively linear dominance hierarchy in some packs, but not in others. [104] As this conclusion was within the same study with the same investigators, we can rule out biases and determine that there are certainly differences between each group.

Interestingly, with regards to this research, these investigators separated leadership from dominance. Leadership involved greeting behaviors and initiators of action, whereas dominance looked at postures during social interactions. Leadership was not concentrated on a single individual, but there were dogs that habitually lead more often.

There was not too much speculation about why there were clear linear hierarchies in some cases but not in others or why habitual leaders did not lead all of the time. It certainly indicated that dominance hierarchies are not a given.

I would guess that the size of the group, temperament and personalities of the individuals, as well as the uniqueness of the relationship might have something to do with it. Like people, dogs have a wide variance of personality factors that influence action and behavior. Some are more curious; some are more alerted to the outside world. While still, others are reluctant to take initiative or are more tuned into social dynamics.

Rather than reflecting a need to lead or follow, it may simply reflect a shifting inclination. Habitual leaders and outcomes as a result of dominance/submissive behaviors may be more habitual as a result of the particular dogs' predispositions and social dynamics, rather than an actual need to enforce an order.

Domestic dogs in the home

Another complication is that the concept of *a pack* in the home is an artificial one. It is often (although not always) made up of different breeds, ages, and sizes and they are introduced at different times. In some cases, the dogs don't appear to care about hierarchies, and in other cases, they obviously do. This sounds remarkably like the feral dogs research.

However, it's possible that we see dominance or subordinate displays only when there is an uncertainty or some kind of tension, however mild. It's also possible that when the social hierarchy is stable, we see relatively few behaviors that indicate a hierarchy. It may also be that, like wolves, when the dogs are of lower rank, the actual status ceases to matter.

Dominance: A matter of perception?

It is widely held that in a dominance relationship, ritualized behaviors are used to manage conflict so that it doesn't escalate into aggression. Some state that dominance refers to gaining access to and retaining resources.[105] Others have written that social dominance theory only applies to conflict.[106]

Still, other authors write that dominance is a characteristic of a habitual outcome of an antagonistic relationship. In other words, where there is a pattern where the outcome is in favor of one, and the other yields rather than escalates, we can see a dominance relationship.[107] This suggests that the dominant role may be defined by those who choose to yield, rather than engage in conflict.

So is dominance a matter of perception then? Dominance theory seems aimed at trying to predict an outcome, so the notion of dominance may really be about the tendency for a certain outcome to occur. But whether or not a dog leads or gains access to something valuable, like a prized toy or affection from a human, the outcome appears to be an expression of the mix of motivations and personalities between the two in the relationship.

So there is no evidence that our trying to be *alpha* and trying to be part of the pack will ensure peace in the home. It is even possible that when we act dominantly, we are really communicating that we experience anxiety about the other, and that maybe we are more like bullies than anything else.

But predicting is challenging. When Shadow, the *alpha* Arctic wolf from the International Wolf Centre, was removed from the main pack, it was difficult even for the ethologists, (scientists that study animal behavior) at the center to determine who would have *alpha* status. Social hierarchies do not refer to *individuals*. There is no evidence in wolves that a wolf is born as an *alpha*.[108] Social hierarchies are about the relationship between individuals.

If nothing else, anything that provides consistency and predictability in those cases where there is human interaction will help reduce anxiety. From this perspective, allowing one dog to go through the door first, get food first, be petted first or any other perceived values consistently may set up a hierarchy-like structure.

By doing so, you are likely setting up an alliance with the dog that is getting it first. You are probably saying, if there is a fight, I will support you. And, are you making the right decision? Have you determined who is the most experienced, the strongest in the case of a physical fight, who is the wisest (that question rules out the dog who has issues)? It is very hard to make this decision without bringing our own biases in, siding with the dog we just like better, or the underdog. Sometimes we just can't tell.

This alone will not resolve aggression problems in the home. *Behavior modification,* teaching the dogs' self-control, reinforcing appropriate signaling and communication behaviors, possibly medication and many of the other possibilities suggested in this book or by qualified professionals may all be required to improve sibling rivalry between dogs.

What can we learn from human social structure?

It is worth putting forth a human social structure analogy to communicate that social structure can be complex and that dominance theories are often unhelpful.

Social organization in people loosely revolves around age, sex, and experience among other things. It is highly influenced by the numbers of people involved, personalities, and motivation for social status among many other influences. It is also fluid and shifts from context to context and not absolute. People can posture to gain social status, and some do this more than others. Some lose status as fast as they get it, and some continue to earn it. Less secure people appear to posture more than more secure people, although it's equally possible much of this posturing is a learned behavior.

Think about the work place: while someone can be your boss, whether you respect them or not may depend on how much experience they have, how intelligent you perceive them, how they treat you, and the kind of relationship you can develop with them. We all know people who seek the attention of others or who want to be perceived as being more knowledgeable or "cooler" than they actually are. We are not always aware of just how sensitive we are to this, but we respond constantly, and probably struggle more often with it than we are aware of it.

On a micro scale, things like manners and on a larger scale, stuff such as the hierarchy of a formally organized group, all work to keep the peace; in other words, reduce conflict and as a result, reduce aggression.

However, social organization really is not organized by people behaving aggressively or by being dominant over us. When it is, we usually recognize there is a problem.

Formally organized social hierarchies – such as those in the workplace, are not always parallel with the true social hierarchy that exists. Our formal social organization sometimes fails (i.e. think of an incompetent boss – incompetence may be a result of poor social skills, lack of experience, or confidence, etc.)

We instinctively follow or pay attention to people who we perceive as being worth following in a given context. We might make this decision to follow someone on our own or we might be influenced by others' opinions. It may be that the other person has more social currency, they are more experienced, or they might provide something we want, such as an instigator role in times of unrest. In the case where there is no one we perceive worth following, we tend to become more independent or even take the lead ourselves. We see this in children and couples frequently. Some relationships are more constant, but overall, social hierarchies in people are fluid and part of an ever-changing social structure. But the roles in each context are not necessarily perceived as equal. And yet, when the structure has been there for a long time, we sometimes become blind to it. Even more interestingly, when the social structures are comfortable, those lines become more blurred. Not unlike dogs.

But in most cases, even when a social hierarchy is imposed, it is really the people who are following that determine who should lead. Just because you tell me you know everything doesn't mean I will believe it. I will choose who to follow.

It appears that dogs have these similar social systems. Depending on the personalities involved and what is occurring at the time, one dog may always get what he or she chooses first, or it may depend on context. In some dogs you see no posturing at all, in others you see much more. You will see much more evaluation between the dogs, and even more conflict when things change in the social dynamic, as opposed to when things have been established for some time. This is why it is often so hard for people to determine who is the dominant dog. It is not as though there isn't some system, agreement, or expectation in place; it's just that whether it's working or falling apart, the system is complex.

 # SPEAKING DOG: INTERPRETING DOG BEHAVIOR

Learning to read behavior is valuable in working with dogs. It is key for reducing anxiety, for de-escalating aggression, and in maintaining dogs' welfare and of course, implementing *behavior modification* programs. Not knowing whether your dog is anxious can cause you to push your dog farther than he or she is ready to go. This can make the situation worse.

But even the experts can't agree

Interestingly, even the experts can't agree what a dog might be feeling at any one time. A study looked at eight experienced dog professionals (including certified pet dog trainers, veterinary behaviorists and applied animal behaviors – all well trained professionals) rating 30 clips of dogs' stress level, arousal, emotions, etc.

While they were in high agreement with 40% of the dogs, 37% were only in moderate agreement, and they were in poor agreement with 7 (23%) of the dogs.[109]

Err on the side of caution

What does this mean for us? It means that accurately interpreting a dog's behavior is not always easy! But you are probably better erring on the side of caution when it comes to interpreting how comfortable your dog is in a situation. In other words, if you are not sure your dog is anxious, assume he or she is and change things so that they can be calm. As said before, probably one of the biggest mistakes dog owners make is exposing their dog to situations that make them anxious and aggressive. This is won't help your dog relax the next time.

Learn about your dog

While we don't recommend you try to make your dog aggressive or anxious to look for the subtle signs it's going to happen, we strongly encourage you to video your dogs in different contexts so that you can train yourself to pay attention to the signs he or she is giving. Videotaping is incredibly valuable when you have more than one dog because you simply can't pay attention to it all, especially when you are just learning, and the behaviors often happen very quickly.

At first you won't know what to look for, or how to read what you are seeing until you can compare their behavior in different contexts. Good times to video may be social situations, natural down times, as well as when you are training your dog to relax.

If you have a video player that can review frame by frame, this can help, but if not, *pause* and *rewind* are your best friends! You do not have to video for long – five minutes will probably do. When you review the video clips, pay attention to each one of these areas, one at a time.

- Posture of the head, back and tail
- Position of the ears
- Activity of the tail
- Piloerection (fur is raised along the neck, back, and base of the tail)
- Eyes and mouth tension (look for tightness, looseness, wrinkling, etc.)
- Vocal and mouth behavior (barking, growling, snarling, lip lifting, snapping and biting)
- Movement over the time (is the dog restless, can't settle or refuses to move? Are they invading others space)
- Approach – how is your dog approaching others? Does he or she go straight for them, do they tend to avoid them, turn their head, walk slow, etc.?

This will help you recognize how your dog holds him or herself and helps you get into the practice of looking for those signs. You will know, for example, that a high tail may be communicating confidence or the desire to assert themselves. Ears turned to the side might indicate some uncertainty. You may see your dog avoiding being petted.

In my case, I had one dog that seemed to be very silly and playful until I came across this book that defined *active submission*. She showed these active submission behaviors in a number of situations, from putting her leash on to go for a walk, to playing with my other dog. Regardless of whether this behavior was in fact *active submission*, it caused me to re-examine my assumptions about what was going on and to really look at her body language. Around this time, I was coming to believe that submissive behaviors in dogs might actually be a result of anxiety rather than of social positioning, or personality. I videoed our interactions and training and reviewing the video later allowed me to pause or shuttle through the video slowly or rewind as needed to that I could focus and concentrate on all the signals. It allowed me to identify those things that happened too quickly for me to catch because I was concentrating on the social interaction at the time.

Although her body posture was lower in nature as compared to the people or the other dogs, it was provoking. I came to realize that it occurred in situations where she was feeling anxious. By the time I took her to a veterinary behaviorist, I already had a very good idea of what was going on, which was confirmed by the vet. My dog-aggressive dog had a generalized anxiety disorder.

She was not a shy dog or really even a fearful dog, but at the vet consultation, she lay with her head on the floor under the couch for a significant amount of time — something she had never done before. Home was okay for her, but this situation was simply more than she could handle and she had no other way to deal with it. It was the equivalent of her covering her ears with her hands and shutting her eyes. But because I spent the time observing her in detail, I already had a pretty good idea that she was not just a silly dog, she was anxious.

Being able to read her behavior allowed me to prevent what I think would have been a terrible accident down the line.

Behaviors occur in sequence

When we are trying to read whether a dog is uncomfortable, it helps to know that individual behaviors usually occur in a sequence when a dog is anxious. For example, a yawning dog does not necessarily mean the dog is uncomfortable. But if he or she has been resting, and now their head is up, their ears are back, they are swallowing or you see their tongue flick out — maybe there is something to that yawn? Actions are not always congruent and interpretation should depend on evaluating all the signs and the context the dog is in. The less congruent the signs are, the less confidence the dog has in signaling particular signs.[110] In other words conflicting signaling suggests that dog is uncertain and may be in conflict.

Behaviors occur in context

Pay attention to the context: what else is happening at the time? What social interaction is going on? Or in the case of aggression between two dogs in the household, what are the things around that the dog might find valuable that may be causing concern? Does it seem to happen around you? What are the other body signals telling you? How are the other animals in the room or the area acting in those cases where the dog is aggressive towards other dogs?

Catching signs early is critical

By the time things become intense, anxiety or aggression has escalated to the point where the dog may be staring, growling, or lunging. At this point, it can be difficult to turn off the sequence, or redirect the dog so that he or she doesn't become more aggressive or actually cause damage. Consequently, catching signs of stress *early* in the behavior sequence, before we see the obvious signs of aggression, is incredibly valuable.

Even though not all experts have the same viewpoint, and although the list that follows is unlikely to be all-inclusive, there are a number of behaviors you can start to pay attention to now.

Signs of stress (must be looked at in context of a situation)

- Yawning
- Licking lips
- Sweaty feet (as seen by paw prints on a floor)
- Pupil dilation
- Tense facial features, including lips and furrowed forehead
- Panting
- Drooling in some dogs
- Fast tail wagging
- Body shaking*
- Crouching*
- Oral behaviors (such as snout licking)*
- Restlessness*
- Low posture*

* These behaviors were associated with acute stress in response to a variety of stimuli.[111] Body shaking was seen less often when humans weren't involved.

Behaviors associated with anxiety:

- Panting
- Pupil dilation
- Ears back and down
- Pacing
- Drooling
- Hiding
- Shaking
- Exfoliation (hair loss)
- Shedding
- Whining
- Destruction
- Urination or defection

Escalation of arousal

The following behaviors might overlap with the stress behaviors or may not be part of a behavioral sequence.

- Hackles are up (the line of fur along a dog's back, at the neck, and/or base of their tail)
- Holding their breath
- Moving very slowly
- Stiff body
- The dog is looking out the corners of their eyes and you can see the whites, sometimes called "cow-eye" or "whale-eye"
- Staring (dogs will sometimes look away just before attack)

Appeasement behaviors that may be associated with anxiety

- Looking away (this often involves a head turn away)
- Urination
- Rolling over

- Paw lifting
- Hunched or cowering behavior

Challenging behaviors to other dogs

- Staring
- Hackles are up (the line of fur along a dog's back, at the neck and or base of their tail)
- Placing a paw on shoulders or head
- Growling, snarling or snapping
- Blocking access to a resting place
- Lying on the other dog
- Stealing resources from the other dog
- Shoving the other dog to get through a narrow area first such as stairs, doorways, etc.
- Posturing in ritualized displays: this can include staring, *standing tall*, circling, approaching the shoulders of the other dog to form a "T" shape with the other dog

Signs of deference that you may wish to reward

- Any behavior that involves making themselves smaller which could include
  - Sitting
  - Lying down
  - Hunching
  - Rolling over
  - Getting below the other dog's nose or muzzle (although sometimes dogs will do this and then poke the other dog to test them)
- Greeting behaviors such as licking muzzle of nose of other dog

Video resources

While we provide lists of things to look out for here, ultimately reading about it is not the same as watching the actual behavior. As mentioned earlier, here are two video resources that may help:

- *THE LANGUAGE OF DOGS - UNDERSTANDING CANINE BODY LANGUAGE AND OTHER COMMUNICATION SIGNALS DVD SET* by Sarah Kalnajs

- *Canine Behavior, Body Postures and The Behaviorally Healthy Dog*, By Susanne Hetts, PhD& Daniel Estep, PhD

WHAT CAUSES DOG AGGRESSION?

The important thing to understand about aggression is that aggression is a symptom to an underlying condition. It is not the problem itself (although it may be in your life!). It is usually the *result* of an underlying problem. From a broad picture view like we described in the overview on aggression, anger is thought to be a secondary emotion by psychologists that happens as a result of a primary emotion that causes the person or animal to feel vulnerable. Anger is a public emotion; it is one that protects us, but it's also action oriented, and causes us to make something happen.

The underlying cause is usually anxiety and sometimes fear-related, but as discussed at the beginning of the book, it can also be other things such as pain or frustration, or any combination. So when we look at what motivates a dog to behave aggressively, we really need to understand what is causing one or any combination of the underlying emotions.

And while a predisposition to aggression does not necessarily mean that a dog will become aggressive, it does indicate that a dog is more vulnerable to responding that way under the right circumstances. Some of the conditions that may predispose a dog to aggression are:

- **Genetic predisposition**: this includes things that the dog has inherited or was born with. Predispositions in breeds only generalize towards what kind of behavior problem a dog might be predisposed to, not whether or not a dog will have a behavior problem. Inherited problems that might affect aggression include anything from learning disabilities to anxiety disorders to ADHD-like disorders. As we get more information from such projects as the Dog Genome Project, we will learn more about genetic predispositions.

- **Physical or mental health condition**: Physical or mental health can be affected by any of the above, but what starts out as one thing may evolve into something more. Aggression may occur at any time and in any condition where the dog feels unwell or is under stress. A non-stressed dog will not be nearly as reactive as a dog that is stressed. In addition there are a number of diseases or conditions that can cause aggression. Seizures and sleep disorders are one of many. Age-related conditions can also influence aggression.

- **Experiences**: A lack of socialization during the critical period of a dog's life can cause problems. Negative experiences during this phase in the early life of the dog are of particular concern as they can cause fear. But negative experiences can happen any time and can cause the dog to develop aggression. The dog learns from these experiences, which then influences future behavior.

  Not only can a lack of proper socialization cause fear as well, but it can also deprive the dog of the opportunity to learn social signaling both from people and dogs. These dogs may not know how to tell if another dog or person is a threat. In other cases, a dog's negative experiences may cause him or her to believe the signaling does not work.

- **Psychological and physical needs**. Dogs obviously need the minimum requirements for survival, but they also need positive social interaction, exercise, mental stimulation, safety, and a comfortable and interesting environment. If these needs are not met, the dog can develop mental and physical issues as a result. These needs may be based on breed, age, sex and the individual. Some dogs, depending on the breed, might be more motivated to chase after certain kinds of things than others, or perhaps have different social needs and may experience frustration when denied.

GENETICS: DNA AND GENES

When we are trying to make sense of our dog's aggression, we often feel a whole host of conflicting emotions, not the least of which is feeling responsible for it and therefor guilty. But how much aggression issues are inherited?

You are probably familiar with at least the terms of both *DNA* and *genes* and may be wondering to what extent it influences aggression in dogs. What about all the stuff you hear about breeding or breeds for that matter, right or wrong?

What is DNA?

Every cell that has a nucleus contains DNA. DNA is a huge chemical information database that we inherit from our parents. It carries a set of instructions for all the proteins a cell will ever need. Although it contains just four chemicals, there are millions of building blocks called *bases*. The order in which the bases appear determines the information (think how letters make words, words make sentences, sentences form paragraphs, and so on.)

What is a gene?

A gene is a segment along the DNA that carries a particular set of instructions usually for a particular protein that initiates action. There are between 50,000 and 100,000 genes in humans made up of thousands or hundreds of thousands of chemical bases.

What do we know so far?

There is a small amount of research that has looked at gene expression in different parts of the canine brain, but relevant to us is research looking at 20 dogs, some non-aggressive and some aggressive to people. They looked at parts of the brain that are implicated with aggression and have indicated that there are gene expression differences between the non-aggressive and aggressive dogs. The conclusion of that research is that the *disposition* for aggressive behavior is most probably *polygenic* (i.e. due to multiple genes) and influenced by several different neurotransmitters (chemical messengers in the brain) and hormonal systems.

The gene that demonstrated the largest differences in expression is the main gene responsible for clearance of the *symptic glutamate*, which is the major excitatory neurotransmitter in the central nervous system. [112] In people this has been associated with multiple psychiatric and neurological disorders.[113] This suggests then, that there may be a genetic component at least with aggression towards people. In all likelihood, there is a genetic component to other forms of aggression as well. So does that means there is nothing you can do about it?

Is my dog's aggression destined?

A genetic mediated predisposition to a behavior problem is just that – a predisposition. It suggests vulnerability, but it is not a prediction of the future. The reality is, knowledge of genetics should be able to help people *shape* destiny. You can teach a dog how to relax if he/she is reactive, teach them how to look to you when they are unsure of how to behave, and/or prescribe them medication if he/she needs it to help make a dog more open to *behavior modification*.

At one time, the idea that what was learned and experienced could not be inherited. However in a study on young mice, it showed environmental enrichment not only enhanced *long-term potentiation* - which is the long lasting strengthening of certain kinds of communication between cells in the brain relating to learning and memory - *but also in future offspring that did not even experience environmental enrichment.*[114]

Studies around gene expression and aggression in dogs so far may provide an indication that there is a predisposition towards certain traits, but the differences in gene expression do not account for the actual experiences the dog may have. Learning will also have an impact beyond genes.

Let go of blame

Aggression is our responsibility to prevent as dog owners, but it doesn't mean we are responsible for a dog being prone to behaving aggressively in the first place. There are plenty of bad dog owners who have done what you have possibly done and worse, and their dogs have not become aggressive. Of course, we can always make things worse, and often do, but whether or not the dog is predisposed to aggression has nothing to do with the dog owner. If you are one of those people who are swimming in guilt, it's time to put that away and let yourself off the hook, and think about how you can change the problem.

It's possible that certain dogs may inherit the propensity for aggression. However, we are not the mere sum of our parts. A predisposition for aggression does not mean the dog is doomed. What we do can often make a difference.

 # HOW DOES THE BREED INFLUENCE AGGRESSION?

There is a lot said about breeds, from the nature of their personalities to what kinds of problems they are going to have. Having owned pit-bulls, I've seen the extreme of opinions with of one side wanting to kill all pit-bulls (and certainly the various bans around the world reflect this thinking), to the other extreme insisting there are no bad dogs, only bad owners. What is true?

Breed Research

There is little research focusing on the differences in behavior between breeds – the classifications by the American Kennel Club are regarded as remnants from past selection during the breed's origin.[115] There have been some pilot studies that looked at the latency and duration of time breeds spent looking at the researcher when faced with an insolvable problem, and while there were differences, the researchers caution against concluding these differences are meaningful as a result of the arbitrary nature of the group classification and the lack of the ethological (scientific study of behavior) descriptions of breed behavior. In fact, the greatest differences seen appeared to be related differences between the ages of the dogs.

One of the reasons why there has been little research is that most dogs are inaccessible to direct behavior observation so the behavior must be assessed indirectly. Alternatively, there would have to be tests that are difficult and lengthy to carry out or data based on owner questionnaires. There is not a lot of confidence in the sensitivity, accuracy, and reliability of both.

Owner questionnaires might be influenced both by their belief and attitudes, but also breed stereotypes that cause them to interpret behavior in certain ways. Other data on breeds comes from bite statistics, behavior clinic caseloads, and experts' opinions, but these may be misleading due to the kind of bites that are reported (i.e. bites to children are more likely to be reported than bites to adults), the size and severity of the bite, the disproportionate representation of any given breed (which also affects the care in which it's bred – more popular dogs have more lax breeding care). And of course, the actual breed may not be verified as actually being a purebred, or even being the breed at all (pit-bulls in particular are mistaken with several other breeds). And with the experts' opinions (i.e. trainers, veterinarians, etc.), it is unknown how much stereotypes and preferences impact viewpoints, or whether there is agreement on what aggressiveness actually means.

That said, it still may be worth looking at research that uses owner reports, since presumably, the owner has more opportunity to observe the dog over time and in a variety of situations. The following charts are based on data that doesn't depend on the number of bites reported; therefor it is likely more representative of all aggression. It does not however, negate any poor standards of breeding due to a popularity of a breed, breed stereotyping, or rejection of breed stereotyping.

But, here in the following charts may be some of the areas that you can look out for if you have a dog that falls into any of these breed groups. Remember at best, these figures only represent possibly tendencies.

In all cases the *majority* of dogs in each breed group do not snap, attempt to bite, or bite. The researchers specifically state, that because of the substantial variation of scores within each breed, **"it is inappropriate to make predictions about a given dog's propensity for aggressive behavior based solely on its breed."** [116]

This makes a lot of sense given that the majority of dogs in each breed category were not reported to bite or attempt to bite.

The following figures based on total number of dogs were 3791, with an average of 115 per breed, although this ranged from 53 (Great Dane) to 349 (Labrador Retriever). The bars represent the percentage of dogs that were reported to have either snapped, attempted to bite, or actually bit out of the entire group surveyed. Dogs that bark or growl were excluded. The reports are subjective as the owners filled them out. However according to the paper, the results are consistent with other reports of breed differences.

The data comes from a paper, authored by Deborah L. Duffy, Yuying Hsu, and James A. Serpell, entitled, 'Breed differences in canine aggression,' published in *Applied Animal Behavior Science*, in 2008. The bars represent a percentage out of the group of dogs in the data set within the category of aggression.

Note that less than 10% of any breed is aggressive toward their owners. Less that 25% is aggressive towards strangers. Less than 30% is aggressive towards other dogs, and less than 12% are aggressive towards dogs they live with in the home (sibling rivalry).

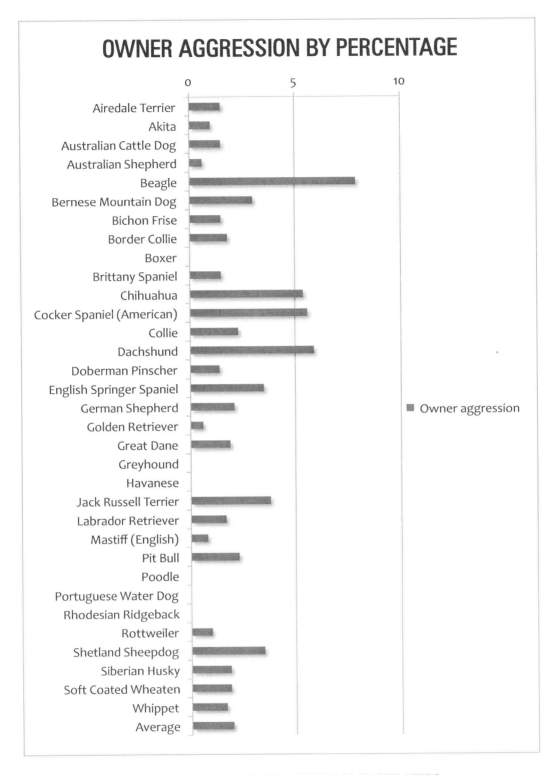

OWNER AGGRESSION BY PERCENTAGE

THE DOG AGGRESSION SYSTEM EVERY DOG OWNER NEEDS

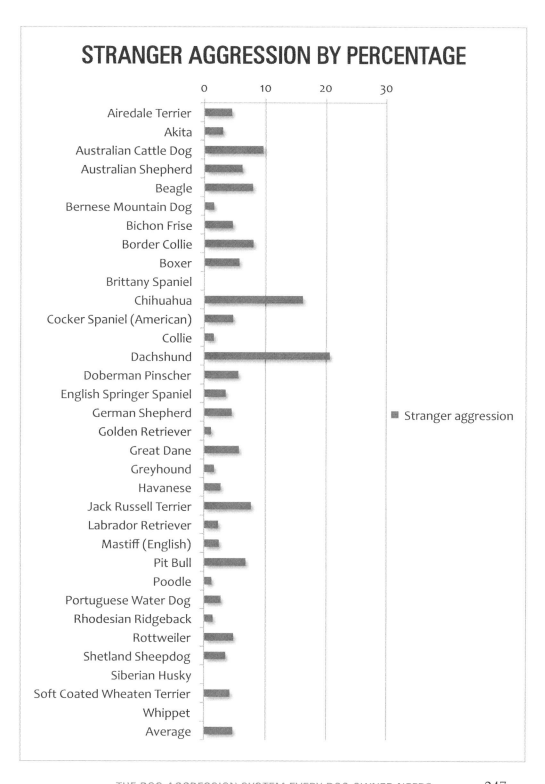

STRANGER AGGRESSION BY PERCENTAGE

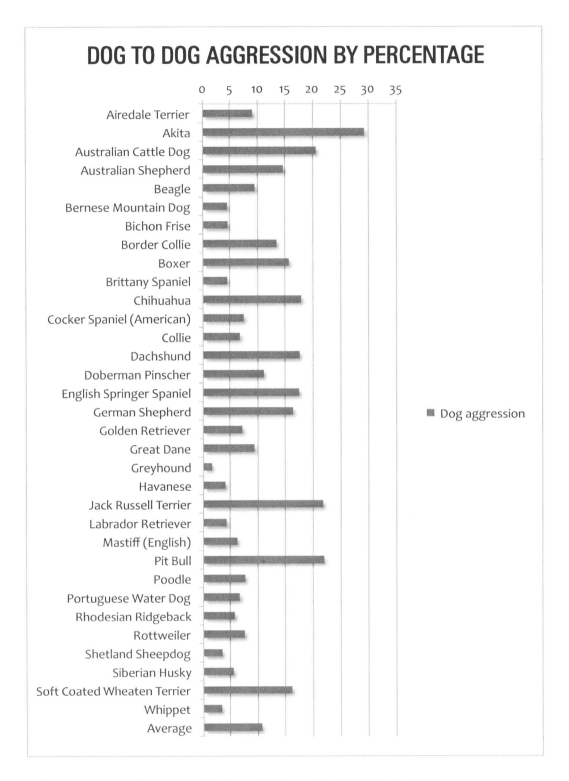

DOG TO DOG AGGRESSION BY PERCENTAGE

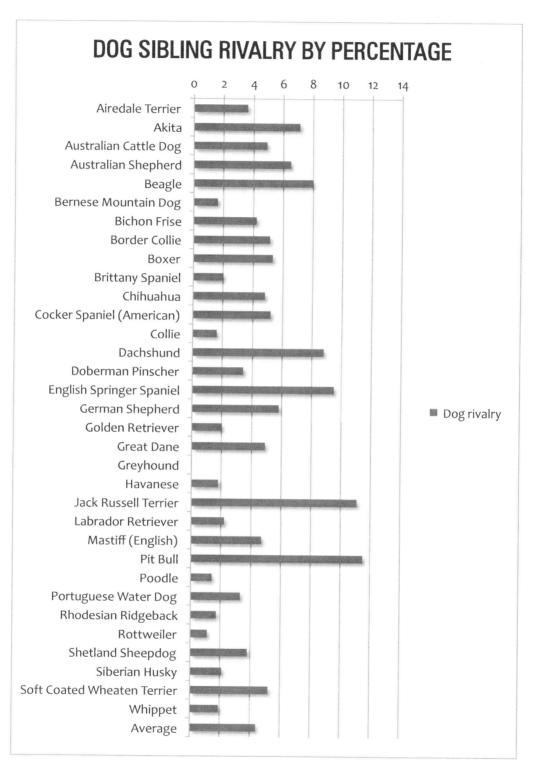

DOG SIBLING RIVALRY BY PERCENTAGE

- Some breeds scored higher than average for aggression directed toward *both* humans and dogs (e.g., Chihuahuas and Dachshunds).

- Other breeds scored high only for specific targets (e.g., dog-to-dog aggression was higher among Akitas and Pit-bull Terriers).

- Aggression was most severe when directed toward other dogs followed by unfamiliar people and household members. Interestingly, aggression towards household members is often the most common kind of aggression that is seen in many behavior clinics. This suggests that many people cope better with aggression towards other dogs, despite that it is most severe on average.

- Breeds with the greatest percentage of dogs exhibiting serious aggression (bites or bite attempts) toward humans included Dachshunds, Chihuahuas and Jack Russell Terriers (toward strangers and owners); Australian Cattle Dogs (toward strangers); and American Cocker Spaniels and Beagles (toward owners).

- More than 20% of Akitas, Jack Russell Terriers, and Pit-bull Terriers were reported as displaying serious aggression toward unfamiliar dogs.

- Golden Retrievers, Labradors Retrievers, Bernese Mountain Dogs, Brittany Spaniels, Greyhounds and Whippets were the least aggressive toward both humans and dogs.

- Among English Springer Spaniels, conformation-bred dogs were more aggressive to humans and dogs than field-bred dogs, suggesting a genetic influence on the behavior. [117]

This particular test appeared to be good for scoring for factors that were good at discriminating between breeds, and conformed to the popular views regarding temperaments. It is still being conducted, (you can find the C-BARQ online) and although further reports have not been made to my knowledge, the database has since grown to 11,000, many thousands more than when this paper was written. Time will tell if this data as reported in this book will still be accurate.

Traits That May Influence Aggression According To Breed Types

Another study looked at traits in terms of boldness and trainability, which may be of interest for some, which we will discuss momentarily. But, it's always wise to not accept things at face value. For example, one of the survey questions from this study is whether the dog understands what is expected from them during playing. That is a fair question.

But play involves a certain amount of improvisation and experimentation. A dog that has been trained with punishment such as leash pops or shock collars may be reluctant to try out any behaviors in case of punishment. Trainers regularly report that crossover dogs, i.e. those that have been previously trained with aversive methods will often shut down or simply not do anything, rather than risk offering behaviors for clicker training initially.

In other words, the dog appears to be too afraid to experiment and try out different things to see what the dog owner/trainer will click for. They are often reluctant to offer up new behaviors for shaping.[118] [119] [120] Is this kind of dog going to be as willing to play as a clicker trained dog that does not fear punishment for doing something wrong? Probably not.

Regardless, the information is statistical. There is a wide variability between individuals within the same breeds. So it is important to look at this information only in terms of tendencies. For example, if you have a non-sporting dog, knowing that they are a little more difficult to train may help to reduce frustration and allow you to be more patient.

- Herding dogs were more trainable than Hounds, Working dogs, Toy dogs and Non-sporting dogs.

- Sporting dogs were also more trainable than Non-sporting dogs.

- Terriers were bolder than Hounds and Herding dogs.

- Breeds with ancient Asian or African origin (Ancient breeds) were less trainable than the Herding/Sight hound cluster and the Hunting breeds.

- Mastiff/terrier cluster were bolder than the Ancient breeds, the breeds in the Herding/Sight hound cluster, and the Hunting breeds.[121]

Explanation of groups	
Ancient breeds	Breeds with ancient Asian or African origin, mainly primitive type dogs
Mastiff/terrier cluster	Mastiff-type breeds or breeds with mastiff-type ancestors and terriers
Herding/sight hound cluster	Breeds used as herding dogs and sight hounds
Hunting breeds	Breeds with relative recent European origin, primarily different hunting dogs
Mountain cluster	Large mountain dogs and a subset of spaniels

Currently, there is a large long term DNA project in research called the Dog Genome project that started in 2004. http://www.k9behavioralgenetics.com/ (we are happy to note that the K9aggression support group had been listed as a Behavioral Resource on their website at the time of writing, but K9aggression.com is not otherwise not associated with the project).

Among some of the things they are interested in are extreme forms of aggression. But unless science eventually proves otherwise, based on all the data available, there is no behavioral problem that is breed-specific. All breeds can have behavioral problems, and researchers vehemently oppose breed legislation.

However, the current beliefs are that some breeds may have a higher proportion of a certain *kind* of behavioral problem, and this may be influenced by how they were selected for certain traits. For example, herders needed dogs that would not actually kill the livestock. They would select and breed those dogs that don't actually commit to the kill. These dogs may be slightly more cautious, or even have some element of fear. It may be this quality that causes them to be more restrained. So when we look at both ends of the bell curve of aggression in these breeds, the bulk of the dogs in the middle are normal. But we may have extremely fearful dogs at the one end of the bell curve, and fear aggressive dogs at the other. Whereas it is possible that in terrier breeds, we have a higher proportion of obsessive compulsive disorders in dogs that demonstrate behavior problems, and more "gameness," which may indicate that some might more willing to fight than to cower.

Dogs who have been selected for their sense of smell might be far more food oriented – and more distracted by all the smells in the outside environment. Dogs selected for other reasons may be predisposed towards other distractions. Fox terriers for example, appear to be able to smell perfectly well, but seem to be uninterested in scent as compared to beagles in some situations. However, research indicates fox terriers are highly stimulated by sounds.[122] If you have a dog that is predisposed to being sensitive towards sound, your dog is going to need training just to be exposed to different sounds. This means their stress load is going to be higher in a noisy environment, which makes reactivity to any stress that much higher, and the ability to learn lower.

Breed traits may help you plan what to think about when considering how to motivate your dog; or perhaps help identify what things to avoid or moderate while training or in stressful situations. Dogs that are sound sensitive or react to movement may be more reactive around busy traffic, or times when school is just being let out, or around playgrounds, etc. and may need extra work in these areas during *behavior modification*, and extra management at other times.

It can also help you when it comes time to understanding how they learn and how you can motivate them. You have seen those dogs obsessed with whatever you can throw for them, yet you can wave a floppy squeaky toy in front of some dogs and they hardly notice it. Others turn their nose up at treats although they are probably simply being fed too much, or you are not using treats THEY find super tasty. Whereas other dogs lose their minds over a piece of dried liver so much that they fall all over themselves trying to get it, and thereby missing the point you were trying to teach (maybe look for a slightly less motivating treat for them).

While it's worth looking into the history of your particular breed to get a sense of what he/she might be predisposed to, you should also consider them as an individual. Breed traits at best are only generalizations on a bell curve.

DIGGING DEEPER: ENVIRONMENTAL ENRICHMENT

Psychological needs probably stem from a survival need over time. The need for mental stimulation probably keeps us learning and exploring so that we have more options to survive when our survival becomes threatened.

Factors in the environment that increases aggression

Research has used manipulation of the environment to cause and enhance (not improve) aggression. These are:

- Stressful experiences, especially early in life
- Social isolation
- Provocation: intense noxious or painful stimuli
- Unpredictable chronic, but mild stress
- Frustration (especially of an expected reward)
- Learned aggression heightens aggression: repeated aggressive experiences that cause an animal to win against another

Other factors that can influence aggression

- Low levels of glucocorticoids (which are typically produced as a result of stress)
- Abnormal activity in the brain
- Genetic manipulations (i.e. breeding)

Environmental enrichment can help to reduce aggression

Animals living under enriched conditions have clearly been shown to have reduced aggression [123], reduction of anxiety, fear and excitability [124] [125] [126] [127], reduction of stress [128] [129] [130], better brain function [131] [132] and better learning abilities[133] than those maintained under standard conditions.

While juvenile rats have been exposed to stress, and this appeared to trigger anxiety and depressive-like behaviors; environmental enrichment was found to be able to reverse these effects.[134] In some situations, environmental enrichment made the animals less anxious, more motivated and they had better learning abilities even compared with animals that have never been exposed to the stress. Because the symptoms in rats caused by the stress appeared to be similar to depressive symptoms in humans, this research was used to speculate that environmental enrichment could help prevent devastating effects in young adults who experience childhood stress.

Why is this important?

All too often when dogs become aggressive, the relationship between owner and dog deteriorates. This is when people pull away, ignore, or isolate the dog. This potentially makes the problems worse. Not only do dogs need mental stimulation, but also major contributors to stress pathology are those situations where an animal experiences a loss of control.[135] Being able to control, explore, and manipulate things in the environment helps this.

For more information on how you can enrich your dog's environment, please see the first section on environment enrichment in Step 3 in Building a Treatment program found in of Part 1 of the book.

We tend to get puzzled when our dogs' reactivity levels change. On the one hand, we feel elated when our dog seems calmer than he/she was before; on the other hand, we are crushed when become more reactive or aggressive.

Dogs will vary in how they feel, react, and process the influences of aggression. They vary not only from each other, and between stimuli (situations, things, etc. that trigger the aggression), but also according to how they might be feeling at that moment. Suffice it to say, there are many factors involved.

 ## FEAR AND ANXIETY AS IT RELATES TO AGGRESSION

None like to experience fear and most certainly if your dog's aggression is coming out of fear, we want to reduce it and make life better for the dog. There is a link between fear of strangers and shorter life spans.

Fear

It is important to remember that fear is important and serves a purpose. It's what keeps us clear of danger in the first place. In fact, the brain devotes the most space and energy to fear out of all the emotions we process. The difficulty for our dogs is that we continue to bring them into situations they would probably have avoided in the first place.

Fear originates in the amygdala of the brain. A woman who suffers from a degenerative condition that left her with brain damage in certain areas was unable to feel fear. It sounds rather wonderful, other than how many times her life has been threatened. From being a victim to hold-ups, death threats, and domestic violence,[136] she has faced these situations far, far more than normal. It seems then, that fear protects us and dictates our behavior early on in a social cycle so that we don't even encounter highly dangerous situations.

Anxiety

Anxiety is like sustained fear. It's less specific, it lasts longer, and it is activated by more diffused cues.[137] It is identified by exaggerated attention to threat. Some differentiate anxiety from fear, with the idea that anxiety is more future-based, whereas fear has to do with what is being perceived in the present. The majority of behavior related disorders in dogs, including aggression, are considered to be related to anxiety or have an anxiety component.[138]

Generalized Anxiety

Some animals with behavior problems have generalized anxiety or situation-specific anxiety. To be diagnosed with generalized anxiety, your dog would demonstrate these signs:

- Increased vigilance and scanning
- Autonomic nervous system hyperactivity (this refers to the involuntary system that governs heart rate, respiratory rate, etc.)
- Increased motor activity
- The above signs must be general and unrelated to immediate changes in the behavioral or physical environment

A dog has generalized anxiety when it has trouble understanding what the appropriate response is to what is going on around them. In an aggressive dog, the dog may be fine with people who ask her to sit and give her good consistent signals, but her responses to all other actions suggest that for each new person, she may have to provoke others and formulate her response based on what they do as a result.

In her book, Dr. Karen Overall suggests that because these dogs can't generalize the good and relaxed aspects of their environment, the anxious part of the behaviors can be self-rewarding.[139]

In *The Trouble With Testosterone and Other Essays on the Biology of the Human Predicament* (1997), Robert M. Sapolsky writes, "People with anxiety disorders can be thought of as persistently mobilizing coping responses that are disproportionately large. For them, life is filled with threats around every corner, threats that demand a constant hyper-vigilance, an endless search for safety, a sense that the rules are constantly changing."

This paints a rather dismal life view for a dog that has generalized anxiety, and indicates without some kind of pharmaceutical intervention in the way of anti-anxiety medication, it may be incredibly hard to make any headway with your aggressive dog.

 ## STRESS AND ITS INFLUENCE ON AGGRESSION

Stress is not an emotion, but a reaction. It is a natural response to any real or perceived threat, and actually helps us to adapt to that threat. As in the *De-stress* section in Part 1 – there are benefits of stress – or certain kinds of stress.

Repeated stress causes more stress

When stress is prolonged, particularly intense or becomes chronic, it may result in abnormal changes in the brain that not only affects us negatively in a physical way, but also makes us unable to regulate and respond to future *stressors*.[140] When stress is uncontrollable, excessive, or prolonged, it can cause a variety of emotional and cognitive changes.[141] [142] [143]

Chronic stress can eventually cause mood disorders or make them worse in people.[144] There is growing evidence, both in mood disorders in people as well as in animal models of stress that chronic stress interferes with neuroplasticity - the very function that occurs in our brains to actually make change possible.[145] It has been hypothesized that physiological resistance to repeated stress might contribute to anxiety-related behavioral disorders in dogs[146 147 148 149 150 151]

In other words, it is like a vicious circle, or worse: a downward spiral where the problem begins to multiply.

1. Stress plays a big factor in many behavioral problems including aggression.
2. Chronic stress in particular has detrimental effects on health and well-being.
3. Stress affects how much we learn and remember, but also how we learn and what we remember.[152]

We all talk about how stressed we are, and use it to explain why we forget things, or lose our tempers, or generally are not ourselves. We have a general idea that stress – at least chronic stress – is not good for us. Few of us realize just how damaging chronic stress is. In summary, stress may be a large player in the development of anxiety that leads to dog aggression both short and long term.

How long does the stress response last?

It is next impossible to determine how long the stress response will last, as there are a large number of factors influencing recovery. However, there is research on the temporal stress response in rats that is worth looking at. Male rats would be placed in an unfamiliar environment with a larger male fighter rat that would attack it on introduction. The test rat was then removed as soon as it showed submissive behaviors.[153] The results are as follows:

- Evidence of sympathetic nervous system activity, such as heart rate, last for 1–2 h after the defeat.
- Corticosterone – the chemical released in response to stress lasts at least 4 hours; testosterone takes at least 2 days to return to baseline levels.
- Different parts of the brain show reduction in receptor binding capacities up to 3 weeks later, other changes in receptor mechanisms lasted for at least a month.
- The circadian rhythm in body temperature takes 8–10 days to recover.
- Body weight of the stressed animals does not catch up with the control

animals, which suggests that set point of body weight regulation may be permanently altered by the defeat.

- Changes in diet preferences have been long lasting and indicates a change in the neurobiological control mechanism and may possibly point to changes in the serotoninergic system.
- Two studies suggest a gradual sensitization to *stressors* over the course of 3 weeks in response to a brief session of acute stress

Given that there are different things happening at different times in response to a single episode of social defeat, one can only imagine how repeated exposures to acute stress might affect the mind and body.

 ## HEADQUARTERS- THE BRAIN

There are probably more similarities in our brains compared to dogs than there are differences. Because of the way dogs have evolved, scientists are now studying the brains of dogs as a way to learn about humans. In fact, we share common subcortical brain structures with all other mammals and much of our brain processing is unconscious and automated.

This occurs because the brain has limited resources. Depending on where you get your information, the brain has the equivalent power of a light bulb[180] (some neuroscientists say about 40 watts, others say about a 100). As a result, the brain needs to be very efficient, and therefore it only processes what it has to.

The brain is a complex system that works on communication between specialized cells known as neurons, and between different areas of the brain. Neurons are nerve cells that can transmit information in both chemical and electrical ways. Neurons connect to each other through synapses. Communication between neurons is strengthened as a result of experience.

This is relevant for behavior because we can only take in limited amount of information, and it is the same with our dogs. We won't focus unless there is a motivating reason to; we won't remember something unless it is meaningful to us, and behavior won't change unless there is a compelling need for it to change.

Emotions, particularly those of fear and anxiety that are particularly relevant to aggression, are a key part of this system. They are part of a system that motivates us to take action and prepares us for action physically. It can then impact how we think about it and how and what we remember, later.

Understanding this will allow you to have some empathy for your dog *and* yourself when you go through the journey of helping your dog.

Parts of The Brain Involved With Aggression

There are several areas of the brain that are involved in aggression, but the brain tissues called the amygdala, frontal cortex, hypothalamus and parietal cortex are reported to be involved in emotional reactions in dogs, including aggression.[154]

Is learning about different regions of the brain important for fixing dog aggression? Not directly. It may help you if you go on to do more research. But, what is important is understanding that dogs are more than simple input-output machines, and that aggression is more than just a result of a status contest. We can't turn on and off feelings like a tap, or change habits over night. Experience is a significant factor in how the brain adapts and changes.

When your dog does not act the way you want them to, remember that there is usually a good reason. But! Never forget! It doesn't mean that change is not possible in most cases. The next sections describe important areas of the brain involved in emotional reaction.

Amygdala

At the base of the cerebral hemispheres is the almond shaped amygdala. The amygdala is a part of the brain that has a central role in processing emotions, especially fear and aggression.

The amygdala primarily operates outside of conscious awareness, and has a direct influence on the brain's cortex where rational thinking takes place.[155] In fact, the amygdala is more likely to influence the cortex than the cortex will influence the amygdala, especially in times of stress. A casual term for this influence is called "emotional hijacking".

In people, stress can cause the amygdala to be more powerful, sometimes even overriding human cortical reasoning. Stress can also make the amygdala faster to process fear over time, as the chemicals that are released during stress cause the neurons to communicate faster.

The amygdala determines how we should respond emotionally based on an individual's stored knowledge. This is why we want to keep a dog's stress level down. If the amygdala starts to rapidly fire, emotional hijacking occurs, and the rational options that the dog has for dealing with the situation will be overridden.

In some people with mood disorders, research has shown exaggerated activity in the amygdala. The effect in some was to be uncertain about neutral faces, or even see them as being threatening.[156] Some medications such as certain antidepressants can help normalize the activation.[157]

Why is this important?

We don't want to encode cells for learning in this area. Why not? Because the amygdala basically limits choices when responding. If we teach dogs to be fearful of humans, we have limited their options,[158] and yet when we train with leash corrections, prong collars, shock collars, and/or alpha rolls, this is exactly what we do.

In addition, our amygdala can activate when we are under stress and we suddenly come face to face with the thing that threatens our dog. This is why we sometimes make bad choices under stress. Aggressive or fearful dogs that perceive threats when there are none may seem to be incapable of determining whether there is a threat and may react even if the other is friendly. These dogs may have an overactive amygdala. Medication may help.

Hippocampus

The hippocampus has many functions. It acts as a gateway through which short-term memories must pass if they are to be converted into long-term memories.[159] The hippocampus also regulates aggression, learning which situations to be afraid of, and transfers information into memory. It is deeply interconnected with the amygdala and the prefrontal cortex, where rational thought occurs. It also is involved with contextual *fear conditioning* (i.e. what cues predict a fearful event is going to happen). It is very good at remembering locations. It is very good at detecting novelty. One of the most famous cases in neuropsychology is the widely studied Henry Molaison who lost both hippocampi during surgery and got stuck in the 1940s because the brain was unable to update newer memories. As he aged, he was unable to recognize himself in the mirror.

Damages to the hippocampus can cause an animal to associate two objects together through *fear conditioning*, but not necessarily the location. Research has shown that the volume of the hippocampus is significantly decreased in patients with borderline personality disorder the longer that they had a history of aggression.[160] There was also a reduced volume in Vietnam veterans with Posttraumatic stress disorder,[161] and adult survivors of childhood abuse.[162] Stress disrupts hippocampal function.[163]

If a traumatic event occurs that is stressful enough to disrupt hippocampal function while enhancing the amygdaloid function, the memory of highly stressful events then becomes fragmented and the memories lack context.

Why is this important?

After a highly stressful event, you or your dog can find yourself in a similar situation later, feeling anxious and fearful without understanding exactly why. This may occur because you were not able to consolidate the memories of the traumatic experience in your hippocampus, but your amygdala autonomic pathways remember. If this happens to your dog, they may feel fearful and simply act on it. Therefore it is important to learn to read your dog's body language rather than assume your dog is fine because there is no threat.

Although I have not yet come across evidence that indicates this, it may also suggest that when you use training methods that cause stress, such as shock collar or other punishment based tactics, your dog may not remember what he/she is supposed to doing quite the way you plan.

Frontal cortex (or Frontal Lobe)

The frontal cortex is the newest part of the brain where rational thinking occurs. It is used to make sense of things, problem solve, and control our responses. It is also the area where impulses, such as aggression are inhibited. The prefrontal cortex in particular is a primary center of inhibition of aggression.

The front cortex demonstrates lowered activity of a neurotransmitter system known as serotonin in both animals and humans showing inappropriate aggression. It indicates that there is a different biological basis between impulsive aggression and appropriate aggression. Control of aggressive tendencies is partly modifiable through re-training generated through the cerebral cortex.[164]

Why is this important?

Aggression can be a very useful response in order to defend food, territory, mates, as well as protect its offspring and defend from attack. But aggression takes up energy and carries with it a significant risk. The frontal cortex is needed to make decisions; often before the aggression sequence even starts. Of course, in order for the frontal cortex to inhibit aggression, activation in the amygdala cannot be overriding it.

Hypothalamus

The hypothalamus is more primitive than the amygdala, and is also involved in aggression in a variety of species. The amygdala discovers the threat and then sends signals to the hypothalamus to go into action.[165] Stimulation of the hypothalamus produces extremes of emotion such as rage[166], accompanied with attack and biting on any moving object. The hypothalamus also has receptors that determine aggression levels based on their interactions with neurotransmitters such as serotonin. The destruction of the hypothalamus results in the absence of all forms of aggression."

Several neurological disorders in humans implicate the involvement of hypothalamus in the control of aggression and rage.[167] That does not unequivocally mean this occurs in dogs as well, although research indicates that partial seizures in this part of the brain can cause sudden unprovoked aggression in dogs.[168]

Why is this important?

Aggression involves many systems in the brain, and most of it is beyond our conscious control. But not all aggression is simply behavioral. Trainers and behaviorists can be essential to helping you with a treatment, but this warrants the need to get a diagnosis from a veterinary behaviorist, rather than rely only on a certified behaviorist or trainer in some cases. Again, medication may help to moderate aggressive responses.

Parietal cortex

This part of the brain is involved in selective attention and integrating information from the senses. It is also associated with recognition of emotion as well as the recognition of noxious environmental stimuli.[169] Lesions (damage) in this area have been reported to impair emotional experience and arousal. In people, this can result in being unable to recognize emotional facial expressions.[170] (Similar findings occur with damage to the amygdala).

Why is this important?

There are several areas of the brain that work together to form complex perceptions, and responses. Abnormality in the parietal cortex could potentially result in dogs having problems with recognizing conflict signals in other dogs or people. Not recognizing signals properly could lead to greater conflict, fear or stress. Abnormal activity in one or more areas of the brain, whether a result of genetic defect, disease, or experiences can impact other areas of the brain, resulting in a complex problem in behavior.

 # NEUROTRANSMITTERS

Mammals have very similar brains. Neurotransmitters, which are chemical messengers, transmit signals in the brain. They are the same as those found in other mammals. The release or the inhibition of these chemicals in the brain are what cause neurons to fire or not to fire – which essentially is how cells communicate with one another.

Mood disorders are often associated with neurochemical levels that are higher or lower than average. This in turn can affect the release or inhibition of other neurochemicals and as a result, change how we think, act, and learn. But they don't act in a vacuum; everything we do changes the brain. The very act of learning alters neurotransmitters and other neurochemicals affect other neurochemicals. The four main neurotransmitters that are involved in mood control, stress, and aggression are serotonin, dopamine, norepinephrine, and epinephrine (adrenalin). The next section goes into more detail on each.

Serotonin

Research indicates that aggressive dogs might differ from non-aggressive dogs in the activities of the serotonergic system and the hypothalamic-pituitary-adrenal axis (HPA axis). [171] HPA axis is a major part of the system that controls reactions to stress and regulates mood and emotions, sexuality, energy storage, and expenditure among other things. Alternatively serotonin differences may be simply another symptom.

The precursor to serotonin is the amino acid tryptophan, which can be found in our diets. Although tryptophan is abundant in protein sources we eat, so are other amino acids that compete in crossing into the brain. This may be a reason why diets in *low* protein and/or *high* in carbohydrates have been shown to have some effect in some kinds of aggression in dogs by increasing insulin. Insulin helps draw the other amino acids into the blood stream, allowing tryptophan to cross the blood brain barrier more easily. Serotonin is thought to influence the activity of virtually every other neuron in the brain.

CAUTION Before you change your dog's diet, consult your veterinarian. Increasing insulin for too long can trigger insulin resistance resulting in lower serotonin levels over time as well as other problems.

Epinephrine

Epinephrine is known by many as adrenalin, and many are familiar with the phrase "adrenalin rush." This happens when we are in highly exciting or stressful situations, whether bungee jumping or in a car crash. Epinephrine gets released in response to stress and prepares our body for action and affects our perception of time when released.

Norepinephrine

Norepinephrine has multiple roles, but is involved in the fight or flight system, as well as influencing attention. It can affect your mood and blood pressure and if the levels are outside of normal, can cause you to feel anxious. There is a close relationship between the serotonergic and noradrenergic systems. It is thought that the presence of norepinephrine in certain parts of the brain inhibits the parts of the brain that suppress aggression. The evolutionary value in this is that you might try to fight something attacking you that you ordinarily wouldn't, thus increasing your chances for survival.

Dopamine

Dopamine is our "feel good" transmitter and is commonly associated with pleasure, i.e. our reward circuits, but dopamine, too, has multiple roles. Dopamine circuits appear to be major contributors to our feelings of engagement and excitement as we seek the material resources needed for bodily survival. It's produced with food, sex, and other rewards. It's also produced when we experience low-stress novelty. As well, it helps us learn better. Dopamine makes connections and makes them stick.

However, it appears the brain processes physical aggression like a reward. When aggression occurs, it produces dopamine in the brain.[172] This further supports the idea that aggression is a coping response in response to the negative experiences of anxiety, frustration, or fear.

Why is this important?

Dopamine is produced with rewards and helps the brain learn better and the learning stick. This supports the choice for using rewards as positive reinforcement when training. Because research also indicates that dopamine is produced in response to aggression, it implies that it is likely that aggression is self-reinforcing and further supports the need to avoid situations that cause the aggression to occur.

In summary, neurotransmitters function in a very complex way and work together in response to many different conditions.

Because they get released at different times and at different speeds (i.e. serotonin is relatively slow acting, while epinephrine is quite fast acting) the response to a stressful or traumatic event can be different over time.

Given the complexity, it is not surprising that the components can get out of whack from time to time, whether as a result of prolonged stress or as a result of other illnesses or conditions that make it more difficult for us to process and cope with stress. Prolonged stress can cause neurochemical changes that then impact perception and coping abilities, which can make it more difficult to cope with challenges. All of this can lead to stress-related disorders, including those that cause anxiety and aggression.

Interestingly, anxiety, fears, phobias, panic disorders, and obsessive-compulsive disorders are neurochemically related, although there are probably different systems and processes that drive them.

 # NEUROPLASTICITY

Neuroplasticity is at the heart of learning and forgetting. It really is a fancy word that essentially means that the brain is capable of changing itself. It is the fundamental reason we are able to adapt to a changing world. Our brains are both flexible and vulnerable because of neuroplasticity.

To understand neuroplasticity is to remember that the brain only has a limited amount of power to process and a limited amount of bandwidth coming in that it can process at any one time (which really makes our brains all the more amazing).

Brain processes that are used get strengthened and more efficient. Those are not used are pruned away. This is why the saying "use or it, or lose it" is so relevant. However the systems in the brain are highly competitive with each other, so a stronger developed neural network will compete against a similar weaker one.

Why is this important?

This can work for us in both positive and negative ways. On the one hand, if you can train a behavior in dogs, practice it, and *overlearn* it, it can become a default behavior, provided the dog has enough motivation to want to learn and practice.

On the other hand, the same could be said for aggression where the dog has compelling reasons to want to practice it. Every time a dog behaves aggressively, he/she has strengthened those neural pathways in the brain. Not only do they get stronger, they get better and faster at it, and it requires less stimulation for those neurons to fire. The more a dog practices the aggression, the more difficult training an incompatible behavior to compete with it will be.

Practice the good stuff. Interrupt the bad stuff and redirect.

 NEUROGENESIS

Not so long ago, it was believed that there are no new brain cells developed once we become adults. Even some academic writing on dog behavior (the author will go nameless) has suggested that the one main difference between neurons (brain cells) and other cells in the body is that neurons are not able to replicate, suggesting that no new neurons are produced shortly after birth. However, this is now considered incorrect. The growth of new neurons in the brain is called neurogenesis. Neurogenesis has been shown to occur in adult mice, birds, and other primates as well as people. It would strongly suggest it occurs in dogs as well.

Neurogenesis occurs as a result of physical exercise, environmental enrichment, learning, and some medications such as anti-depressants. A new neuron takes over a month to be able to send and receive messages. Unfortunately, stress and social isolation can restrict neurogenesis.[173 174 175]

Why is this important?

Neurogenesis may be important in certain kinds of learning and memory. Stress and social isolation can have a negative impact on your dog's ability to learn. Exercise and an interesting environment to stimulate continual learning are all important for your dog to learn and develop new memories, which is essential for treating your dog's aggression. At the time of writing, more recent research suggests that neurogenesis may play a larger role in treating depression than originally thought. By extension, a lack of neurogenesis may possibly play a larger role in the development of inappropriate aggression as well. Only future research can confirm this.

COGNITIVE PROCESSES

Learning is the process by which we gain information or acquire skills through experience, and in many cases, by practicing or being repeatedly exposed to it. It can be either passive or active learning. Passive learning seems to occur without our putting much effort into it. Active learning is where we deliberately acquire it through effort.

The degree to what we learn and how much is moderated through attention, which acts both as a filter and a focusing mechanism. Our abilities to perceive and therefore learn or react appropriately may be compromised by anxiety.

Self-control actually uses up energy in the brain that can cause us to have less self-control later. But it can also be practiced so that we can develop greater self-control and can regulate our emotions better.

We use these cognitive processes when we use *behavior modification* techniques to change behavior and attitudes a dog may have towards their *stressor*.

 ATTENTION

When we are teaching a dog something new, we obviously need them to pay attention to us. But attention is a cognitive process that actually involves two forms: *orienting* and *attending*.

Orienting is when we first notice something. It's usually caused by something particularly intense or unusual, such as a sound or strange smell. But, it might also arise from someone waving at you in a crowd, for example. Most people in a crowd don't wave their arms around. If one person does, it catches our attention.

Some term this passive attention, because it's largely involuntary. We can get our dogs to orient to us when we call them or startle them with something. Sometimes, we can't get them to orient to us when the anxiety or aggression process has begun. Other times, we can get them to orient to us, but once they determine it is not worth paying attention to, we have lost them – we can't seem to keep their attention. A dog owner might call their dog's name, the dog looks over, sees that there is nothing interesting enough to keep their attention, and goes back to what he/she was doing.

Attending is attention that occurs at the point at which we decide something is important enough for us to consciously focus on it. For example, we might orient to an unusual sound that we hear outside at night, but when we realize that it's just the wind knocking some branches against our window, we stop paying attention because it's not important. We are not attending.

However, when a young dog sees another dog in the distance, he/she might focus on that other dog perhaps out of the desire to socialize or perhaps out of apprehension. As the dog approaches, the young dog probably tries to assess the other's size and strength, as well as the other dog's inclination to be aggressive or play. The same way when the dog senses you might start preparing their dinner, he/she *attends* to you, looking for all the signs it might happen.

Some call this active attention, because it is primarily voluntary. It includes alertness and focused concentration. Because it requires mental energy, it is often motivated by needs such as curiosity or hunger.

When we work with our dogs, we want them to attend to us. We don't want to them to just pay attention for a brief moment because they heard their name or happened to notice us moving around.

Why is this important?

Attention is not just important for learning; it is key in *retaining* what we have learned. We want our dogs to be deeply interested and attending during training and *behavior modification* in order for the learning to stick better.

Shifting attention

The act of paying attention is actually partly shifting attention from one thing to the other. This can be a struggle for some. In people, this is largely considered to be a more or less stable trait. Some people get easily distracted; others have difficulty making transitions, such as putting down a book. Dogs are the same.

But thankfully, it's a skill that can be developed. People with generalized social-phobia that have been trained to pay attention to non-threatening positive material and ignore threatening material, showed significantly greater reductions in self-reported, behavioral, and physiological measures of anxiety than did participants from those who were in groups either required to pay attention to the threat or pay attention to both.[176]

However, it appears that the real benefit is not in focusing on something non-threatening, so much as *disengaging* in the threat. This is where the deliberate *shifting* of attention becomes important. Functional areas of the brain expand or shrink as a result of how frequently and how intensely they are used. Phobias and anxieties become worse the more a sufferer focuses on it. Telling the brain that they are no longer by thinking of something else helps make this shifting easier. Our economical brain repurposes the neurons to be used for what the brain is more regularly occupied with. So the *Sit, Attend and Wait (SAW)* training, while seemingly unrelated to aggression, can actually help dogs cope with anxiety.

The essential thing is to keep in mind what the dog is actually paying attention to. Your dog does not improve at a sit-stay simply because they are practicing it; they get better at it by paying attention to the request. He/she is more likely to pay attention to it when they are motivated, and in particular, they will be motivated by curiosity or hunger.

There are often multiple things going on in our lives at the same time, but what we pay attention to, is what will become more developed in our minds. For example, a woman might be trying to solve a word puzzle while there is jazz music playing in the background. She is focused, thinking about the music she hears and listens to the instruments and rhythms closely. Her neural networks are optimizing, making her better at understanding music and hearing subtleties within a melody.

But if she is focusing on the puzzle, regardless if the music is playing, those neural networks are optimizing, making her a better puzzle solver. Or, she might actually be focusing on the pain her arthritic hands are causing her, making the pain more intense, easier to feel, and harder to ignore.

Attention training can improve emotional regulation

In research on humans, attention training to reduce vigilance and responsiveness to social threat resulted in decreased stress.[177] This suggests that it's possible to lower reactivity simply by manipulating attention prior to perceiving the threat and this, in turn, reduces stress overall. In addition, the benefits of training attention, just like practicing self-control, could extend to greater emotional regulation of behavior.[178]

Signals of threat demand our attention

We want our dogs to let go of paying attention to something else, and voluntarily shift their attention to us. But research shows that signals of threat hold our attention more than other emotional information and that we are slower to shift our attention away from information associated with danger.[179] This means that it's going to be challenging trying to get our dogs to pay attention to us in any situation where they perceive a threat. But because paying attention – or *shifting attention* is a skill that can be learned, we help our dogs do this better, especially when we make it important to do so.

The more a dog STOPS paying attention to those things he/she is threatened by, the more the neurons involved in that process will get co-opted to do something else. So, it's essential that we give them a reason to want to pay attention to us. Getting a "Good dog!" and a pat on the head simply may not be that important to a dog. In addition, in the process of *desensitization*, it is important to work at a distance where the dog is not too concerned about danger.

Things that interfere with paying attention

- Feeling anxious, sad, or depressed
- Feeling tired
- Feeling sick or not feeling well
- The degree to which the thing that we are attending to is perceived as important

Should our dogs pay attention to us or to the target during *Targeted Behavior Modification*?

Some people have theorized that getting your dog to pay attention to you while working around their *stressors* is not actually doing much to change the dog's response to the *stressor*. Some feel the dog should pay attention to the thing and learn to associate it with good things. Which is right?

While learning to associate positive things with your *stressor* is desired, we have to take the process one step at a time. What we want to do first is enable a dog to become a much less reactive dog and a dog that is able to control their reactivity. We see this on the online K9aggression-support Yahoo group all the time: people continue to put their dogs in situations they simply are not prepared for. This is usually because people simply don't know any better, but unfortunately; it sets the dog up for failure rather than success.

Having your dog pay attention to you first and take your cues about what they should be doing is the first step. The second step is to allow them to pay attention to the *stressor* – PROVIDED they are not going above threshold. In other words, they are not getting anxious, and we are not seeing the licking of the lips, yawning, hyper focusing, or any other indications that your dog is worried.

PERCEPTION

Because our brain can only run on about 40-100 watts of power[180] to deal with at one time, our sensory system, which includes those receptors and neural pathways involved in common systems such as vision, hearing, touch, taste, smell etc., is only capable of processing a limited amount of information at a time.

Take the visual system for example. The bandwidth of an optic nerve is considered to be able to transmit 1 MB per second.[181] That was the equivalent of a cable modem for Internet several years ago. When we think about just how much video could be delivered on a cable bandwidth of 1 MB per second, was the best quality and certainly not enough to be considered adequate video streaming. Regardless, the video we would be watching would be nothing like the reality we perceive in our brains.

We only update what we perceive when things change

Because we can only take in a limited amount of information at one time, our brain updates information only when things change. In other words, I don't need to keep reprocessing that a room is blue, or a certain size. I only need to update if something changes in it, for example, if there is a person who has just entered the room. So while it feels like I am looking at a blue room of a certain size, I'm not actually. My brain is storing that information for me. My visual system is actually now processing the movement of the person.

What our brain then takes in depends on what we decide is important to pay attention to. For example, we might pay closer attention to whether or not we recognize the person and what the face and body are doing that will give us some kind of idea of what the person's mood or intent is. In this way, our brains are incredibly efficient. But of course, this also allows for errors. Once we decide we have enough information to provide us with the answers we need, we move on to the next thing we decide is important.

Is anxiety inferring with perception?

Unfortunately, we can miss things. Like people who experience social anxiety, a larger part an anxious dog's brain may be concerned with being on the look-out for threats and coping with the resulting anxiety. That can mean that the brain is less available for other kinds of processing, and this is something that we need to keep in mind with dogs. They may be less capable of truly knowing whether something is a threat or not because the brains of highly anxious dogs are continually attending to hyper vigilance and coping.

In some cases, this can make the occupied brain a little less tuned into the social norms. They may have simply never learned because they were focusing on other things that were deemed far more important. Alternatively, this challenge may be temporal and only related to the present situation.

Perceiving the presence of social norms means all is ok

When we sense that social norms are not being followed, red flags are raised internally signaling all is not normal. Humans and dogs naturally use norms and systems to communicate that there is nothing to worry about, all is safe. That is why we *follow the crowd* and want to be similar to others – it is inherent in our sensing that all is ok. The absence of social norms causes us to become anxious. The need to fit in to the group is so ingrained into both humans and dogs that negative emotions arise when we don't fit in. Humans lose self-esteem; we feel lonely, and so on.

When this occurs a kind of feedback loop happens as now the anxious one senses the other is uncomfortable. This perceived discomfort in the other conveys to the anxious one that there really *is* something to be worried about.

Anxious people and dogs can have difficulty learning or paying attention. It's not that they are not just as intelligent as anyone else; it's just that their brains are already processing things that non-anxious people are not processing.

So one of the things we do when we teach our dogs to sit and wait is to make other people and dogs more comfortable around our dog and this in turn can help calm our dog. An inappropriately stiff, staring or lunging dog is not following social norms, and this can cause the target to feel anxious and react. We want our dogs to be calmer, so they can perceive a situation more accurately to the extent that they are able to do so.

In non-anxious dogs, perception still occurs the same way, and the brain is still only capable of taking in a limited amount of information at any one time. The direction of where they focus is largely determined by attention and what has been determined as highest importance according to the dog's interests and motivations.

Why is this important?

A dog will only pay attention to what it has to and feels the need to. This is not so much a choice as a necessity, since paying attention uses up brain resources. Most of the time, we are simply not that interesting to our dogs. If nothing changes, then there is no need to update the brain with new information. In fact, it's far easier and more economical for a dog to keep on believing and behaving as he or she has always done. This is not because your dog is stubborn or stupid. It's because the dog's brain - just like ours, decides on a regular basis what is the most important thing to pay attention to right now.

Anything that delivers on biological necessity will have the highest priority. That means a food treat will be more valued by a hungry dog than the chance to play. And, it means that the survival instinct will always trump a food treat.

A dog will only update their perceptions of the world if something changes. If their belief is that all other dogs are bad, then there is no reason to spend extra processing power on determining if each and every dog is bad. He or she will simply act on the fact.

 ## SELF-CONTROL IS A LIMITED RESOURCE

Self-control is the ability to control emotions, behaviors, and desires. It is theorized that exercising self-control uses up resources (glucose which is produced from both carbohydrates and proteins) in the brain, which are limited whenever we control our impulses. Even when we know we are not supposed to behave aggressively, self-control becomes more difficult when we are cognitively taxed.[182] [183]

Engaging in activities that require *executive functioning* uses up brain resources. This includes using the part of the brain that controls and manages other cognitive process, such as attention, problem solving, inhibiting (preventing ourselves from doing something), and decision-making. If your dog is learning, processing a new environment, coping with stress or holding themselves together, the resources in the brain that are responsible for self-control will get used up.

When these resources are temporarily depleted, it becomes more difficult to control our emotions and behavior, which means there is a risk in acting out when you might normally inhibit this behavior.

Luckily as said before, self-control is like a muscle: the more you practice, the better you get at it.[184] There are several studies that indicate that when you practice self-control over a period of time, your ability to self-regulate improves. Better yet, it appears to improve overall, rather than on a specific task.[185] So asking your dog to sit that extra bit longer before getting their treat may help them stay calmer when requested in other circumstances.

It is a good idea to practice, but at the same time, be aware of how any kind of brain processing can you or your dog to be vulnerable to losing their cool.

LEARNING AND MEMORY

Learning and memory is a function of neuroplasticity and neurogenesis. Most of the research in the past few decades has focused on memory that is dependent on the hippocampus, but memory is actually made up of several systems that may interact with each other.

Learning and memory is a process. When we learn things, our neurons start to fire. This firing continues even after the initial learning and experience to turn it into different forms of memory. The brain can start to re-wire itself in response to change in just a few days, but it takes less than 12 to 24 hours to revert back to its former state.

Conditions that impact learning

Learning is complex and variable and extends beyond classical and instrumental conditioning. There are several factors involved and can impact both how and what we learn. Stress can impact learning at the molecular level for example. What we actually retain is also impacted by the extent to which we are motivated to learn, believe that's what we are learning is important, and then opportunities to subsequently practice it.

Conditions that impact learning in dogs:

- The degree of attention paid.
- Motivation and interest in what is being learned.
- Stress or distress.
- Factors that affect olfaction (the ability to smell)
- Age and effects of breed.
- Nutritional factors including that which may affect available brain energy.[186]

Memory is fragile

Each time we remember something, it's like taking a file folder full of paper out of a filing cabinet. And while the file folder is out, we might lose some papers, or file some more papers inside, changing the contents. Memory is much the same; each time we remember, the memory becomes fragile and we re-encode it when we store it again. What we learn and remember becomes even more distorted by the things we learn after it, especially if the content of that learning is similar. As soon as six hours later after training, memories become less vulnerable to interference.

Why is this important?

When our dogs are learning or something new or practicing something new, we want as little as possible *after the fact* to interfere. In fact, if we can get our dogs to have a snooze after a training session, so much the better. Their brains will work with those memories rather than other experiences that might interfere (so you students should study your toughest subject before going to bed).

But if our dogs have a bad experience, we want to interfere with the consolidation of that memory as much as possible. We can do this by providing *stimulus* that he or she will react to, provide new learning, or provide a novel situation. We would do this as soon as possible to interfere with memory consolidation of the bad experience.

Learning, memory and stress

Learning and memory can be affected by stress, in some cases by enhancing memory, and in other times, impairing memory. It is thought that stress enhances memory when the stress is related to what is being learned. This makes sense as it helps us to remember the particulars of a threat for next time.

But stress impairs memory when the stress is experienced outside of the learning context – in other words, if you are trying to learn something, but are stressed for a completely different reason, it will be harder to remember what you learned.[187]

The same could be said for acquiring information – if we are paying attention to a situation that is going to help us deal with whatever is stressing us out, we are more likely to remember what that is, than if we are not stressed. On the other hand, if we are stressed by a family event and are trying to learn how to solve difficult math problems, it's going to be much more challenging to learn the math when stressed.

It is almost as if the body and brain are set up to make stress a high priority, meaning that whatever is stressing us out, whatever we have determined is threatening us, is going to be the top priority for the allocation of our brain's resources.

Why is this important?

When we are trying to teach our dog any of the foundation training work, such as *SAW (Sit, Attend and Wait)*, we are going to have a more difficult time getting our dog to learn and remember if they are stressed by anything that is going on around them.

On the other hand, the technique of getting the dog's attention, leaving the scene of stress, and getting to safety (and causing the dog to experience relief – a natural reward) may actually stick quite well. Assuming, that is, that your calling them and getting them to safety becomes associated with relief. If the calling and tugging on the leash does not convince the dog that paying attention to you will serve their interests, it may just serve as an irritation. The difference may come down to how well learned the foundation training was before you experience the stressful situation.

Fear Learning

Fear learning happens quickly. It involves the amygdala, and the memories are rapidly encoded into long-term memories. The circumstances surrounding the event may also get remembered even if they are not directly related. For example: imagine a dog attacked another dog. The circumstances immediately preceding the attack or other details that may predict the attack happening again may also get encoded. If it there was a car alarm that went off just before the attack, the alarm may spook them next time.

If the owner had pulled up tight suddenly on the leash just before the attack, the next time the owner pulls up tight on the leash may set the fear response in motion. The fear response includes defense responses, changes in physiology (heart beating faster, raise in blood pressure, etc.), as well as hormonal releases that prepare the dog to flee or freeze, or fight. In addition, there is usually an emotional activation that is uncomfortable (such as anxiety, fear, etc.) that compels the dog to act.

The same could be said for dogs that have been abused, scared or hurt. If the dog formed other associations that occurred at the time of the abuse, these associations may be associated with the fear.

Overlearning and habits

Overlearning occurs when an already learned behavior is practiced so much that it becomes almost automatic. The behavior then requires very little conscious thought to perform. This is what we want to achieve when we want to teach our dogs how to behave appropriately and calmly.

Unfortunately in many cases, undesirable behaviors such as aggression can also be *overlearned*. Overlearning can result in automatic behavior so that a dog uses fewer and fewer warning signs. It is important in this case to look at the initial incidents for clues.

How long does it take to create a habit?

The million-dollar question! In the case of aggressive dogs we want to know, exactly how long is it going to take to improve behavior? Well, according to the Internet self-help gurus, you might think between 21 and 28 days. But we need to be clear on the difference between making a change, and then making the change so solid that it requires little conscious thought to perform.

In reality, the time it takes to learn something can happen quite quickly, and forgetting can happen just as quickly. One research study demonstrated that habits – learned behavior that no longer requires self-control - can be picked up in as few as 18 days for people, but also can take as long as 254 days – which indicates just how much variability there is.[188]

Looking at dogs, one study that used a CD-based *desensitization* and *counter conditioning* program in combination with DAP (Dog Appeasing Pheromone) to deal with a fear of fireworks saw most of the change within the first month of training, with no significant change the second month. [189]

Things that impact the formation of new habits is the strength of old habits and the cues that are associated with old habits such as time of day, location, activities, and behavior of those around us. If this seems discouraging, just remember that learning occurs quickly. You should be seeing results in a matter of days. After that it is a matter of practice, and avoiding other situation that interfere with that.

The ability to learn a habit – behavior that occurs subconsciously - really depends on:

- What other habit is the new developing habit is competing with – and how strong the neural pathways of the old habit are.
- How frequently it is practiced.
- How important the dog or person considers it to be (and how motivated he or she is to practice it).
- The power of situations to trigger past responses (rather than the new habit).
- The rewards of practicing the old habits vs. the rewards of practicing the new. Remember, inhibiting bad habits and rehearsing new practices requires work.

Why is this important?

Establishing new behaviors for aggressive dogs that are in direct opposition to the old habits (for example, we ask our dogs to sit and relax, instead of becoming anxious and reactive) is extremely important for changing problem behavior. But we have to keep in mind that actual habits take time. We need to continually practice, we need to avoid ANY opportunity for the old habit to get practiced, and we need to keep motivating our dogs to perform the new habits long after we think they've learned it.

Thankfully this is not nearly as difficult as it sounds when we know what we're facing. It merely means avoiding putting our dogs into situations where the aggressive behavior sequence starts. If we DO find ourselves in a bad situation, get your dog learning something else right away, and get that dog happy! Keep treats with you and practice every day. Practice does not need to be long, just ' fearfrequent. Incorporate it into your daily life: walks, exercise, play, etc.

BEHAVIOR MODIFICATION EXPLAINED

 ## BEHAVIOR MODIFICATION TERMS AND TECHNIQUES

Behavior modification is the process where we systematically change behavior – usually problematic responses to a particular situation or trigger. Essentially, this is a learning process that involves learning a set of responses that are incompatible with the old problematic response. It can be helpful to look at *behavior modification* as a re-training process.

When people use terms we are unfamiliar with, not only can it be intimidating, but also we actually have to work harder at figuring it out and learning it. It can help to get familiar with the terms if you want to continue your learning and understanding of *behavior modification*. Understanding the techniques will allow you to better customize your program.

TERMS

Stimulus – is a thing, event, or circumstance that causes (or stimulates) a reaction. People often use the word "stressor", "trigger", or "target" to mean the same thing. The word is useful is that it allows you to identify whatever it is by how it's affecting the dog. It can be substituted for anything easily.

Stressor - is generally a thing, event or circumstance that causes stress.

Conditioned – The average dog owner doesn't usually talk about *conditioning* their dog when they are talking about training, so this word can help us become confused when a dog professional uses words like "*Conditioned stimulus*", "*unconditioned response*", etc. But you can more or less exchange the word *trained or learned* for *conditioned*.

Conditioned stimulus and conditioned response - In the famous experiment where Pavlov was able to get dogs to salivate when a bell was rung, the dog learned that food would arrive shortly after the bell. In this case the bell is the *conditioned stimulus* because the bell stimulates the response as the dog learned (was conditioned) that the bell predicted the arrival of food. The *salivation* response at the sound of the bell is the *conditioned* (learned) *response*. That the dog salivates at the appearance of food would be an *un*conditioned response, because this response occurs without learning.

TECHNIQUES

Classical (or *Pavlovian*) *Conditioning* is a type of *learning* that directly involves associating occurrences, objects, or people with basic drives such as hunger and responses to threat. These responses are primarily involuntary. Although we can rationally control some of the responses to a certain extent with relaxation exercises, meditation, etc., they primarily happen below the consciousness. They include changes in heart rate, pupil dilation, sexual arousal, appetite, etc.

Again, the most common example given is the Pavlov experiments where a dog is fed every time after he or she hears a bell. In time the dog links the sound of the bell with the fact that food follows. This caused the dog to start salivating when they hear the bell. It is the result of learning, but it is largely involuntary.

Sympathetic nervous system response

There are two sides or two main states to the nervous system that *classical conditioning* can exploit that are very important to understand. One state is commonly referred to as the "fight or flight" state, where when a person or dog becomes threatened they might typically run or fight. The official name of this state is the *sympathetic nervous system* response.

In reality, we have more than the two reactions: fight or flight, in response to threat, such as freezing. You will see prey animals, such as rabbits freeze frequently, and this helps them become *invisible* to hunters that primarily pay attention to moving objects. We also experience it when we freeze under stress and don't know what to do.

Regardless, the nervous system responds in a very generalized way that is meant to help our chances of surviving a threat. These changes include the release of various chemicals in our body in a variety of ways that make us more physically prepared to handle and survive threat.

Parasympathetic nervous system response

The flip side of the *sympathetic nervous system* response is the *parasympathetic nervous system* response, which is what we experience when we are relaxed. It's during this state that our body tends to repair itself. It is also the state that is associated with appetite. This state is generally considered to be incompatible with the sympathetic nervous system response ("fight or flight response").

Classical conditioning can be used to link an occurrence or presence of something with food. With enough repetitions, the anticipation of this occurrence can cause the dog to salivate, thereby kicking in their parasympathetic nervous system response.

Because cla*ssical conditioning* does not tend to reduce anxiety at the trigger itself, it is generally used to just reduce aggressive arousal by triggering the incompatible response.

For example, a sequence of events naturally occurring in the home may start with a knock at the door or a doorbell. Without having any scary or threatening people coming in, since the sound is not truly threatening, it is possible to reduce the aggression by pairing the bell with food. Simply by changing the association the dog has with the knock or bell from threat to food helps reduce the aggressive arousal with several repetitions.

While the actual threat (the person) is not any less threatening, the parasympathetic nervous response has kicked in, which is incompatible with the aroused aggression. Overtime, the dog aggressive arousal is reduced. In a situation where it is difficult to calm the dog, *classical conditioning* may help reduce the dog's arousal level in order to make learning – *operant conditioning* – possible.

Operant (or Instrumental) Conditioning

Operant (or Instrumental) Conditioning is a type of learning that involves associating a response or an action to a reward. For example, by rewarding a dog with a treat for sitting they associate the sitting with the reward. A rat in a maze can learn that every time he or she presses a lever, they get a food pellet.

This learned association causes the behavior to repeat (and to occur more often) if the reward is rewarding enough. The main difference between *classical conditioning* and *operant conditioning* is that in operant conditioning, the dog has to do something. In *classical conditioning*, the dog doesn't need to do anything to get the reward. As a way to remember this – associate *operant with* the word *operate*. The dog needs to operate to get the reward.

We want to use *instrumental* or *operant conditioning* to teach a dog to relax when we give them the cue to relax. We teach them this by rewarding them for relaxing. We then have them associate a cue word with the process of relaxation, followed by a reward. We stop rewarding them for relaxing when we don't give them the cue word, but continue to reward them for relaxing with the cue word, and there we have set up a process that can be used for *counter conditioning*.

Clicker training

Clicker training uses both *classical conditioning* and *operant conditioning*. A clicker is simply a device that makes a distinct clicking sound. It doesn't do anything else.

The click is *powered up* (fancy dog industry phrase) by a process of clicking and then giving the dog the reward immediately after (for doing nothing! Lucky dog!). This is repeated several times. Once the dog makes the association between the click and the treat, and learns that the click predicts the arrival of a treat, *both* the sound of the click and the delivery of the food will cause the dog to salivate.

Then the clicker sound can be used to *mark* the desired behavior. Or in other words, the clicker can be used to identify exactly *when* the dog is doing something that will cause a treat (the behavior you want them to repeat). As soon as the dog hears the sound, the emotional and physiological response is the same as if he or she is about to be delivered the treat and the dog has the desire to repeat the behavior that caused the click to earn the reward.

While you could theoretically not follow up the click sound with a treat, you risk extinguishing the association between clicker and treat, and thereby extinguishing the positive association the dog has to the sound. This would cause their motivation to pay attention to the clicker to diminish. Then, he or she would be less likely to repeat whatever they were doing at the time to cause the clicker sound to happen. So it's best to continue to deliver the treat after the clicker sound every time.

Clicker training does not require a clicker. You can use any *marker* and pair it up the same way, such as a whistle (used to train marine animals), or even a word. The benefit of the clicker is that it is a distinct punctuating sound, which appears to have a better response than voice. The delivery of a word may vary depending on the mood you are in, and it may be easily muddied by other words you use. But the advantages of using your voice are that you always have your voice with you. It is possible to use both but clickers have the bets response overall. If your dog is deaf, you might try a visual marker such as a flashlight or a specific tap, for example.

Shaping

Clicker training works in baby steps and involves a process called shaping. *Shaping* refers the process where you subtly modify a dog's actions to be more and more like the final behavior you want to see. Shaping is done in baby steps. It is like starting with a lump of clay and slowly molding it into something you like. A simple way to do this with clicker training is waiting for the dog to consistently offer the behavior to get clicks/treats. You then stop clicking, and wait for a change in the behavior. Often the dog will do an exaggerated form of the behavior, which may be closer to the end result that you are looking for. Dogs that are familiar with this training look at it as a game and are motivated to try many things if something is they are doing is not earning the click. You can train dogs to do complex behaviors by shaping and linking behaviors to other learned behaviors.

Desensitization

Desensitization is the process where we become less sensitive to something by exposure at a level that is manageable – so it involves an emotional component – usually anxiety or fear (as compared to habituation). We do this by getting the dog used to the thing that he or she finds bothersome by allowing them to experience the thing at a scale that is not too overwhelming. Either that means using a less threatening but similar substitution of the threat, or working at a distance where the thing is not all that threatening, or exposing your dog to the trigger for a very short duration at first. As the dog becomes less sensitive you gradually get closer and closer to the real threat while rewarding for relaxation.

In all cases, the dog should not be so anxious that they are unable to relax when their handler calls their name and asks them to sit and look at them happily.

But there is a subtle difference between distracting the dog so that they are unaware of the trigger and actually having them be aware of the trigger and then following it up with relaxation and *counter conditioning*. The first would be considered part of a management plan. For *desensitization* and *counter conditioning* (re-training) to occur, the dog must be aware of the *stimulus* (the thing that causes them to be anxious or aggressive) and yet still be able to relax.

The progression of these exercises uses a number of variables. Each trial should only deal with changing one variable at a time and only slightly so that the dog can *easily succeed*. As part of your treatment plan, plan what you will do first and what the incremental stages will be. The act of doing this will help discourage you from moving too fast or demanding too much of your dog. It will also help you to learn to stay calm. Bonus!

Plan for safety. Also, have an Emergency Response Plan for worst-case scenarios.

EXAMPLE OF VARIABLES

Distance

Distance refers to the distance between the dog and the *stimulus*. We always start at the farthest point and gradually move closer as the dog indicates they are able to remain relaxed and happy.

Duration

Duration refers to how long you ask your dog to stay in the presence of the *stimulus*. We always start with the briefest exposure to the *stimulus* and gradually extend the length of time we ask them to be calm.

Distractions

Distraction refers to other things that the dog is likely to orient his attention to. In particular, we want to focus on the dog's sense of smell, movement, and sound.

Intensity

Any element can be made more intense: louder voices, more or faster movement (as described below), bigger social responses, etc. These are just some elements to consider. Break it down for your own situation.

Stimulus characteristics

This may relate to size, height, age, etc. You start with something that is only slightly like the actual thing he or she is afraid of. For example, a dog fearful of thunderstorms might listen to a very quiet CD of thunder sounds. A dog fearful of strangers might start with a familiar person first.

Movement

Your dog is hardwired to pay attention to any kind of movement – in fact, we all are. It served us hunting food, as well as in being alert to threats.

So it is inevitable that your dog will be alerted to movement in the environment. The more things that are moving around them, whether it's people, vehicles, bicycles or other dogs, the more challenging it will be for them to remain on task. The type of movement of the *stimulus* will also be of concern. You may need to work with a variety of speeds. For example, if your dog is aggressive towards strangers, you need to do set-ups with the person moving in different ways at different speeds.

Examples of types of movement:

- Standing up
- Sitting down
- Squatting
- Walking – slow pace
- Walking – fast pace
- Skipping
- Jogging
- Running
- Jumping
- Dancing
- Bicycle riding
- Stopping
- Raising hand up
- Reaching towards the dog

Your positioning can also be confusing if you are always in the same position when training, vs. doing something different in real life.

Practice asking the dog to sit, attend, and be calm (*SAW*) when you are:

- Standing
- Sitting
- Facing him or her
- Turned to the side
- Facing away from him or her
- Walking at different speeds

Sound

Dogs are sensitive to the different kinds of vocalization from other dogs. The ones that are fluent in *dog* know when a growl is a play growl and when it's not. Dogs can be just as in tune with us. But a cue word that is usually given in a relaxed way might be confusing the time that it's shouted in panic. It's a very good idea to gradually expose your dog to a variety of ways you can request an action from them. Vary your vocalization from stressed to excited to relaxed during practice.

In addition the sound of the environment will have an effect. Dogs in an urban environment will be far more reactive simply from the noise of the traffic alone. Sudden appearances of large vehicles can be startling both visually and aurally. Wind can interfere with their hearing and make them more on edge as well.

Always start in the least distracting circumstances and only introduce one distraction at a time for the least amount of time and farthest away as possible. Gradually increase the proximity of the distraction and separately increase the duration if you can.

If your dog is afraid or aggressive towards people, be creative and think of all the different sounds that people often make from the sound of keys jangling to singing to gasps and build this into your plan.

Social

Dogs are social animals just as people are, although they may not be good at it. But social signals can be more loaded than other distractions, particularly for those dogs that may be fearful or aggressive. People will reach for dogs, squat, wave their hands, make direct eye contact, talk to the dog, etc. Other dogs might approach, stalk, play-bow, stiffen up, stare, bark, growl, etc. During *desensitization*, it's important to be aware of these factors. Your dog should not be getting anxious and should always be at a level where you can get your dog's attention. If you can't, you are too close to the subject or your dog is experiencing more stress than usual.

Novelty and familiarity

Pay attention to how familiar the dog is with the environment, person, animal, or any other variables. Your dog will do much better in an environment he or she already knows about. Always start in the most boring well-known environment and gradually move to more challenging environments. Your dog will have greater challenges in new situations. In the case of aggression between two dogs that live together, the aggression may appear to be controlled, but then when a new situation occurs that you have not trained in, the chances of lapsing back into aggression is higher

Counter conditioning

This is often confused with and occurs at the same time as *desensitization*. But *desensitization* can occur on its own – just like when we get used to a noxious smell or sound in the room. *Counter conditioning*, on the other hand, helps make new associations or links between things or circumstances *that replace* old learned associations or links. Consequently, the old inappropriate response is substituted with a new appropriate response.

If we equate the word *conditioning* for training or teaching, and the word *counter* with the concept of *acting in opposition to* we can understand that we are looking to teach/train a response that is *incompatible* with the way the dog usually responds. In this way, we can extinguish a behavior by teaching an incompatible behavior for the dog to do instead. For example, you might teach a dog to sit and relax when they see their target and be rewarded. The behavior and response is fundamentally incompatible with aggression.

Of course, you need to set up the situation in such a way that teaching the dog to do this is actually possible. This means working with the dog when the dog is below "threshold", in other words, the aggressive arousal sequence has not begun. Keeping the dog below threshold can usually only be done by reducing the intensity of the threat to the extent this is possible initially and then increasing the intensity tiny steps at a time each time the dog experiences success and is rewarded for remaining calm.

This relaxation and rewarding allows a dog to make new positive associations where there may have previously been bad ones. It's important to understand that fear learning is very powerful, however. It will take patience, many repetitions, and consistent positive outcomes for this learning to occur. The dog needs to believe that the new conditions are permanent. This means the positive experiences happen for so long and so consistently that their suspicions actually reverse. It helps to understand this from a human perspective. Imagine your spouse has cheated on you – how long will it take for you to be able trust that person again? In this case, a lack of trust translates into a state of apprehension or fear. Or, imagine that you got into a few car accidents with a particular unsafe driver – how long will it take before you can trust that the driver is now, in fact, a safe driver? How about an alcoholic who has finally got sober – how comfortable will you feel when you know they are going out with friends to a bar? It takes time and repeated positive experience to trust.

Unfortunately, if your dog is put back into the same stressful situation again, you have undone a lot of your hard work, because you have just taught the dog that the negative situation still has the potential to occur at any time. Using the human situations above, it's possible that should your spouse cheat again after a long period of being faithful, or the driver drives unsafely, or drinker drinks again, you may find it all the harder to trust them the next time. We need to safeguard our dogs and ensure we don't break their trust in us.

Habituation **and** *Flooding*

Habituation is the process whereby we get used to a situation. *Habituation* is very similar to *desensitization* except the thing(s) or situations are generally non-threatening. For example, in the earlier *desensitization* examples, it is a good idea to get the dog used to an environment where there are no threats before working on *desensitization*. A good example might be letting the dog get used to a busy street. Eventually, the brain realizes that there is no need to pay attention to the things in the environment. This is different from *desensitization* in that *desensitization* deals directly with a threat. Relaxation must be encouraged.

Flooding is exposing the dog to their triggers for long enough that eventually he or she gives up. [190] This can be a dangerous technique as it can cause greater fear. Unfortunately, many dog owners use *flooding* instead of *desensitization* without realizing it.

Extinction burst

When you remove reinforcement or a reward from a behavior, the behavior doesn't usually decrease right away. Usually, the dog tries harder at trying to get the reward or reinforcement. This burst of activity is called an *extinction burst*. But eventually, the dog realizes that the reinforcement (reward) is not coming and the dog gives up; the behavior becomes extinct.

Extinction

Extinction is the gradual weakening and disappearance of a *conditioned response*. And by *conditioned*, we mean learning that has occurred in the presence of something else that causes you or the dog to develop an association between the two things. For example, if every time a particular light went on just before you received a painful shock, you will come to develop a response – usually fear and apprehension – to the light.

Extinction occurs when you learn to disassociate the two things. For example, what happens when the light gets switched on, but the shock stops happening? In time – a much longer time than it took to pair the association between the light and shock, we start to de-couple the two and experience much less fear, or perhaps experience no fear at all when the light is turned on.

Extinction can happen relatively quickly or may take a long period of time. For example, in the famous experiment where Pavlov was able to get dogs to salivate when a bell went off, he started to play the bell and did not supply the food after. Eventually the bell was *unpaired* with the food, and no longer represented food coming. The *conditioned response* (trained response) of salivating at the bell became *extinct*. In other words, the dog stopped associating the sound of the bell with food and the dog stopped salivating when they heard the bell.

A fear response that has thought to become *extinct* can re-appear under stress, over time, or if the part of the brain that is involved in inhibiting the fear response is otherwise occupied on another mental task.

The techniques of *desensitization* and *counter conditioning* can help certain associations to become extinct by causing the dog to learn that the previous associations are no longer linked.

But *extinction is not forgetting!* Research has shown that we don't forget our fearful memories, but learn to inhibit them as we come to see that certain associations are not actually associated. *Extinction* really is a matter of learning new behavior that takes over.

In other words, the animal learns that the signal of the untrained *stimulus* now predicts that it will *not* occur. It is a relearning process – what is defined as *inhibitory learning*. Unfortunately, it takes longer and is more fragile than fear learning. This is why it is so essential that we avoid situations that produce anxiety and aggression.

Why is this important?

Why does understanding how *extinction* works important for people working with aggressive dogs? Because the response tends to come back under stress or in different contexts. This means if you *condition* a dog to not respond anxiously to one person in the house, he or she still may respond anxiously when under stress or after a lengthy period of time. This can be why we have relapses in aggression. If a different person comes in, then the context has changed and the dog is likely to become anxious again, and possibly become aggressive.

PUNISHMENT

For the average dog owner who doesn't have a back ground in learning theory, punishment is punishment. In other words, your dog does something wrong, so there are consequences: you follow up by doing something that the dog really doesn't like, in hopes that this will discourage your dog from repeating the behavior because he or she fears being punished again.

But the word punishment has a technical definition as well. I would say you could skip the definitions, but unfortunately there are people who will exploit these definitions to confuse dog owners into believing that even the positive dog trainers still use punishment.

Good trainers know that for punishment to work in average dogs, it actually has to be severe enough to cause the dog to avoid it from then on. Normally, owners do not punish that hard to discourage the dog from doing the behavior almost immediately. So when the dog repeats the thing they are supposed to not do, and then the owner has to increase the level of intensity of the punishment. This is how dogs get used to punishment. And how owners get frustrated.

> **TIP**
> For more information on what "positive punishment" and "negative punishment" is, please refer to the end of punishment section. Using this lingo as a way to confuse dog owners can be a tactic to justify the use of fear-based punishment.

It is far better to manage the situation so the dog does not have the opportunity to behave undesirably and then train desirable behaviors, than to actually punish him or her for doing the wrong thing.

But it is also important to look at the situations that cause you to withhold treats, too. Withholding treats can cause some frustration, so this should be used judiciously. If you find you are withholding too much, it means you are asking for more than the dog is capable of at that time. Withhold too much, the dog will start to feel so frustrated that they give up or simply loses interest. Unfortunately, they will be less likely to want to work with you next time.

Lots of people do it

You wouldn't be alone if you have scolded your dog, yanked on their chain, or worse. Many people punish their dogs, and are probably more likely to punish their dogs when they are being aggressive. In fact, many people have a hard time accepting that they *shouldn't* punish their dogs for showing aggression. Things like flipping your dog over (*alpha rolls*, etc.) are even recommended by so-called experts. But should we do it?

Does punishment work?

It is dangerous to use punishment on aggressive dogs. There are all those trainers who insist on using it as part of their obedience training, however in most cases, it is unnecessary to use punishment. There are many obedience situations that punishment can work to decrease a simple behavior, but it is often just as easy and more humane to manage the situation (i.e. put the garbage out of reach) and teach the dog what he or she should be doing instead.

Punishment affects learning

Research in humans show how negative emotions cause and impact on cognitive processing – producing more errors and showing less activation in brain areas associated with task performance, suggesting that negative emotions actually compete for brain resources.[191] This means under the best of circumstances, the brain is not *all there* to process what is going on when negative emotions are produced even when relatively minor. The dog might be able to better process the learning involved and remember, as it relates to fear, but you cannot control exactly what the dog is associating with the fearful situation.

They are less likely to remember anything that does not relate to the fearful situation. Because our brains are so highly focused on avoiding circumstances that cause us fear – our brains rapidly take in all the things that may predict this event happening again. This will include you, too. It is important to remember that from the dog's perspective, aggression is a response to an anxiety or fear-producing *stimulus*. It is designed to be a coping response to fear, and not a predictor of fear.

Aggression itself is also self-rewarding. [192] As mentioned earlier the neurotransmitter dopamine is produced in the brain in response to aggression and this helps the dog cope with the highly aversive condition of the anxiety it was experiencing just prior to the aggression.

If you were to punish the aggression, you have to ask yourself whether the punishment is worse than the sense of dread and impending doom that the anxiety produces. Unlikely it is. At best, it suppresses the aggression. At worst, he or she goes all out when their anxiety levels become unbearable.

So if your dog is behaving aggressively towards another dog and you punish them, they are more likely to associate the other dog with the punishment, than they are likely to associate the punishment with their own behavior.

Because we know that the so-called stress hormone *cortisol* disrupts hippocampus functions in the brain, we know that in higher stress situations memories are fragmented, not unlike dreams being fragmented (for the same reason – cortisol produced late at night in the brain disrupts hippocampus functions). This means the direct cause and effect aspect of memory – or the narrative aspect of memory to string things together into a sequence that makes sense - is disrupted.

It is dangerous to use punishment on aggressive dogs.

It is worth repeating: it is dangerous to use punishment on aggressive dogs. Don't do it. In some cases, where it appears to work, all it is doing is temporarily suppressing the aggression. The key word is *temporarily*, here. Usually the result of punishment ends up removing all the warning signs of pending bites as well cause the dog to be even more anxious around the thing or situation that caused the aggression in the first place. This makes a dog dangerous to be around.

In some cases, the argument is that aggression is not always a serious thing, but just that the dog is misbehaving, and consequently punishment should work. However, I witnessed something as mild as minor warning growling at a toddler get worse the more the dog was scolded. In this case, the scolding was not likely a severe enough punishment to stop the growling. But had it been, the dog *might* have suppressed the growling. Is that the answer to your problem? No. The underlying anxiety would have never been treated. Instead, an increase of anxiety would have been associated with the child's approach or proximity. The dog would have been quieter, but more dangerous. What happens in the case where the toddler grabs the dog when the adults are not looking? Sadly, many children get bitten this way.

In this mild case, the problem was quickly resolved simply by giving a treat each time the child started to approach. This not only reduced the growling, but also made the dog look forward to the child's approach. This dog lived almost another decade, well into old age, with no further aggression towards children.

Punishment negatively affects behavior and the human-dog bond.

Studies have indicated that dogs owned by owners that favored punishment were less likely to interact with a stranger. Not surprising. They also tended to be less playful.[193] Owners that used punishment-based collars reported less satisfaction with their dog's overall and leash-walking behaviors.[194] Higher heart rates in dogs are associated with people associated with punishment as compared to lower heart rates with those associated with petting.[195]

These findings implicate that using punishment negatively affect the dog's behavior, as well as the human-animal bond.

People have the tendency to punish for the same reasons that dogs might behave aggressively: they are fearful, in pain, frustrated, or it has become a habit. Needless to say, the likelihood that a person is experiencing fear, pain, or frustration when a dog behaves aggressively is much higher than it would be in ordinary circumstances. In the section ahead on Emotional Arousal in People, we discuss how using punishment can result in repeat behavior partly because of this arousal.

Shock collars

The popularly of shock collars depends on the speed and permanence in which fear learning occurs to deal with behavioral problems such as aggression. In addition, it is a punishment device that can be used over a longer distance. Theoretically when the dog behaves in a certain way, and the dog is shocked immediately after, then he or she will come to predict the shock will happen whenever the dog behaves that way. This is supposed to encourage the dog to inhibit their behavior to avoid the shock.

However, any benefits of shock collars are outweighed by the problems. Outside of collars malfunctioning, there are the very real problems of timing, emotional arousal in the dog handler, and emotional arousal in the dog.

Timing

It is not uncommon for dog owners to have poor timing when providing both rewards and punishments. Ask any positive-based trainer who teaches clicker training, and they will tell you just how poor inexperienced people are at responding immediately when they need to. In clicker training, exercises not involving the dog are often recommended, such as practicing clicker training people (fun party game or to practice clicking at the very moment a bouncing ball hits the floor. Poor timing is not all that problematic since receiving a treat – even when the dog can't predict when they are coming – is still enjoyable.

But when it comes to shock collars, the lack of timing can prove to be very problematic if the dog is unable to figure out why he or she has been shocked and subsequently, incapable of escaping shock. Maier and Seligman who wrote a paper on *learned helplessness* in dogs, state that between 1965 and 1969 the behavior of approximately 150 dogs were studied that had received prior inescapable shock. [196]

Two-thirds of these dogs (about a 100 out of the 150) demonstrated *learned helplessness* in response to the shock. That is to say, 100 dogs failed to jump a barrier to escape shock. In other words, the motivation to respond in *any* way to the shock seems to decrease.

Even in those that did respond in similar conditions and their response provided relief, the subject often had difficulty in learning that the response worked. They wrote that the *learned helpless* effect in the dog occurs in a variety of situations and is easy to produce. It did not matter about how frequent or intense or how long the shock was or whether there was a signal letting them know the shock was coming.

Learned helplessness appears to be common among species that learn. Depression and anxiety may predominate.

Stress

Shock at a medium level (i.e. level 8 out of 15 possible levels) has been shown to be particularly stressful for dogs, shown both by body postures and elevated cortisol levels in later studies.[197]

In other studies, being unable to associate the shock with a specific *stimulus* leads to insecurity and extreme states of anxiety. One study looked at three conditions in which hunting dogs received a shock: when they touched something like a dummy prey (dummy rabbit fixed to a motion device), when they did not comply with a recall command that had already been trained, or were randomly shocked. [198] It should be noted that hunting, while mimicking aggression, does not have the same fear and anxiety levels associated. Consequently, learning to inhibit a response under these conditions should be much easier in the conditions where the shock was clearly associated with touching the dummy prey.

Based on the earlier discussion on *learned helplessness* in response to inescapable shock, the randomly shocked in this study had very high stress levels. When dogs are unable to associate the shock with a *stimulus* that allows them to predict the shock the next time, dog owners set up a situation that mimics this problem.

But even those dogs that were shocked when they did not comply with a command in the study – in other words, they should have been able to predict the shock - saw an increase of cortisol values up to 160%. Those that received the shock when they touched the rabbit – something that was clearly associated with the shock, still experienced an increase of cortisol up to 31%. However, it would be difficult (and unethical) to shock a dog within seconds of attacking another person or dog just so that the dog could make the connection between the two events as a way to deal with a dog aggression problem.

However, trainers in the field using shock devices are more likely to shock a dog for not complying with a command for example. Theoretically, the command could be for a behavior incompatible with aggression, and the use of the shock early in the training could make compliance very solid. However we have the same issue of anxiety being highly disturbing and largely involuntary. It is a mistake to assume that dogs find the experience of shock worse than the experience of anxiety. If an act of aggression can momentarily replace the dog's anxiety, a dog can be willing to tolerate the shock under highly arousing and motivating circumstances.

Emotional Arousal in People

The average dog owner is more emotionally invested in their dog behaving than an experienced dog trainer. Feelings of frustration are uncommon in dog owners when the dog isn't motivated to comply.

Studies have indicated that aversive stimuli evoke the desire to do harm.[199] Frustrations can create aggressive inclinations.[200][201] This means the risk of abuse is higher. In addition, studies on catharsis demonstrate a reduction in stress symptoms after the opportunity to shock someone who had caused them to feel frustrated.[202] This means that we are more likely to repeat the behavior in similar situations because to behave aggressively is self-rewarding. Obviously, the same tendency to abuse a shock collar exists for other forms of punishment.

Why do some people, including some trainers, support these techniques if they are so problematic?

Science has proven that punishment works under certain circumstances. But the decision to use punishment methods when there are other methods that are just as effective is usually not an entirely logic-based choice. There are many reasons why dog owners and dog trainers still continue to use these methods: values, belief systems, other influencers, etc.

Average dog owners usually resort to physical punishment for these reasons:

- Anger and frustration
- When everything else they have tried seems to have failed
- Because someone else seen as having more experience has advised it
- Because it reflects their values (i.e. "bad" behavior should be punished).

In some cases, people may have poor impulse control and/or low tolerance for frustration themselves. They are usually not aware of the emotional aspects that may influence the desire to use punishment.

If you or someone you know tends to be reactive or volatile, it may be worth talking to a doctor about it, especially if there are other signs of problems such as the tendency to abuse, drink heavily, use drugs, depression, or there are other control issues.

We also experience social pressures. When our dog misbehaves, other people expect us to punish. Most don't want to see you give a dog that has just growled a treat. But when it comes to dog ownership, just about everyone has an opinion. That you have an aggressive dog causes others to assume you are doing something wrong, and they will often be happy to tell you what.

Behaviorism influences

B. F. Skinner was a pioneer in the field of behavior and has influenced many. Many theories have been validated today and are almost accepted as common knowledge, at least in an extremely simplified view, which is: rewards increase behavior; punishment decreases behavior.

Skinner's work here primarily focused only on behavior, rather than cognition and emotions. This appeals to both average dog owners and trainers since we can't get inside the head of a dog. This philosophy provides a basic science in which to increase or decrease behavior.

While his ideas were rooted in credible, verifiable evidence, Skinner's experiments generally dealt with basic behaviors - not aggression. The theories do not account for the many complexities that are specifically involved with aggression. It's one thing to teach a dog a behavior to avoid shock; it's another thing altogether to improve the underlying problems of aggression, thereby reducing the tendency to behave aggressively.

Social dominance

The role of *alpha* and dominance theories is discussed more in the next section, but it is enough to know that some gravitate toward aversive methods because of the belief that canine aggression is rooted in 1) The need for social dominance, 2) That social dominance is attained through force-based behavior. Dog trainers may have used these methods for years and may be relying on past experience that punishment can inhibit behavior as a general application. There are two problems with this. One is that aggression is complex and involves the dog's physiology and emotions the way typical behavior such as heeling or jumping up generally doesn't. The other issue is that trainers don't always follow up. The dog may revert back to past behavior. Most clients don't know if a failure is the dog's, or of the training methods, or a weakness in their own training abilities.

The influence of so-called authority figures

Unfortunately, celebrity influences many people, and average dog owners are no exception. There have been TV celebrities, as well as dog businesses online and in real life, which still communicate the myth that methods using pain and/or fear will fix dog aggression. People who appear as experts in the media seem credible because they appear to have been vetted by the media.

In reality, producers and editors are looking to build audiences, particularly with the growth of the Internet. Charisma, drama, and even conflict are often what drive people to watch television and video and this is what producers and editors use to attract people. Without viewers, they go out of business.

Television in particular can be a powerful communicator because it reaches so many people, and even while it competes with the internet, a single show certainly reaches far more people than a veterinary behavior website or specialized symposiums whose audiences include the already converted. Regarding dominance, punishment, etc., you can search for the *American Veterinary Society of Animal Behavior* for their position statements.

Some of these television shows communicate that if a dog is lunging and out of control, a collar such as a prong collar should be used, or that the dog should be flipped over on their back, that showing a dog who is "boss" or being a strong 'leader" is all you need to do. As the average dog owner, how are you supposed to know this is a bad choice for an aggressive dog?

Temporarily suppressing behavior

It is possible to *temporarily suppress* behavior through punishment. From the outside, it looks like the aggression has been terminated. When done right, it is possible to temporarily suppress behavior quite quickly. This is incredibly attractive to a dog owner who wants a quick fix. Combine frustration with a sense of urgency to stop aggression and you have a person who may be willing to put aside their own ethical values to stop aggression.

Again, the key phrases are *possible* and *temporarily suppress*. Punishment is much more likely to suppress behavior (although likely unnecessary) on normal non-aggressive dogs and puppies if done properly. But it can just as easily backfire making your dog worse.

In truly abnormal dogs, which many of our aggressive dogs are, the techniques not only cause problems for the dogs by making them even more anxious and less trusting of you and other people, but there is a high risk of the dog becoming aggressive in a more intense way when their back is truly up against the wall (i.e. when the dog is so stressed, and feeling threatened).

Average dog trainers work mostly with normal dogs.

The average dog trainer tends to work with normal dogs for the most part. Normal dogs tolerate punishment better. But trainers are quick to recommend euthanasia for those dogs that are viewed as having "weak nerves" or "poor breeding" or whatever else when punishment methods don't work. Like the vets, the suggestion of euthanasia protects them. But for trainers who use punishment as part of their tool box when treating aggression may actually be hiding the fact that not only are their techniques inhumane, but ineffective when actually dealing with this kind of problem. A good trainer knows where their abilities lie and will recommend clients to a veterinary behaviorist in serious cases of aggression.

Many dog trainers are trying to run a business.

Unlike doctors and vets, there is no licensing system as of yet to provide any kind of checks and balances. Anyone can hang a sign out and claim to be a trainer, behaviorist, or specialist.

It is important to keep in mind that many dog trainers are running a business and it's a business where there is often a lot of competition. There is not necessarily a lot of repeat business, and does not pay especially well overall. They need clients and they need immediate results for those clients. Repeat business is not a given, as most dog owners feel confident to continue the training themselves when they are dealing with obedience issues.

If a trainer is open to using punishment, the need for speed may justify their use of punishment in aggression cases. In those cases where punishment doesn't consistently work, clients may continue to search elsewhere for answers and may find another resource so the trainer is not getting the opportunity to see the results. If a trainer does see that the dog's aggression is worsening, it may be more comfortable to shift the blame to the dog or owner rather than question the methods. Thankfully the force-free approach is gaining momentum.

The difficulty in determining whether a dog trainer can help your aggressive dog or not

A dog trainer can tell you how experienced they are, but it is hard to know how successful they have been at treating aggression for a few reasons.

- There is no licensing system for dog training even if there are certifying bodies.

- The trainer may not have enough experience with the kind of aggression problem your dog is experiencing.

- The trainer may simply not be good enough.

- It is good business sense to screen former clients to be passed on as references, which means you are not getting an objective picture.

- Past clients' dogs may have their aggression suppressed short-term if punishment methods were used and would be willing to give a good reference. They may be unaware of how the underlying problem has just lead to different symptoms. If punishment does work to suppress the aggression long term, punishment still may backfire for your dog.

- People who have aggressive dogs that don't get any better move on. Rarely do they come back to the trainer if they have lost confidence in them (or feel scammed) especially in the case of trainers with intimidating personalities.

- There is so much conflicting information available that dog owners don't know how to decide. We may just choose based on who we like, who is the most persuasive or who talks with the most authority.

See the section on Professional Help in Part 3 to understand more about how to find someone who can help.

Positive punishment? Negative punishment? What's that?

In the behaviorist world, Positive Punishment means a punishment that has been applied - in other words, something you are adding to the situation to decrease behavior. But there are other ways to punish that include taking things away - such as yourself; you walk out of a room, you remove food, or take away a treat. This is called negative punishment, because you are taking something away from the situation.

Some people will argue that there is no way to avoid punishing because if you are withholding a treat for a dog not performing the behavior you are looking for, this withholding could be interpreted as punishing to the dog (in this case negative punishment – something has been removed). Some people claim that clicker training works on this principle. For example, if you withhold a treat when your dog sits instead of lies down when asked, you are withholding something that they want. Whether or not it can be defined as negative punishment may center around which specific behavior it is supposed to be eliminating and whether withholding is the same as removing. Regardless, the resulting frustration is usually mild and motivates the dog to try something else.

Removing your attention short-term from an obnoxious dog trying to get your attention or control your behavior might be considered negative punishment because you are removing something of value to decrease the dog's obnoxiousness. But outside of those dogs who experience severe separation anxiety, most dogs' fear and anxiety states are unlikely to be mobilized, nor is the human-dog bond likely to be compromised.

It is all about the response

The most important thing to keep in mind is that **anything that causes the dog to be fearful, anxious, causes acute stress or affects the dog's welfare needs to be avoided**.

It is very easy to get lost in the definitions and analysis. Be aware of this if anyone uses these definitions as a way to convince you positive-based trainers still actually use punishment, and therefore so should you.

 REWARDS

Rewards are anything that the dog would like to have or experience. Rewards vary in how rewarding they are and how much the dog wants them at any one time, and vary from dog to dog and situation to situation. For example, a dog may be more willing to work for food before dinner than after dinner. They may also be more interested in certain types of food. Your dog may be willing to eat kibble at any time, but they may be more motivated to pay attention to how they can get a piece of chicken or cheese, than a piece of kibble. He or she is more willing to work for play when they have the energy to play and the play style suits their breed. They are more willing to work for praise and attention when they haven't been showered with love all day.

Advantages to using food for rewards

The most common and effective reward to use is food because all dogs have to eat. Food is also easy to give quickly, and the dog can consume it quickly. In addition, dogs are often more motivated to work for food than praise or petting (many dogs are ambivalent about both, or even dislike petting).

There is another advantage: The body appetitive system is in conflict with the system that is involved in the fight or flight response that triggers aggression. It's not a simple thing to take advantage of since most dogs will not care about food when they are aggressive, but it can be used in *classical conditioning* set-ups to help prevent the body's system from switching over quite so fast. Also, because food is a necessity, the body is designed to anticipate and respond to food more than other rewards.

Finally, another advantage: food is very pleasurable to dogs and as a result the neurotransmitter dopamine is produced in the brain. Dopamine enhances learning. See the Neurotransmitter section for more about dopamine.

Timing

Timing is important and rewards should be delivered within 30-60 seconds to be effective and need to be consistent and predictable (i.e. the dog is rewarded every time until they have learned the behavior very well in every circumstance and then after that rewarded intermittently).

Intensity of rewards

Rewards should be something more enticing than the usual kibble for each new change in what he or she is learning, but not so fabulous that the dog gets over excited. They should not be rewarded when they are not calm, nor should they be rewarded when their behavior starts to slip. This is much harder for new trainers than it seems. At the same time, you need to make sure you are not asking for too much. Dogs get confused and tired. If you see this happening, end the session with something that the dog can be good at. You want to leave them feeling good about training.

The more complicated the task that you are asking the dog to do, the less motivated he or she will be to do it, so don't demand too much.

But my dog will get fat!

In the wild, a dog's dinner would not happen to pass by waiting to be eaten. The dog would have to forage and hunt for food. In fact, research has shown that wild African Dogs spend about 3 hours a day tracking down food, and rest the remainder of the time. So feeding your dog dinner by giving small portions of it as rewards during training can be an excellent way to keep your dog challenged without adding too many extra calories to the dog's diet. It also ensures that a dog is hungry enough, and therefore motivated enough to work for the treat. Also keep in mind that when dogs are learning new things, their brains consume energy. Training uses up calories. But also keep in mind, that dogs may pay attention better and focus better when they have been recently fed.[203]

- Canned food can be frozen in chunks or baked
- *Jackpots* are extra amounts used to let the dog know what they did was

extra good. Use high value food for *jackpots* or when the dog does something or learns something new in their training; use cooked chicken, freeze-dried liver, hot dogs, cheese, etc.

- Cut the pieces up in approximately raisin-sized pieces, depending on the size of the dog.
- Stuffed Kongs or other food-based toys can be given at the end of a training session.

Other rewards are often just given away for free such as:

- **Attention** (play, praise, petting)
- **Access** through a doorway, hallway, or outside, to a favorite person or dog, etc.
- **Toys**
- **Freedom**

Instead use the SAW program and ask your dog to sit, attend and wait for a moment before giving these rewards.

 PROGNOSIS

This is always a difficult area, because there are so many factors, the biggest of which being owner compliance to the treatment program that is prescribed. There are no guarantees. Temporary relapses are more likely to occur in homes where the owners believe the dog is cured and stop reinforcing the appropriate behaviors.[204]

According to Dr. Karen Overall and Dr. Lore Haug here are a number of things that influences prognosis:

- Owner compliance to the (right) treatment program

- The age of the dog at the onset of aggression
- Predictability of the outbursts
- Duration of the condition
- The pattern of the behavioral changes in response to environmental, behavioral, and pharmacological intervention
- The dog owner's resources (financial, emotional, time)
- The willingness and capabilities of the owners and family
- The environment the dog is in

This means the earlier the problem developed, the less predictable the outbursts (and this could change once the owner is taught how to recognize the signs), the longer the condition has existed, and the more frequent and intense the rate and extent of the outburst, the worst the prognosis. If the owners are physically or emotionally challenged, if there are people in the home that won't comply with treatment recommendations, etc. then this will affect how much the dog can improve.

These elements may be key factors in how you decide to handle the aggression problem, particularly if you are unable to predict or anticipate when the aggression might occur. A veterinary behaviorist should be consulted in this case if possible.

Many people want quick fixes that don't require a lot of work. If you are one of these people, you are at risk for rushing through the program and expecting too much from your dog before they are ready.

If you really want to make an improvement: work hard, stay consistent, but don't get burnt out. Expect that this is a journey. If you are hyper-focused on the end goal, you are more likely to give up. Instead, pay attention to the progress you are making. And of course, manage and prevent the aggression so you are happy to live with your dog in the meantime.

PATHOLOGY

Studies now indicate that all mammals are capable of sharing emotions of others.[205] But what is going on with a dog that behaves aggressively when there is no threat against them? It appears to be particularly puzzling when dogs are aggressive to people who just want to be friendly to them.

Pathology refers to a disease component. This is not always a pain related condition. It can also be related to such things like an imbalance of neurochemicals. This might be something that a dog is born with, or has developed as a result of stress or other conditions.

In most cases, the underlying cause of aggression is fear or anxiety (more about fear and anxiety in the next section). In other cases, it can be a result of pain or frustration, which may be considered normal.

Dogs may have had a learning experience that leads to aggression or they may have something more related to disease (pathological) that indicates that the aggression is not normal or appropriate for the situation.

If the dog's aggression is considered to be inappropriate given the context that it occurred in, and there are other behaviors that seem to be out of the ordinary (such as hyper-vigilance, separation anxiety, etc.), it may suggest that there is something more involved than the aggression than simply a result of a learning experience. However it is not inconceivable that in the wrong kind of environment disease can develop in an otherwise normal dog (i.e. a normal dog living with an unhealthy aggressive dog). In such cases, medication might be warranted to allow *behavior modification* to work, regardless of whether the issue is a result of genetics or a learned component.

Here are some questions to help you explore whether your dog may need additional help possibly in the way of medication or other medical interventions. A veterinary behaviorist will be required to make the final diagnosis.

Questions	
How quickly does the aggression appear? Aggression that appears with little warning can suggest pathology. But a shortened warning sequence may also be the result of repeated opportunities to practice aggression.	• Is there any other posturing or growling, etc. that tried to resolve the conflict first without aggression? • Are there any warning signs that the dog was becoming stressed? • Has there been a progression of aggression over time where the dog did show warnings, but no longer does? • Does the dog seem to have a *hair-trigger temper*? • Is it possible to predict situations where the aggression will occur? • Are there other behaviors that indicate the dog is generally anxious or frustrated?
How intense is the aggression? Uninhibited biting can suggest pathology.	• Does the dog tend to snap, rather than outright bite? • Is the dog resorting to skin punctures or full pressure bites before any other aggressive strategies were used such as growling, snarling, lunging, etc.? In other words, has the dog used a "sledgehammer when a feather will do"?

How long does the aggression take to dissipate?

Aggression that does not resolve or a dog that continues to attack another dog after it has submitted can suggest the dog is not normal.

- Does he or she continue to lunge on the end of a leash, pant, or show any other intense related behaviors after an aggressive episode?
- Is your dog responsive to cues from you, i.e. will they pay attention to you, sit calmly when asked after the threat is gone, etc.?
- Does he or she appear to use post-conflict appeasement signals if the aggression is toward household members?

Is the aggression appropriate?

Inappropriate aggression suggests pathology. However a caution here is that many people do not know how to behave appropriately around dogs or how to read a dog's signals that he or she is becoming stressed. A veterinary behaviorist can help determine if there is a pathology.

- Does the dog have a reason to be fearful, anxious, frustrated, or in pain given the context?
- Does the dog have a real reason to be afraid or is the dog using a pre-emptive strike?
- Are there any signs indicating that the target of their aggression is, in any way, threatening the dog?

 INTENSE DOGS

Some dogs respond either more intensely or more quickly than other dogs. This hyperactivity may indicate the problem is pathological (again, pathological in that it relates to disease and is not only a learned behavior). These dogs may be impossible to interrupt once they reach that level where the brain begins to fire indiscriminately. According to veterinary behaviorist, Dr. Karen Overall, anticipation of these behaviors that signal early concern are critical for the treatment of these dogs for the treatment to be at all successful.[206]

Other animals may be intense but still can respond well to treatment. Behaviors that can be associated with intensity can include:

- Alertness (hyper-vigilance)
- Restlessness (motor activity)
- Vocalization
- Systemic effects (vomiting, urination, or defecation)
- Displacement or stereotypical behaviors
- Changes in the content or quantity of solicitous behaviors

 # AGGRESSION VS. VIOLENCE

Some scientific literature is interested in violence in animals as a way of shedding light on violence in humans. Here aggression in animals has been categorized into two types, differentiating normal adaptive aggression from violence[207]. However, these distinctions seem limited, when violence on the one hand is seen as maladaptive and cold-blooded vs. adaptive aggression that is seen as a form of social communication, where the goal is acquiring *resources*, (food, shelter, mates, and status).

This view does not seem to take into account the aggression that appears to be motivated by the need to cope with anxiety or fear. And while the need to cope with anxiety of fear may be adaptive, the *reason* the animal is experiencing anxiety or fear may be maladaptive at least in terms of its results, i.e. aggression towards its owners may eventually result in re-homing the dog or putting the dog down, or in the case of another dog, may result in death or severe injury.

I would argue in this case that this kind of aggression is not cold-blooded at all and that signs of sympathetic arousal (i.e. the nervous system response that is responsible for the freeze, fight, or flight response) is in fact, activated. While we may see a condensed or absent behavioral sequences, there may be subtler signs of stress that we can detect that indicate emotional arousal. It may simply be how we decide what is actually adaptive or maladaptive and it may be a sliding scale between the two.

For discussion sake, it is worth looking at these large picture behavioral sequences that largely comes out of a review paper, called "Animal violence demystified", appearing in the *Frontiers in Behavioral Neuroscience* journal differentiating violence and adaptive aggression.

As a quick overview, adaptive aggression primarily occurs within a behavioral sequence, but violence may have a disordered behavioral sequence (more on this later). The violent *cold-blooded* aggression is observed without any emotional arousal. This is seen in a variety of animals from rats to horses to humans. Bites aimed at vulnerable parts of the opponent's body are considered characteristic of violent aggression. It is uninhibited and happens out of context. In dogs, some might consider this rage aggression. Rage aggression is thought to be rare. In rage aggression, or as it is sometimes called Idiopathic aggression, the attacks are not frequent and can be spaced out by a months or more.[208]

BEHAVIORAL SEQUENCE LEADING TO AGGRESSION VS. VIOLENCE

Intent

This is the stage where the dog is sizing up its opponent, and you may only see this as a series of pauses or movements over a brief time-period. In some cases, a dog might show signs of stress such as yawning, lip licking, sniffing the ground, looking away, or shaking the body. Some trainers describe this as calming signals, although they may simply be signs of discomfort or anxiety and while dogs respond to those behaviors in various ways, they may not actually be intended as communication.

Dogs that would be considered abnormal or violent would ordinarily not show any signs of the sympathetic nervous system arousal - the system controlling the freeze, flight, or fight reactions, which activates heart rate, respiration, etc.

This paper argues that in order to resolve conflicts effectively, animals must assess the opponent, and that this results in a series of pauses or movements over a brief time-period. That this has been truncated or absent in violence suggests an intention to attack without this appraisal, and suggest that the intention to attack is different.

Ritualization

These are antagonistic behaviors and are used to resolve conflicts *without* fighting and there is a progression of these behaviors. These behaviors serve to increase the apparent size of the animal or expose their weapons.

In normal dogs, the ritualization is usually all that is needed for one animal to back down and aggression doesn't occur. Dogs that bear a stronger physical resemblance to wolves (e.g., the Siberian Husky) apparently show a larger repertoire of agonistic behaviors – i.e. behaviors that occur within a possible conflict including threatening, aggression, retreat, appeasement, or submission - than dogs that do not look like wolves at all.[209]

You might see an example of antagonistic ritual behaviors in the dog park when you see dogs *stand tall*, their ears and tail stand up, they appear to be on their toes, and they slowly circle another dog. When that dog looks away, lowers their head or tail, the challenge is over and they interact in other ways (such as sniff or play) or ignore each other. Alternatively if neither dog stands down, it might progress to other antagonistic behaviors.

Abnormally aggressive dogs may actually *bypass* this phase. Their motivations are not necessarily to resolve the conflict, but to actually cause harm.

Pre-escalation

These are threat displays and may involve low growling and/or hard staring. It might include a threatening sound or guttural bark. The dog is often stiff and still or moving very slowly. It might involve the *whale eye* or *cow-eye*, which involves the head turned away, but the eyes are faced in the direction of their target and the whites of the eyes are showing. The dog might snarl. Again in abnormal dogs, these behaviors may be completely lacking or inadequate.

It is helpful to remember that average dogs do not want to cause harm, *unless absolutely necessary* (as they perceive it). From this perspective, the benefits of aggression must be weighed against costs.

Note: The result of punishing the early warning signs of escalating aggression such as growling or baring teeth is that this ritualized behavior often becomes inhibited in dogs. Therefor a lack of ritualized behaviors is not necessarily an indicator of an abnormal dog; we simply have taken their tools away to resolve conflicts. For these dogs, owners need to keep a close eye on stress indicators or any kind of staring or stiffness.

Escalation

This may include striking out and biting, and are usually short and rapid. According to the ASPCA, some of the behaviors you might see in order of escalation are:

- Lunging forward or charging at the person with no contact
- Mouthing, as though to move or control the person, without applying significant pressure
- "Muzzle punch" (the dog literally punches the person with her nose)
- Growl
- Showing teeth
- Snarl (a combination of growling and showing teeth)
- Snap
- Quick nip that leaves no mark
- Quick bite that tears the skin
- Bite with enough pressure to cause a bruise
- Bite that causes puncture wounds
- Repeated bites in rapid succession
- Bite and shake

In adaptive aggression, conflicts can still be resolved by one retreating at any point. This may not occur in abnormally aggressive dogs. Abnormally aggressive dogs might target an opponent and its vulnerable body parts regardless of its subordinate or submissive status. Dogs that are at the repeated bites stage or bite and shake may be too frenzied to back off.

Bites that cause any kind of damage such as tears or bruises are in fact still somewhat inhibited aggression and indicate some self-control, but certainly indicate that the dog is less inhibited that the dog who merely snaps or bites with no mark. Dogs that have inhibited bites certainly can progress to uninhibited bites at any time, however, particularly as they practice the aggression and become more stressed, anxious, frustrated, etc.

In abnormal aggression, the aggression may not be related to the context; in other words, it may not matter who the opponent is or what is happening in the environment.

Post escalation

In normal aggression, dogs display affiliative behaviors (behaviors designed to reconnect the relationship) during this phase. There is a lack of any post-conflict appeasement behavior in violent dogs. In fact submission by the victim may provoke further violence in dogs that are abnormally violent.

The importance of signaling

We have a tendency to punish our kids for not being respectful, and escalate that punishment when our kids become aggressive. But, we do our dogs a great disservice when we punish dogs for growling or not being "nice". While these signals are not friendly, they are in fact part of the proper way to communicate. Punishing dogs for growling means we have taken away a very important part of their communication, which can only serve to frustrate them when in conflict.

Violence is rare

Thankfully, violence as defined here and in the paper we have referred to, is relatively rare in wild populations as it is in humans. But it is not inconceivable that aggression could proceed to violence.

 # MEDICATIONS

To go into medications in detail is beyond the scope of this book. But it is important to dispel some myths about the use of medications in treating behavior problems.

Prescribe now if needed

- If your dog needs them, it is actually better to prescribe medication as soon as possible. Unfortunately due to the stigma of behavioral medications, many people prefer to exhaust all other options before resorting to medicating. Unfortunately, this means that the dog is anxious for longer and will be harder to treat and owner burnout is likely to occur.

Personality changes and addiction

- Behavior medication does not "dope" up your dog, make them "high," change their personality, or anything else that causes the dog to not "feel like him or herself." It does not make them unnaturally "happy" or on another planet. In fact, many people who are prescribed SSRI medications say that they finally feel "normal" (some SSRI medications are also prescribed to dogs). People prescribed SSRI medications tend to experience emotions in the same way that healthy people do. They may have a series of side effects when ramping up on the medication or off the medication that can cause them to feel strange. Yet, most side effects are minor and go away once the body adjusts to the medication.

- Common behavioral medications such as SSRI's (Prozac is part of this family) are not addictive! Again, these medications sometimes cause side effects ramping on and off (i.e. starting and stopping the medication which should be done slowly) as mentioned above but are not signs the medication is addictive. These effects can include sleepiness or hyperactivity, lack of appetite, etc. It is usually temporary. This is not the same as dependency or addiction, but simply a result of the brain and body adapting to the changes. In some cases, people see their dog's sleepiness and worry that their dog is "doped up" or their personality has changed. The neurochemical serotonin, which is commonly targeted in aggression cases, does regulate sleep and appetite so it's common to see temporary changes in these areas. However in many cases what people are actually seeing is the dog being able to finally relax for the first time.

Wait until the medication has its full effect before working with the targets of their aggression

- Many medications take several weeks before they have the desired effect, so exposure to the circumstances that had caused the dog to be anxious or aggressive should wait until then. You can use this time to work on training and foundation exercises. Behavioral medications should never be stopped abruptly. Consult your veterinarian if you have any concerns or feel you need to discontinue the medication.

If they need it, it works. If not, it doesn't.

- If your dog *needs* medication, then *behavior modification* will be an uphill battle without it. This is a dog that is unable to cope in a normal way. These are often dogs that see threats everywhere, and sense that the rules are constantly changing. This greatly interferes with their ability to learn how to relax, and how to respond appropriately to uncertain situations. If there is an improvement as a result of the medication, it suggests that your dog needs the medication.

- If your dog does *not* need the medication, it will not work. Some medications affect a neurotransmitter called serotonin for example (others target different neurochemicals or areas of the brain). This may go without saying but some people still think these kinds of medications are like Valium where it makes you dopey whether you need it or not. They aren't. A shortage of serotonin may be what causes problems so the medication might help deal with that. It allows serotonin to be more available for the brain to use. But if the brain has enough, there is no effect; everything is already working as it should. *Excessive* serotonin causes other issues, but your vet can discuss these issues with you and determine whether this is a risk and if so, whether it is an acceptable risk with the medication being prescribed.

Medication is not a panacea

- Medication alone will not *solve, cure, or eliminate* your dog's aggression or behavior issues. There is always a learning component with aggression, especially the longer it has gone on. The neural pathways in the brain that have been formed are likely habits now. In all cases, while the medication may make your dog less reactive, or less impulsive, they still need behavioral help in becoming less sensitive to their triggers and to learn new associations and new ways to respond that are incompatible with the aggression. The medication helps this learning take place. Regardless of the medication, it will still be easier for your dog to react in the way your dog always has because it is simply easier and more efficient for the brain to do so. Re-training helps tackle this.

Dosing and prescribing is dependent on the individual

- There are guidelines, but no exact answers on how much to dose. The ability for your dog to absorb the medicine entirely depends on their physiology. The right dose is partly determined by how the dog responds.

- There is no point in comparing different medications prescribed for dog aggression, because aggression is only a result of an underlying cause. The brain is enormously complicated and the biological reasons for the aggression may not be the same. Veterinary behaviorists will look at the whole picture and make the decision based on a variety of indications, taking other symptoms or behavior besides the aggression into consideration. It may take some time to find the right combination of medications.

Some medications help the brain develop new neurons.

- Good news! Recently, we've seen a bonus effect of some behavioral medications: neurogenesis. Some behavioral medications used to treat dog aggression have been shown to help the formation of specialized brain cells, known as neurons.

  As of the writing on this book, new research suggest that SSRI antidepressants used for treating dog aggression as well as treating depression may actually act by increased gene activity that promotes synaptogenesis and neurogenesis. It could be that serotonin levels may simply be a byproduct of the brain no longer making new neurons and/or no longer making connections between neurons.

  Therefore it's possible that in the future a drug targeting this process could help those who do not respond successfully to current medications.

Alert: a side effect can be lowered inhibition

- Some behavioral medications can cause more aggression because their effect lowers the dog's inhibition to bite. They should never be prescribed without the dog owner knowing what to look for and knowing how to keep the situation safe. The vet prescribing them should have a detailed history of your dog and a good idea of what your home life is like to help determine whether this is an acceptable risk. For example, are there children around? Has your dog caused physical harm? These and other factors are important considerations for prescribing medications.

PROFESSIONAL HELP: WHO TO CHOOSE

Not everyone needs professional help, but everyone is vulnerable to advice. Sometimes you don't know what to think – what YOU think. Good professionals help can make the difference. When you are on this roller coaster, it can be a huge relief having someone on your side, someone who says: hey, we can handle this together. Suddenly things are not so overwhelming. You take a deep breath, and you sit back and accept what they offer.

But there are some very good professionals, and there are some not so good professionals. There are many more who will have you convinced they know what to do about dog aggression. On top of which, your breeder, groomer, friends, neighbors, and even complete strangers will all have advice for you, about your dog, about you, and about who or what can help.

Some of the advice out there is way off the mark and potentially dangerous; some is just not that effective. But what people don't tell you is that after the third or fourth professional you consult, you start to feel a little hopeless and you are less likely to trust.

So the best thing is to find the right people first off. Let's have a look at the various professionals that help dog owners with their dogs.

Veterinary Behaviorists: Board Certified Specialists

Owners are more likely to continue to consult a trainer because they are more accessible, and generally are not nearly as expensive. But dogs that are a risk to others are not "normal" dogs. To treat them as if they are simply being naughty or bad and that need to be corrected harshly can make the problem worse.[210]

The advantage of these professionals is that the requirements to become board certified are high. They can fully evaluate your pet both medically and behaviorally and are trained to know whether psychotropic medicine is warranted.

They have extensive access to ongoing studies both published and in process, but also access to the experience of other veterinary behaviorists in an "ad hoc" basis that is unfortunately not available to most other trainers or behaviorists. They deal with the most serious cases and usually have several years of learning, education, and experience behind them.

Unfortunately, the number of board certified veterinary behaviorists are limited, and although there are some certified in different areas of the world, are mostly concentrated in the US. However, a number of them do consultations with vets across the world. It is always worth asking your vet if he or she can refer you to a veterinary behaviorist, or at least consult with one on your behalf in serious cases.

As of writing this, Tufts University offers PETFAX, which does remote consultations, meaning people from all over the world can have access to a veterinary behaviorist.[211] As well, there is VETFAX for veterinarians anywhere in the world. Remote consultations in some cases have proven to be just as effective as personal consultations.[212] Personal consultations are always far more preferable, but sometimes you don't have a choice in options.

As of writing, Dr. Gary Landsberg in Canada does remote consultations for vets in other parts of the world, and there are probably several others.

Those that undermine veterinary behaviorists

The dog training industry is a contentious one. I can only guess that it is strong-minded, opinionated and passionate people who are drawn to the career of training dogs and people, but whatever it is, there seems to be a lot of confrontation and in-fighting within the industry about which methods are right and which professionals know their stuff.

But it is also a good business tactic to try to undermine the competition. With the waiting lists that veterinary behaviorists have, their practices thrive and I have not seen underhanded tactics.

Some claim that veterinary behaviorists are not trainers. True. Most of them aren't. Nor are they meant to be. The difference between a veterinary behaviorist and a trainer is like comparing a psychiatrist with a teacher. Good teachers can reach children and teach children how to behave. To be effective doing this is a skill and a talent. But teachers are not going to be diagnosing and treating attention deficit disorder or impulse control disorders, even if they have opinions on it.

Another myth is that veterinary behaviorists don't work with or want to recommend trainers. This is absolutely false. In many cases a dog owner will be recommended to a trainer as a good qualified trainer can help with *behavior modification* and help adjust the program as you go when needed.

At the same time, it is just important to keep in mind that in serious cases, aggression is not a training problem. A dog that is a threat to people or dogs outside of an appropriate context are generally not misbehaving. Aggression is not common for average dogs, nor is it common for other canids, such as wolves. Evolutionary speaking, aggression is risky and uses up valuable resources.

Obedience may help *manage* a problem, and even improve self-control at best but will not *treat* the underlying problem. Veterinary behaviorists will look at and provide the big picture view that not only includes training methods, but look into the environment, health issues, medication considerations, diet, and whether the aggression is a pathology (disease based). This is not something any other professional is qualified to do.

Vets

Vets are well known to dog owners of course, since dog owners have been consulting them for the health and welfare of their dogs since they first acquired them. There are even veterinary behaviorists who feel the first professionals that should be consulted when you have a dog with a serious aggression problem are veterinarians.[213] However, most veterinarians are the equivalent of general practitioners (GPs). They are not usually specialists in behavior and are often under-educated when it comes to behavior.[214] Caution is warranted when it comes to accepting advice about aggressive behavior *unless* the vet giving the advice is a veterinary behaviorist (discussed prior). An anonymous article on an online veterinary site admits that average veterinarians have a low tolerance for aggression because they have seen so many *nice dogs* put to sleep.[215]

To complicate matters for the aggressive dog owner, in Australia, for example, vets can be taught to recommend euthanasia as a way to prevent them from being sued for any type of aggressive event that the animal might have had.[216]

Some vets are wonderful, as my vet is. She recommended me to a veterinary behaviorist years ago when I needed to consult one. She did not pretend to know more than she did, she worked together with the veterinary behaviorist, and more importantly, never judged my dog or me.

Vets with an interest in behavior

There are other vets who have a great deal of interest in behavior and have continued their education, although may not have completed the training necessary to become a behavior specialist. They may be familiar with the latest knowledge and research. These veterinarians may be able to help you, although understandably do not have the background that a board certified veterinary behavior specialist does. If you are in the US, you can find one at the American Veterinary Society of Animal Behavior (AVSAB) at www.avsabonline.org.

Behaviorists, trainers and other specialists

Some trainers, behaviorists, and specialists are excellent; they combine a thirst for knowledge and education with a very real experienced understanding of dogs. They live with them, they work with them, and they pursue credible scientific education that helps them further. One of the best things about working with a good trainer is that it can go a long way to staying committed to treating your dog. They can answer your questions when something has come up that you don't know how to handle, provide you with guidance when you are making the wrong choice, help ease your resistance, or challenge you when you can't help but look at your dog as a child (one that can't speak, has four legs, and is furry).

But some trainers are successful because they are actually successful business people and can be persuasive and convincing. They have learned how to market their services, and sell a good story. The best are highly persuasive, but unfortunately, none of these qualities determine whether they are actually good for the dogs.

Good trainers are excellent communicators and teachers and strive to continually learn. Bad trainers can simply decide one day they train dogs and hang a sign up and away they go. Other trainers may be competent, but use punishment (as the lay person understands it to be) because that is what they have learned, that is what they are comfortable with and what they have a history with. It's not that punishment doesn't work to inhibit certain behaviors as that it is usually unnecessary and in the case of aggression very problematic.

However, while good trainers may know what normal and abnormal behavior looks like, they can't fully diagnose behavior disorders. A true professional trainer will recommend you consult a veterinary behaviorist in the case of any aggression where people or other dogs are at risk.

> WARNING: Anyone can call him or herself or herself a dog trainer and anyone can call himself or herself a trainer, specialist or behaviorist.
>
> Trainers often get their clients from word of mouth, in other words, recommendations from past clients. Unfortunately, past clients really don't know how to accurately determine whether the trainer knows their stuff when it comes to aggression. A successful dog trainer is often one who is successful in convincing people to hire them.

The veterinary behaviorist will prescribe the treatment plan, and it's perfectly appropriate and even desirable for a trainer to help implement that plan and even make adjustments to it if the triggers or *stimulus* prove to be too much for the dog to initially handle.

Unfortunately those that use force-based tactics (such as leash "pops", *alpha rolls*, scolding, pushing, etc.) may be reluctant to work with the treatment plan prescribed from a veterinary behaviorist as these tactics are heavily discouraged.

A behaviorist often implies a veterinary behaviorist or a *certified applied behaviorist*, but not always. They may have a training background, a psychology degree, or nothing. A *certified applied behaviorist* does have a lot of education and usually experience.

Making a Decision

It is important to keep an open mind, and do your research. But note, that it can be hard to make a rational, considered decision when you want help immediately. Sometimes the sense of urgency pressures us to make a decision quickly, sometimes we just like the person; they make us feel they can help. Find out before committing.

There are trainers and behaviorists that go on to get certification by reputable organizations and the certification usually requires a number of hours of direct experience and a variety of knowledge based tests. Ensure they are not supporting members as I am, but actually certified meaning that they need to have a number of hours in the field and usually go through some form of testing. These include (but are not necessarily limited to):

- The Animal Behavior Society (ABS)

- International Association of Animal Behavior Consultants (IAABC)

- Certification Council for Professional Dog Trainers (CCPDT)

But there are also other organizations that support trainers who use coercive methods. We won't mention them here, but you often have to dig through their websites, and read between the lines. Usually those that encourage force-free methods, which are the kind of methods you want to use, will be very clear about the fact.

In general, there is a huge range of expertise and experience. Only vets are licensed; no one else is. When anyone is free to call themselves a trainer, behaviorist or specialist without knowing much of anything at all, you need to do your research.

It is well within your right to ask if they have been certified in anything and to ask for proof. Always double check by contacting the certifying organizations directly and contact the professional via that site. Always do your research on the certifying body as well.

Being part of an organization does not necessarily mean that they follow the organizations requirements, or that they are skilled enough to help you, however. **It's buyer beware!** Hopefully this book has provided you with enough information that you have some idea what to look out for and what questions to ask.

There is a larger list of organizations you can consult on the K9aggression.com website here:
http://k9aggression.com/treatment-methods/who-can-help/

 MYTH BUSTERS

Giving treats will reward aggression – myth?

It is a common misconception that giving food after a dog has been aggressive will only increase the likelihood of aggression. Treats will *not* reward aggression. Why?

Biological preparedness plays a role in some forms of training and learning. In a study of chaffinches (a kind of bird), it was learned that recorded chaffinch songs are an effective reinforcement to get them to perch in a certain spot, but not for training them to key-peck. Yet, food was an effective reinforcer in training them to key peck, but not for training them to perch in a certain spot. Rats are more likely to learn to press a lever to get food pellets, but not to avoid shock. However, they do readily learn to freeze or run to avoid shock. Pigeons will learn to fly from one perch to another to avoid shock, but won't learn to key-peck to avoid shock.[217]

What we learn has an adaptive logic – in other words, we make those associations with situations that are most likely to help us survive *given the context* of the situation we are in.

Food is needed to survive. So a dog hunting or performing any kind of trick that will get us to give up food to them makes sense. But outside of hunting, which is not the same of aggression, gaining food as a result of an aggressive or fearful social event does not make any sense. Instead, disabling or avoiding the threat is more likely to enable a dog to survive. Therefore, what is most likely to cause a dog to repeat their behavior is whatever will gain them what he or she needs to survive, given the context.

Rewards that are tightly coupled to their evolutionary value are going to be the most effective rewards.[218]

Using food to reward a dog means you are dependent on using food forever – myth?

We use rewards to help dogs learn, but once a habit becomes automatic (the technical definition is *overlearned*) you can reward intermittently, and reward with other things such as lower value rewards such as play or praise – unless there is a self-rewarding reason to perform.

It is not unlike paying someone to work. Most of us are unwilling to work for free, but are capable of a lot when we are paid. Given that dogs have not chosen to be in our lives; we keep them locked in our houses, crates, on leashes, etc., with little choice of whether they can leave us to join some other pack; it is probably only fair that we continue to provide motivation for them to take us seriously.

On the same vein, if you only use punishment or negative reinforcement to motivate a dog to behave, you will be dependent on those techniques in the same way. The problem is that unpleasant reinforcers such as punishment do not put our dogs in a happy place. That means they are less likely to pay attention. Worse yet, unpleasant situations can cause anxiety, which interferes with learning.

Why do we use food instead of other rewards?

The key reason to use food is that working for a tasty treat keeps our dogs more motivated to pay attention, and attention. Interest is key to retaining what has been learned. While there are other rewards that can be used, like a toy, play, and/or petting (if your dog likes this), food is small, can be quickly given, and does not take up a lot of time in a training situation. Other natural rewards are used as part of the *Sit, Attend, and Wait* programs. The dog learns to sit, attend, and wait (*SAW*) to get affection, time outside, their meals, etc.

Remember, rewards need to be given consistently and predictably until long after the behavior has been learned and practiced under a variety of conditions, after which intermittent rewards will keep the behavior reinforced.

My dog knows he or she did something wrong; he/she looks guilty – myth?

It's common for people to identify a guilty look after their pet has done something wrong. But research shows that dogs show the so-called guilty look in response to scolding, regardless of whether or not they had been obedient. In fact, this effect is even more pronounced when the dogs had been obedient than disobedient.[219] In reality, dogs are unlikely to have the same sense of right and wrong that we do since their value systems are different from ours. The guilty look we see is most likely an appeasement behavior when they are threatened or anticipate being threatened by our behavior

It's obvious when dogs are anxious – myth?

Unfortunately, the average person does not recognize when a dog is feeling uncomfortable even when the signs are obvious. Things like stiffening up, yawning, licking lips, etc. just do not get recognized as anxiety. This happens frequently, especially when dogs get hugged or kissed on the head. Sadly, not recognizing the signs results in people being unnecessarily bitten.

The fact that anxiety is not obvious should be a concern. It puts people at risk. Other people have no idea what is going on with the dog and the dog gets put into these situations that he or she shouldn't be put in. It even leads dog owners into saying, "My dog is great with kids," when it fact the dog is not comfortable at all and has been holding him or herself together all this time. It leads people to do all sorts of things to dogs they don't like and are uncomfortable with, and yet when the dog bites, it seems as if the bite has happened, "out of the blue".

Thankfully, there is information available on how to recognize the signs (look at the section called *Speaking Dog* in Part 2 of this book for more information on how to tell if a dog is anxious).

Sudden or unprovoked aggression – myth?

Aggression can appear to be very impulsive, and happen with little warning; however, true unpredictable aggression is rare. Punishment or other aversive interactions may have caused this dog to become more dangerous because the warning signals have been repressed and aren't there to read. Often looking at the history of the dog's aggression will indicate what some of the triggers are. Owners are strongly recommended to respond immediately to anxious behaviors, rather than wait for the aggression to occur. Any time an animal or people are at risk, a veterinary behaviorist should be consulted.

Unfortunately, the more impulsive the dog, and the more difficulty there is in predicting when the aggression will occur, the riskier it is to deal with the dog. True idiopathic aggression, i.e. aggression that is truly unpredictable, is very dangerous.

Rage aggression – myth?

Rage aggression is not considered a clinical problem – only a description according to one scientist who has studied the occurrence of this kind of aggression in springer spaniels. She notes that the most common reason for this kind of aggression is "fear (self-defense), along with a physiological "fight or flight" response and a revving up of the HPA (hypothalamic-hypophyseal-adrenal) axis." And while it can be very serious and needs life-long management, it is probably not a disease.[220]

A wagging tail means a happy dog – myth?

Wagging does not automatically mean a happy dog. Some believe that it means that the dog only wants to interact on some level, but does not indicate how. Dogs that wag their tails when they see their owners wag their tails differently when they see a stranger.

A playing dog is a happy dog – myth?

In the case of playing, dogs are often at a more physiologically aroused level than they are at rest. Play requires cooperative behavior, but it is also an arena where the ordinary social rules are broken. This means at any time there can be misunderstanding between the players. Some dogs will overlook it; others start to feel irritated. Some dogs are confused and will grow anxious. Some dogs know how to get out of a play situation simply by stopping and other dogs will respect it. But other times, dogs don't always know how or when to start and when to stop; others may overstep by biting too hard, or do something the other dog finds really offensive or irritating. These can be cases where conflict can arise.

Dogs like to be petted – myth?

Not all dogs like to be petted! Dogs that like petting may not like to be petted in all ways. To pat a dog on the head and sometimes the back can be threatening to certain dogs, especially when it is a stranger doing this. In many cases, dogs that don't like it will tolerate it, (but not always) rather than actually enjoy it. They have learned we have good intentions.

But in cases where dogs are unclear about what is going on, or are prone to anxiousness and aggression, a head pat may be a bad thing. When approaching a strange dog, don't face them head on. Stand side by side with the dog so you are not facing them directly (otherwise they will perceive they can't escape). Wait for them to make those last few steps to approach you.

If he or she allows you to touch them, then a pat or scratch on the shoulders is best until the dog gets to know the stranger or confusing human better.

Dogs that like to be petted make no secret about it. Here is a test you can do to determine if your dog likes it:

Call your dog over and pet them like he or she is the most wonderful dog in the world. Then, stop and take a step back. What do they do?

- Leans on you, nudges you, or moves closer to you?
- Moves away
- Ducks their head, avoids your hand, or moves away as soon as you start to pet them?

If your dog moves away, they probably tolerate petting, but it is not rewarding to them. If they duck away as soon as you start to pet them or they move away, not only is petting not rewarding, but he or she actively doesn't like it and it may either provoke anxiety or frustration.

If this is the case, your dog may prefer a different kind of petting, such as a scratch on the shoulders or around the neck. Some like to have the base of their ears stroked. But some don't like any of it. If so, your dog *still* may enjoy physical closeness like lying against you or on your lap, but the physical sensation of petting may just not feel good.

You might try to *counter conditi*on and *desensitize* them to petting so that he or she feels better about it, but you have to keep in mind they are only tolerating it. It is not a reward for them.

Dogs treat us like we are other dogs – myth?

The idea that dogs perceive the world through a dog's eyes and with a dog's understanding certainly makes sense.

But to what degree does a dog's understanding of the world color everything that is in it? Are they necessarily going to assume that we are part of a pack? If so, do they really design their interactions and expectations with us based on behavior of dogs? In other words, does this assume we need to act like top dog (see the section on *alphas* and dominance for more on this)?

Scientific evidence suggests that they are capable of adapting to how we are different and so moderate their own behavior accordingly. But science aside, there are some very obvious differences that dogs between us:

- We don't have ears and tails to communicate with. They learn to read our body language on other ways and have learned by context which behaviors mean what.
- Dogs learn to interpret our smiles other than baring our teeth or as submissive smiles.
- Dogs can learn that our gazes are not threats despite for the length of time we hold their gazes (but not all aggressive dogs do).
- A hand on the head or back is not the same as a paw from another dog on the head or back.
- Lots of sounds come out of our mouths, most of it meaningless.
- Wet stuff comes from our eyes sometimes.
- We always control the food, but we give them entire dinners. Every day!
- They must think we store our food in garbage cans and can't figure out why we won't eat it – how crazy is that!

- We don't mark our territory nor express any interest in checking out what other dogs leave behind in this regard. They must find this exceptionally puzzling, but it certainly leaves us out of the whole dog social society thing.
- We never sniff their butts or genitals. Or, at least I'd like to think most of us don't.

Scientifically speaking, studies with dogs learning taught us that dogs read us in ways that they don't read other dogs as mentioned earlier. Emotions are more faithfully reproduced on the right side of our faces. Humans tend to look at the right side of others' faces. And, so do dogs. Studies looking at where dogs look indicate that they will look at the center of our faces, and look left - to the right sides of our faces. However, they don't do this with other dogs. [221] They also play with us differently and read play cues differently than they do with other dogs. And as mentioned earlier in this book, play between dogs and play between dogs and humans are structurally different and accordingly, motivationally distinct.[222]

From all of this, we can assume they are very clear on the fact we are humans and not dogs, and that they change their behavior consequently.

MANAGEMENT AND TRAINING TOOLS

Learning dog body language

- *THE LANGUAGE OF DOGS - UNDERSTANDING CANINE BODY LANGUAGE AND OTHER COMMUNICATION SIGNALS DVD SET* by Sarah Kalnajs
    - http://www.bluedogtraining.com/products.html

- *Canine Behavior, Body Postures and The Behaviorally Healthy Dog*, By Susanne Hetts, PhD& Daniel. Estep, PhD
    - http://animalbehaviorassociates.com/program-canine-behavior-posture.htm

Video camera

Any video camera will probably do, but one that is not too obtrusive or that you typically don't hold in front of your face is probably best.

Keep in mind that some dogs are uncomfortable with cameras. Maybe because it mimics someone staring at them, or paying attention to them and they aren't sure what it means. It may help to set up a camera on a tripod, although you may not always get what you want in a shot as the dog moves around.

Journal

Keep a journal of your progress and anything else you notice. You will need to look back on things to gain perspective at times. Keeping the journal where you can easily see it, such as a kitchen counter, helps you maintain it.

Head-halters

While they don't prevent bites, head-halters can provide you with a lot of control. The dog should be *desensitized* to wearing one, and instructions on how to do this are on the K9aggression.com site in the bonus area. They are useful tools for dealing with aggressive dogs. The Gentle Leader is probably the most popular and recommended head halter by certified behaviorists and veterinarians. There is a fitting guide on the Gentle Leader site that should be heeded, as the fit is very important. Halti and Snoot Loops are other popular brands – although they all vary slightly in their design. They are like a horse halter that straps around the nose and neck. You can find these in pet stores, or on Amazon.

- http://Gentleleadercanada.com
- http://Halti.co.uk
- http://Snootloop.com

With all head-halters, muzzles, and harnesses, using shaping through clicker training can be really helpful to encourage the dog to willingly put their head or legs in and *desensitize* them to wearing it. Head-halters are not appropriate for every dog or every situation.

Easy Walk Harness

The Easy Walk™ Harness is designed to gently discourage your dog from pulling while walking on a leash. It's so simple – easy to fit, and easy to use. There is very little acclimation time.

Unlike traditional harnesses, the Easy Walk Harness never causes coughing, gagging, or choking because the chest strap rests low across the breastbone, not on the delicate tracheal area.

Here is a YouTube video demonstrating how to put it on that was online as of the time of writing this: http://youtu.be/69rPBfh8GIA

Ultimate harnesses

Produced by the same company as the Gentle Leader, the Ultimate Harness may be an additional alternative. It allows you to have some control, it eliminates chafing that is caused by other conventional harnesses, and it is non-punishing and non-choking, just as the Easy Walk harness is. There is also a fitting guide on the site.

- http://gentleleadercanada.com/product.html

Keep Away Shirt for dogs

One of the challenges dog owners face is keeping people and dogs away from their own dog when they are working with them. For whatever reason, there are certain people who simply find it impossible not to approach your dog. Others are so intent on proving their dog is perfectly friendly that they ignore your panicked look, shaking head, and gestures to keep away. For this reason, K9aggression.com designed a t-shirt your dog can wear that uses a universal sign to keep hands off that even children will recognize. You can find this shirt via the web site in the shop area.

Dog Training clothing for people

If you are wearing a shirt that says Dog Trainer or Dog Training, people will understand you are working with your dog. This will help convey the impression that you are a responsible person (and not someone who abuses their dog!) You can order a Dog Training shirt through the K9aggression.com site shop area.

Audio for desensitization

There are a number of CD's and sounds you can download on the Internet. Here are just a few CDs.

- Sounds Good Audio Cd Series by Terry Ryan, Find on Amazon
- Calm Pet - Desensitizing Sounds for Animals Series
  Find on Amazon

- Scared No More Canine Audio Therapy System
  http://www.scarednomore.com/order.html

Treat n' Train Manners Minder

This is a remote control feeding tray for dogs and includes a training DVD. This can be used to teach a dog to run to a remote location or reward them when they are away from you. Check the K9aggression.com for links or use this.
- http://www.amazon.com/Premier-Manners-Minder-Behavior-Training/dp/B0010B8CHG

Clickers

Clickers are inexpensive and can be found in many pet shops now, including PetSmart. But you can also find them online on a variety of dog sites, as well as on Amazon. Check the K9aggression.com site for links.

Feeding Tubes

Feeding tubes are similar to a toothpaste tube, except you can fill it with your own choice of food for your dog such as spreadable cheese, ground meat and gravy, etc. These are great for dogs that snatch treats and tend to bite fingers accidentally (especially those excitable dogs). It also is good for those of you who work with your dogs in colder climates and prefer to keep your gloves on.
- http://humanedogtraining.com/products.php

Window Clings/Film

Window clings or film are sheets of plastic that let in light, but provide privacy.

Some are simply applied by using water and a flat plastic surface to smooth out the bubbles, which make them easy to apply and remove. This can be useful for those dogs who bark a lot and/or tend to be hyper vigilant about whatever may be going on outside.

Word of caution however, restricting the ability to see outside may be also restricting some important stimulation for those dogs. Those dogs who are left home alone during the work day and do not get that worked up by what may be outside may benefit be seeing outside.

You need to use your best judgment. The important consideration is to what degree your dog is able to relax. Some dogs can never relax knowing there may be something outside. For those dogs who find it challenging to relax, or who tend to bark incessantly at everything that goes by or when the wind blows, it may be of some help. Search online to find them in your area.

Drag lines

Drag lines are essential lightweight leashes with no handle that can be dragged around by your pet. It allows them to range free, but gives you the opportunity of picking up the leash. This is handy for dogs that are aggressive towards their owners. You can find draglines in a variety of places, but you can also purchase a lightweight cat leash and cut the handle. You don't want a handle getting snagged on your furniture.

Hitches

This is a temporary anchor in the form of a hook that you can mount on a wall to use in your house to tether your dog to. You might want to use this to keep a dog away from other people or for situations like opening a door. You might also want to use it for dogs that fight each other indoors and you need to quickly get one of them contained while you deal with the other. Using it this way depends on the dog wearing a leash with a handle, which is not always a good idea in doors. You can usually find hitches at http://Petedge.com

Gates

Gates can be used to separate dogs from other dogs or people inside the home. Many people use baby gates, but caution should be exercised since many gates can be jumped over or destroyed. We went through several of them before finding the E'longate Pet Gate found at Petedge.com. It expands from 48 inches to 60 inches wide and can be adjusted to the width you need, and was easy to open with one hand. You can even add 4 extra panels of approximately 13 inches for those extra wide doorways. We used it right at our front door for a dog that used to escape when we opened the door, as well as in wide openings such as our dining room. It's metal so dogs can't chew through it. Your dog may not be accustomed to jumping gates, but if motivated enough, they may try it.

It also allows the dog to be able to see you so they don't feel as socially isolated. On the other hand, if you are separating dogs that are aggressive towards each other, it's probably best that they can't see each other, so using some kind of material to block sight may help.

- http://Petedge.com

Basket Muzzles

This should be used for a safety device only. It should not replace avoiding the situations that cause your dog to behave aggressively. It should also be considered a short-term tool and not left on for too long. But if you are in a situation where you can't control exposure, safety should be your number one aim. Muzzles tend to frighten other people and that can work both against you and for you. It may cause people to shun you, but it may also help to keep people away. You will want to purchase a brand that fits your dog's muzzle.

Basket muzzles are considered to be the most humane for dogs as it allows them to pant and drink. It should not affect your dog's breathing, it should be adjustable, and it should allow your dog to open their mouth. Typically, you measure size by measuring from between their eyes to the tip of their nose. Then measure around her snout approximately an inch below the eyes. You can buy wire basket muzzles from a variety of dog sites online such as Morrco, as well as through Amazon.

- http://www.morrco.com

Citronella spray

Used to be called Direct Stop, but is now called Spray Shield Animal Deterrent Spray. Hopefully you will never have to use this, but sometimes you will want to keep an off leash dog from approaching yours if your dog is aggressive, or interrupt a pending dog fight. It does not cause pain, but dogs don't like the smell. You can get this from a variety of suppliers, including Amazon.com. Check out the K9aggression.com for links.

Break or breaking sticks

Sounds worse than they are, but this can be slid in the gap behind the teeth to pry open a dog's jaws that may be holding on very tightly without breaking the dog's teeth. Generally they are used with breeds whose bite style is to bite and hold opposed to multiple biting. Those breeds that are not likely to hold may turn and bite you if you use a break stick. Hopefully, you will never need to use one of these.

- http://pbrc.net
- http://wildboarusa.com

Snarem Noose

These can be harmful if not used correctly, but this tool may allow you to catch a dog without getting your hands too close to their mouth.

- http://Petedge.com

Sleeves and Gloves

If you are breaking up a dogfight, then you probably won't have time to put these on, but someone such as a helper might. You can purchase different sleeves and gloves to protect your hands when dealing with biting and scratching at Pet Edge.

- http://Petedge.com

Online training resources

Protocols for deference, relaxation, and how to *desensitize* your dog to wearing a head halter or muzzle are all available on the Internet. You can find copies of this on the K9aggression.com site as the resource links were not consistently kept up to date and the website suffered from many dead links as a result. All credit must be given to the original authors. Check the Bonus section earlier in the book for the URL.

- Dr. Karen Overall's **Protocol for Deference: Basic Program**
- Dr. Karen Overall's **Protocol for Relaxation**
- Dr. Lore I. Haug's **Desensitization / Counter conditioning for Muzzles and Head-halters**
- Dr. Lore I. Haug's **Desensitization / Counter conditioning for Veterinary Visits**
- *Core Behaviors Training Guide* Booklet

 ## TOOLS FOR ENVIRONMENTAL ENRICHMENT

Flirt poles

Are poles with a rope attached and something tied to the end (it might be a piece of leather, rag, old toy, etc.)

- Start with short sessions (a few minutes at a time). Your dog might be out of shape so as with any kind of exercise program, take it easy and build up.
- Be aware that if you get the dog over aroused, they may get nippy. Take frequent breaks to calm them down if he or she is the type of dog to do this. Put the pole down when you end the play session because if you simply take it away, they may continue to jump on you.
- Encourage chasing.

- Be very careful of jumping as the dog may become injured
- Play on a soft surface such as grass.
- Remove it if you are not around.

Boomer Balls

These are a little pricey and having them shipped were quite expensive, but for those of us who have pit-bulls or other dogs who seem to be able to chew through anything, these balls can be invaluable. Initially designed for enrichment for zoo animals, these are hard plastic balls that seem to be impervious to destruction because they are too large for the dogs to get their jaws right around. They have drilled holes on either side, that allow you to put kibble or other small pieces of food inside, and the dog pushes the ball around with nose or paw to get the food to fall out. If you feed your dog kibble, you can feed your dog their entire dinner this way. Great for dogs who are bored inside the house or need other kinds of activities to do.

- http://boomerball.com

Food puzzle toys

Food cubes, Kongs, etc. can provide something interesting for your dog to do. In some cases you can feed your dog's entire meal using a food puzzle toy. There are many creative things you can do with Kongs in particular, such as coating the inside with peanut butter, stuffing with large biscuits or freezing chicken stock to chew on during a hot summer's day. Food toys should be alternated so it's a good idea to invest in several types. Always check them, and if your dog is the destructive type, don't leave him or her unsupervised with them. Here are just a few toy suggestions to get you going:

- **Kongs**: http://www.kongcompany.com/
- **Buster Cubes** (can find these at pet stores were dog products are sold) http://www.ourpets.com/products_smartertoys.html
- **HomeAlone** (Aussie Dog Toy) balls (dog pulls rope/bungee cord to release a small amount of food in the ball from above – expensive, but popular) http://www.ozpetshop.com.au/product_info.php/products_id/626

Music and Sound CDs

In addition to the various desensitization CDs available, you may also want to try classical music to help calm your dog. Look for music that has slower rhythms, fewer instruments and simple melodies. Be sure to play it low.

THERAPEUTIC TOOLS

DAP (Dog Appeasing Pheromone)

DAP is meant to mimic the natural pheromones that nursing mother dogs give off. There is some evidence that it helps dogs that have separation anxiety, and can help fearful dogs relax. [223] [224] The advantage of using DAP is that there are no side effects. It is available as a plug in unit, a collar, or a spray. Talk to your vet about it.

Pressure Wraps

These wraps or shirts tend to be used for anxious dogs. Some of the brands are Thundershirt and The Anxiety Wraps. Some people have even used tensor bandages.
- http://Thundershirt.com
- http://AnxietyWrap.com

Tellington Touch or TTouch massage books/DVDs

TTouch tends to be the most well known massage program for dogs and has been recommended by veterinary behaviorists. They carry both books and DVDs on their site.
- http://www.ttouch.com

The biggest challenges that people tend to have are setbacks in behavior modification. But there can be other struggles, too. Trainers can be a great resource because every situation they deal with is unique, making the good ones creative problem solvers. Even if you are not sure you want to commit to several teaching sessions, many trainers are willing to do telephone consultations and may be able to help you with something you are stuck on. In the meantime here are some of the more common challenges.

 ## SETBACKS DURING BEHAVIOR MODIFICATION

There may be a number of things going on here. Look at the list and see what might be a contribution and then look up the information that follows:

- Too much, too soon
- The dog has not been *conditioned* in the situation that you were in when he or she relapsed.
- The stress load on the dog was too high.
- There were a number of other distractions involved and the dog had not been trained to deal with them all at once.
- The dog was not feeling well.
- You missed signals that the dog was anxious.
- There may be a biochemical component to the aggression.

Too much, too soon

This is constantly a problem for people who really want their dogs to do well or for those that are fixated on the goal of eliminating the aggression entirely. If you are an over achiever, a top A-student, a type A-personality, lean towards anxiousness, bend to social pressure, have a low tolerance of routine or boredom or are a high energy kind of person, or want quick fixes you might be at risk for this. If so find someone to help you.

There is a tendency to put our dogs through a pace of training that is simply more than the dog can handle. Our abilities to read dog behavior is usually much less refined than a dog's ability, so while they may have been giving us all sorts of signs, we may have been missing them.

When in doubt, do less. Make the change simpler, smaller, and if it's not working, go back to the circumstances in which it *was* working.

We must not lose sight of the fact that learning can be stressful, and certainly hugely demanding on the brain's resources. The brain's preference will always be to follow the path of least resistance, and in this case, the behaviors that are most habitual. If there is too much going on for the dog, they will automatically revert back to what they know.

Instead of being discouraged, realized that you have done too much, too soon. Take a step back, train for shorter periods of time, let slightly longer durations between sessions elapse, and let the dog recover. Go back to your relationship building exercises. If the setback involved aggression, give your dog time to de-stress.

The dog has not been conditioned in the situation that you were in when he or she relapsed.

This is a common mistake many dog owners make even in regular training situations. Humans are different from dogs in that when we learn something, we generalize better than dogs. That means if we learn something in one circumstance, we can apply it to other situations. The skill becomes transferable. Dogs are not nearly as capable of this as we are.

Instead dogs discriminate more than we do. So what they have learned under a given set of circumstances does not transfer over that well.

So a dog that is aggressive towards other dogs will not learn to be calm around all other dogs by only working with a few. They will more likely learn that those few dogs they have been working with are not a threat. But other dogs may still be perceived as a threat (and in some cases, they actually are).

A dog that learns not to be aggressive to strangers on the street may still react badly at the door. A dog that has come to accept another dog within the same house may become aggressive with the same dog under a new situation.

The best way to handle this:

- Train the dog in as many conditions as possible - only varying just one element at a time and only moving on when the dog is successful most of the time in that situation.
- Be alert to any new situation.
- Be alert to any stresses the dog may experience.
- Learn to read their anxiety signs, and teach others to as well.
- Make sure your *Emergency Cues* and other management strategies are firmly in place and are being *overlearned* (in other words, they need to be practiced so often, the behaviors have become automatic).
- Keep delicious treats nearby in a variety of places to use any time.

The stress load on the dog was too high.

Fear is not something we can eliminate entirely. It depends on the pre-frontal cortex of the brain overriding the response so we can definitely manage fear. However, if the pre-frontal cortex is occupied with other tasks, the fear response can come right back. Stress can occupy many of our brain's resources; as well can cause us to be reactive when we might ordinarily be calm. In some cases, the stress is so acute that the amygdala in the brain hijacks the frontal cortex. Solution: take a break. Try to be aware of what else is going on in the dog's life that might make their stress load higher. Changes in schedules, people coming and going, trips to the vet, holidays, even the fact that it's nighttime and dark out can cause additional stress.

There were a number of other distractions involved.

The brain can only deal with so much at a time. Things that are scary, intense, new and unusual, or otherwise simply more rewarding in some way are things that are going to distract your dog.

If your dog has *overlearned* something (in other words, it has become habit), it becomes far easier to deal with distractions. It is also much easier when your dog has learned to develop their self-control, as well as learned to shift their focus to you and then keep their focus on you. This too takes practice and what the sit-stay-wait exercises should help with.

An easily startled dog may have a high stress load. It is worth talking to a vet to see if he or she tends to be more jumpy or more vigilant than the average dog. It may indicate that there is a need for medications and without them, the dog will find it very difficult to concentrate on the training.

The dog's ability to control him or herself had already been taxed by a prior activity.

Brain resources for self-control are limited, although will eventually be replenished. This means in any given situation there is a limited supply of brain resources and we can use it up.

This is why we are more likely to yell at our children at the end of a hard day than we are when we are relaxed and well rested. Brain energy can also be affected by what is available in the body nutritionally. Luckily you can strengthen your dog's ability to control themselves, which means your dog's ability to control themselves later will likely use fewer resources in the brain.

The dog was not feeling well.

Unfortunately, dogs can't tell us what's going on. Like us, they probably have moments when food is not digesting quite right, or there is something stiff or sore, or perhaps they didn't get a good night's sleep. Maybe they even get moody just like us. If you sense your dog is under the weather, don't work on anything challenging with your dog that day. You want your dog to be feeling positive –

this is the best condition where learning is internalized and absorbed.

You missed signals that your dog was anxious.

Unfortunately for us, we are not always that tuned in with the body language of dogs and it can happen so quickly. Sometimes we are projecting what we want to see on our dog. Sometimes we just don't recognize it or interpret it as something else. Try spending time really looking at their body language (check out the section on Speaking Dog in part 2 of this book).

Also, learn to be aware and trust yourself - if you can get your of your own way, it's amazing just how much we know instinctively when we are paying attention. Sometimes we don't trust ourselves, but you probably know your dog better than anyone. In other cases, we simply don't know or do not pay enough attention. Make sure that you know the signs, but also make sure that *your* stress load is low, and that you are in a situation where *you* can pay attention. If you are going for a family walk, the other people might distract you for example.

Your dog needs medication.

Unfortunately, a dog with wacky levels of neurotransmitters is going to have a very difficult time learning and moderating their mood. This could be something he or she was born with, or it could have developed. Being under stress can lead to an imbalance of the neurotransmitters in the brain that can affect the dog's mood, and even their perception, and certainly interferes with learning and memory.

The best way to determine if there is a problem and deal with this is to get a consultation with a veterinary behaviorist, whether it's direct or through your vet. Keep in mind most vets do NOT have a good education in behavior (see the section on professionals in part 3).

- Consult a veterinary behaviorist if possible.
- Ask your vet to consult a specialist if they're not one themselves.
- Understand that medication will not eliminate the aggression without some kind of retraining or behavior modification.
- Step up your management and safety practices.

How to manage a bad session or unexpected encounter

This was a question I consistently asked of trainers and never got much of a response to. Essentially, you want to manage a situation so your dog never has the opportunity to become aggressive. That was the feedback I got and it's good advice. You will undo the work you have done to *desensitize* or make the response *extinct*.

BUT let's say you have made a terrible mistake, and your dog has just become aggressive. What is the best thing to do? Go back to part 1 and get really familiar with the *Emergency Response Plan*. Be sure to check with your dog aggression specialist if the *Emergency Response Plan* is best for your dog, first.

Getting discouraged

Every time our dog has a setback, we get discouraged. It's only natural. But the more setbacks you have, the more discouraged you can get. It may lead you to consider giving up. While there may come a point where you must ask if whether or not you are making a difference and if it's worth it to continue, here are some suggestions you might try before making a big decision to stop.

- Find support (you will find like-minded members on the K9aggression-support yahoo group). It's hard to go through something like this alone, but often your friends and even your family don't understand.

- Hang out with optimistic people. It makes a difference!

- Read the other reasons for setbacks and make sure you are setting your dog up for success.

- Make a conscious effort to do things you enjoy doing with your dog. So important.

- Go back to relationship building. Sometimes we over focus on fixing the problem that we forget what we like about our dog. But if we have a hard time liking our dog, it will be hard to keep going.

- Take better safety measures and just manage your dog for a while. Give yourself and your dog a break.

- Accept that each time your dog becomes aggressive, you too will be under stress – another good reason to take a break.

 ## TREATMENT IS NOT WORKING AT ALL

There may be a number of reasons why treatment is not working. Here are some of them:

- **You have not reduced the dog's stress load enough overall**: Go back to Step 1.

- **The dog is in need of medication, or is not getting the right medication or the right dose.**
  Consult your veterinary behaviorist again, or consult one if you have not seen one.

- **You are inconsistent**.
  Devise a plan. Review it every morning before you do anything else. Use reminders to help you whether it is through calendar alerts on your computer, or yellow sticky notes on your fridge. Join a support group to help you stay motivated. Write a blog about your progress. It may help you to find a really experienced trainer to help you with this. They will see things you won't.

- **You have not practiced the foundation training enough**.
  Realize that you may be rushing because your dog's aggression is not managed well enough. You might also find the work too boring. In that case, work for shorter sessions, and provide yourself with rewards for meeting your goals. Find ways to avoid the aggressive situations.

- **The dog is still being punished.**
  Figure out why you are doing this. This book makes a good case for not doing it so review those sections again. Alternatively, you may be

struggling with being under stress yourself and are finding it hard to keep a lid on your frustration. Find a way to take a break and address your stress load: chronic stress is a real hazard to your health and state of mind.

- **The dog has an underlying condition that has not been treated yet (for example, seizures, pain, etc.).**
  See your vet, and ask for a veterinary behaviorist referral or consultation.

- **The aggression has a long history and it is well practiced and established in your dog's brain**.
  This is a real challenge, as it will take a lot of work to compete with those established neural pathways. You will need to really step up your prevention and management.

- **Your dog is still anxious during Targeted Behavior Modification so he or she is becoming more sensitized, rather than less**.
  Go back to learning about how to read and interpret dog behavior. Use a video camera to learn. Find a really experienced professional who knows the signs well to help you. Get the videos recommended in the book. Find less threatening targets. Consider medication.

- **You are unable to adequately control your dog's environment**.
  If your dog is constantly being exposed to the things that trigger the dog's aggression and you are unable to do anything about it, you need to ask yourself if your dog is in the right environment, and is the environment the right thing for the dog.

 YOU ARE TOO EMBARESSED OR SHY TO SEEK HELP

You should not feel embarrassed about your dog's situation – join the K9aggression-support Yahoo group – you will see just how many great people have problem dogs. And how many people have made mistakes. Aggression is the most common behavior problem in dogs. Most of us know next to nothing about it when we get a dog. Enlist someone to help you find a good credible dog aggression professional and have that person come to the consultations with you. Two people can remember more than one person in any case.

YOU CAN'T AFFORD TO CONSULT A PROFESSIONAL

You would not be alone worrying about money. What is even more worrying is paying a professional for information that doesn't help. I've been there. The reality is, you will be the one working with your dog regardless of who you consult. If you consider yourself to be very in tune with dogs, and you are already clicker training, and the situation is not all that serious, with some research and education you might be able to improve your dog's problem yourself, *provided* you follow the right kind of treatment plan. You will not get a diagnosis or an objective point of view of course. If your dog needs medication, then your dog is likely not going to be a very happy dog, either. You must also remember that dealing with aggression can be dangerous and unless you know you can recognize when your dog is truly stressed or anxious, and act on that, then you will risk making your dog worse and a lawsuit.

If your dog is already at the snapping or biting stage, you need to ask yourself can you afford not to seek help? Try calculating what you will spend on your dog over his or her lifetime (try adding up all the food you buy, and trips to the vet, etc.). You will find that the cost of a consultant is not that much in comparison. And yet getting good help can last for the lifetime of your dog. Just make sure you do your research first to ensure you are getting the right help.

YOU FIND IT HARD TO STAY MOTIVATED

Granted, at times it is not easy, especially if you are just starting out, have been through the ringer with a number of trainers, techniques, etc. or if you have had high expectations to begin with. Are you under stress? Are you burnt out? It is okay to take a break as long as you can avoid the situations that cause your dog to behave aggressively. Ask how important solving this issue is for you or how committed you are to your dog. You might be discouraged, or in need of some inspiration, in which case a support group such as the K9aggression-support group on Yahoo! Groups might help you as mentioned before. Motivational books and audio/video may also help you.

Remind yourself that your dog is not happy either and depends on you for your help. It is not their choice to be in this world living the way we do. Health problems, poor socialization or poor breeding is not their fault either. However, it is much easier to stay motivated when you focus on what is in it for you to do the work, what the positive outcomes would be and why these are important to you.

If you simply can't commit, and you unable or unwilling to control the aggression either, then you need to ask yourself if this situation is best for the dog. You may have to consider rehoming if the dog is not too aggressive or euthanasia.

YOU ARE AFRAID OF YOUR DOG

If your dog is aggressive towards you, it's natural to be fearful. If you are committed to your dog, improve your ability to read and interpret dog behavior. This will give you more confidence. Learn everything you can about what your dog's triggers are so that you can avoid them. Take a break. Figure out if your fears are warranted.

But in some cases, people can't manage their fear the way some dogs can't either. This may be a result of your own genetic make-up, personality quirks, what have you. If you are afraid of your dog and are unwilling to work with them, you may have to consider rehoming if the dog is not too aggressive or euthanasia.

YOUR DOG GIVES NO WARNING BEFORE THEY STRIKE

If you are not seeing any signs of stress, discomfort or anxiety, and your dog is not giving you any warning signs, like stiffening up, staring, etc. there may be something else at work and you should consult a veterinary behaviorist. You will have to use management and prevention to handle your dog until then. Be aware that no warning signs results in a more dog dangerous.

YOUR DOG IS A PEST: JUMPING, GRABBING, ETC.

We are assuming that if your dog is being a pest, they are not actually biting you to threaten you, but perhaps chewing the way puppies do or grabbing you when they can't get their own way or want something. Let's see what might be happening.

Some situations can cause frustration for your dog, and this can occur on walks, during training, or any number of situations. Sometimes this is because they don't know how to get what they want or what is expected of them. In this case, you can have the dog sit to calm themselves or stop what you are doing. For example, if your dog is biting the leash, you stop walking until they stop biting the leash. But be consistent. If your dog starts being a pest to get a treat or your attention, you can ask him to sit, attend and wait before the pest behavior starts so note when it happens so you can predict it. If that doesn't work withdraw yourself immediately. Alternatively, if your dog is an eager beaver, you might ask or teach him to lie down and stay while you go about your business.

If you are running into this during training, it might be because you have gone too far forward and they don't understand what you want. Again, dogs don't generalize well. If you change something too much for them, they no longer see the connection. In this case, break your sequence down into even smaller steps.

But if they are truly being obnoxious, stop looking at them, stop talking to them. Walk away to another room if you have to. They try it a few more times but will eventually get the message if you are consistent.

In some cases, we encourage pest behavior when the dog wants attention and we continue to talk to the dog (perhaps asking them to stop), waving our arms around (perhaps pushing them off of us, or moving our hands away from the teeth). Sometimes we allow it to happen at certain times for a little while before removing our attention, or whatever it is they want. We may feel guilty, or maybe we are not paying attention to what we are doing.

When we are inconsistent, they will try much harder to get what they want. It is a little like a slot machine situation: if they persist, it might pay out at some point. If this is you, and you want to be more consistent, enlist your family to help, or post reminders, or go into every situation with a plan on how to handle it. It will also help you to read about extinction bursts. It will get worse before it gets better – just persist.

 # HOW TO DEAL WITH YOUR FAMILY AND FRIENDS

Regrettably, members of the family are not always on board and this further adds to the conflict experienced in the home. This is really due to the connection that the family member feels with the dog, or to the extent that the family member is fearful. But it can also be influenced by unresolved conflicts as a result of other issues. It can also be heavily influenced by our childhood experiences. Many couples experience conflict in how to rear children and the same happens with how to treat dogs.

Have empathy

The majority of any interactions we have are based on an 80/20 rule. That is 80% of what you are feeling in response to the interaction is actually rooted in *your* past. This is the same for everyone else. When people get upset, most of it is being triggered by past experiences and it is mobilizing feelings in the present. Whenever you get into a conflict or feel judged, remember to respect their feelings, but also be aware that you are not entirely responsible for them all. You may be at fault, but you can't blame yourself for everything the other person is feeling. And remember that about yourself. Sometimes we get very upset with people in our lives, but not everyone would react to the same situation that way you have. By appreciating where you have come from, you can take ownership for your feelings and learn to have empathy for yourself.

Strengthen your relationships

The best way to cope with this is with understanding and communication. Sometimes groups of people or couples pick a position in reaction to the other. In other words, if one is more cautious, the other will take more risks almost in frustration or to prove a point. Historical enactment may make these roles even more pronounced. What is the way forward? Well according to some studies, active listening is not actually related to marital success. What pattern did emerge for heterosexual couples tended to be this:

Women tended to bring up the problem, the analysis of it, and presented some solutions. The degree to which the men were willing to accept some of these ideas correlated with marital success. The degree to which the man stonewalled tended to predict failure. So the real question to the female in heterosexual relationships may be: how do you get your male partner to be open to some of your ideas? It may be as simple as rekindling your love for each other first.

Research indicates that couples feel more attracted to each other and in love when they take part in leisure activities that involve both partners and are relatively unpredictable, exciting, and active, rather than passive. So before you have your problem solving communication, try going on a date where you are experiencing something new and exciting together.

This can also be applied to family members and friends. Spend more time together doing new and interesting things. Get more physically affectionate. Appreciate each other and let them know why. Another solution is to look at the more effective ways to influence others by encouraging them to discover why they might want what you want. An excellent book about this is: *Instant Influence*, by Michael V. Pantalon, Phd.

Try for your children and communicate

It is important for any children involved that you do everything you can, even for the child who may have been bitten and who is probably in conflict about it. Children may not articulate this, but they may become concerned that they too will be made to leave the home if they act badly. After all, they see similar things with children on the schoolyard. The dog is seen as a beloved family pet and may even harbor fantasies about the dog in ways we don't even think to imagine. In many cases, they do not see the situation from your point of view. But obviously safety is the first concern.

HOW TO DEAL WITH NEIGHBORS

Your neighbors are not always your friends. But we are often stuck with them in our lives. We are hardwired to be sensitive to what others think of us because historically our survival depended on being accepted in the society we live in (this is even more so for females).

We are also hardwired to pay attention to animals – both you and your friends and neighbors. A study indicated that there is more activity in the amygdala part of the brain in response to animals, whether they were aversive or cute to look at. This was not the same as the response to people or landmarks.[225] Possibly the evolutionary reason for this is that animals were important to us, either as prey or predators. So your dog is attracting attention whether you like it or not. But when your neighbors judge you because of your aggressive dog, some very ugly situations can arise.

It is important to understand that there are many people in the world who don't like dogs. Period. They may have had a negative experience with dogs, or know of someone else who has. They may simply have no experience and a good measure of fear of them. Then there are others that know dogs, but are quite willing to write off a dog that is aggressive. And then there are those who believe there are no bad dogs, only bad people.

If your dog has shown aggression

If the neighbors know your dog is aggressive, this fact could become a legal issue down the line. Dog aggression is a very hot issue. No one will sympathize with you or your dog should anyone get hurt. You cannot rely on people around you to do the right thing, whether it's your neighbors or your immediate family. You must be extra careful that all safety precautions have been taken.

Leashes can break or get dropped when the dog suddenly pulls. In fact, there was a person on the K9aggression-support yahoo group whose dog charged at a person right through their glass door and attacked a child years ago. Dogs can escape through doors, over or under fences, or other people can inadvertently leave a gate or door open.

Perception is everything.

If you have a dog that isn't aggressive, it's easy to be judgmental of those who do. Until it happens to you. Try to understand.

Communication and responsibility are key.

If your dog is aggressive and your neighbors are aware of the fact, you can't assume they will be willing to talk to you about it. Instead, they may stew and wait for the first opportunity they can get to facilitate the removal of you or your dog from the neighborhood. Nor are they likely to let you know if they are judging you for being irresponsible or abusive.

If you have neighbors or friends willing to listen, explain that the aggression is a result of an anxiety issue and assuming that the triggers are specific, identify what they are to your neighbor in hopes that it won't cause your neighbor to feel even more worried about the situation. But if your dog is only aggressive to strangers or other dogs, your neighbor may breathe easier. But may not.

- Assure your neighbor that the peace of mind and safety of the neighborhood is the most important thing to you (assuming that you have not been negligent in any way that they perceive).

- Explain you are training the dog to be a calmer and safer dog and that the most important part of the program is avoiding any situation that will set off the anxiety that could lead to the past behavior.

- Detail what cautionary measures you are using to make sure safety is the utmost concern (i.e. muzzles, crates. etc.) if your dog is a threat in any shape or form.

- Explain that you don't intend to walk your dog when your neighbors are around or leave your dog unattended in a backyard. Let them know that their concerns are recognized. But do it in a calm way.

- Make sure to communicate that your dog's past behavior is not because of any abusive or punishing techniques you are using. There is still the myth around that there are no aggressive dogs, simply bad owners who have caused their dogs to be aggressive. If you *have* used abusive or punishing techniques in the past, you need to realize that there are still recommendations by supposedly educated professional dog people who suggests this is the way to treat dog aggression. At the time of writing this, it was still possible to enter "dog aggression" into the Google search engine and on the very first page of results get a site that appears reputable that suggests that dog aggression should be controlled with prong collars and the like.

- If your neighbor offers you advice, you can either choose to listen, or politely let them know you are seeking professional help. But stay aware that they most likely are not experts themselves and their recommendations can potentially be harmful.

- Provide clear tips on how they should act around the dog when you are out with the dog. But be aware they will probably forget them all and if your dog is out, they will pay attention to your dog more than they will to you.

- If your dog has any issues with people, you should definitely explain that your dog has anxiety issues and how important it is to keep people away from him or her to help them get better.

- If the neighbors have children, let them know you are aware of the fact children being children don't always follow the rules so your intention is to not let your dog out when they are. But don't judge their children!

In most cases when people feel they have no control over a situation, the stress level goes up. People will always be most concerned about their children, because children's brains have not developed to the point where they can make the right choices and animals are usually highly attractive, interesting, or scary to children.

Your neighbors are likely your biggest threat in terms of having your dog reported. Neighbors don't want to feel your dog is threatening them through the fence when they are in their own backyard. Their home is supposed to be a shelter, a safe place. People feel that if the dog has charged them or charged the fence at their child there is reason to be very concerned and are on high alert.

How your neighbors greet you on the street may not at all reflect what they are saying about you and worrying about in the inside of their homes. If other neighbors feel the same way and they talk together, then there is a risk of the talk reinforcing what they feel even more strongly. Unfortunately with breed bans and dangerous dog legislation, your position is not strong.

Your biggest risk is that people will do what they want. Neighbors let their friendly dogs off leash, even when they shouldn't, and parents may tell their children to leave your dog alone, but it's a toss of a coin whether that child will be listening to their parents or testing the boundaries of childhood. Even adults sometimes cannot help themselves but approach your dog.

As mentioned earlier K9aggression.com had a special dog shirt designed to communicate that people should not touch your dog using familiar symbols that the majority of people understand. You can buy these shirts through the k9aggression.com website.

If your dog has never shown aggression in front of your neighbors

One of the worse things you can do is pretend as if your dog is just fine and hope he or she won't do anything when people or other dogs are around. Another bad thing to do is use your neighbors for any kind of *behavior modification* unless they know exactly what the issues are and they are willing to go along with it. But if your neighbors are unaware that your dog is aggressive, you are probably better off not revealing it because it will cause unnecessary stress for everyone involved.

If your dog is likely to be aggressive towards your neighbors or neighbors' dogs, you *should* reveal that your dog is afraid of people or dogs and if they keep away from them, he or she will feel more comfortable.

If you are in a situation where you didn't anticipate the approach of a neighbor and you are out with your dog, move away from them and tell them your dog has a fear or anxiety issue. People are often more than willing to give you the space. Again, the dog t-shirt was designed to help communicate to people that they should not touch your dog.

You must take every safety precaution so that your dog has no chance to escape or show aggression. Dog aggression can have very serious consequences.

Using Muzzles

People are sometimes concerned that if they muzzle their dog people will automatically assume the dog is aggressive and change their attitude about your dog, and potentially create a problem where there wasn't one before. However, if your dog is known to be aggressive, having your dog wear a muzzle will likely reassure people that you are being responsible.

If your dog is not known to be aggressive, you could try explaining that your dog is anxious and that by using a muzzle, you can keep people who insist on approaching your dog and frightening them at a distance. But at the end of the day, if an accident happens, the muzzle could be the difference between whether your dog lives or dies.

Muzzles often keep people from approaching your dog, but not always. So don't rely on them to do so.

 MY STORY

I put this at the end, because frankly, I often skip this part in other books, at least at first and I fully support you skipping mine. But we all have a story, and mine is the reason why I care so much.

I have always loved animals and been interested in psychology and how the brain works. But it wasn't until I owned my own aggressive dog that I learned just how confusing it is for dog owners to deal with dog aggression.

We went down the path of trying to find trainers that could help. All of them at that time recommended punishment based techniques such as leash corrections, spraying water in the dog's face, or excessive crating and isolation. With the first serious incident, my husband found a board and train based trainer who claimed that he had been able to fix all of his clients dogs but one. If he could not fix our dog (and he used the word "fix") then he would find a home for her. He had been on national television and had a full two page spread in one of the cities top newspapers. He appeared to be credible.

Well, as it turned out, he was not able to fix her. She had only got much worse. He told us he would adopt her himself and we could see her whenever we wanted. A few months after that when we saw her she was skin and bones and a nervous wreck. We were told it was because she had cancer. She tried to climb in our car when we were leaving and he had to pull her out. We never saw her again after that.

A few months later in an email he pronounced her cured and reported that he was sending her to have guide dog training with a friend out in BC. No, we could not keep in touch with this man, as he was a recluse. Case closed. She was never seen by anyone again.

The sad story is that other past clients started to come out of the woodwork with stories of neglect and cruelty. He has since gone underground. It made me question what happened to the dog he had supposedly adopted from us. Did she really have cancer? Did she really go to another home? I would say without a doubt, this situation is the emotional impetus that has driven me ever since.

I was now on a mission. I wanted to get to the bottom of what had happened, including learning about dog aggression. Was anything I had been told about dog aggression and its treatment backed up by credible scientific data? Could any of this been avoided? Was it true what I heard that dogs should not play with other dogs? What about punishment?   What about excessive crating and isolation we had been encouraged to do? Valid? Or invalid?

What I actually learned was that anyone can call him or herself a dog trainer, a specialist, or a behaviorist. That even if someone appears to have years of experience and comes with recommendations, and even if they excel and persuade you to believe their recommendations are best, they still may not actually know the right way to treat dog aggression. And even with those that do, they can't always agree on whether a dog is safe to approach, stressed, or how the dog might be feeling, suggesting that even 20 years of experience and learning does not mean they know everything.

Serious dog aggression is not the result of poor training, "weak nerves," or being a poor leader.   That while you can make dog aggression worse through punishment, inconsistency, poor socialization or an unstable environment, it's not usually the owner's fault the dog is predisposed to aggression.

Aggression is a symptom of an underlying issue – usually anxiety related.   All dogs will need a systematic approach to re-training; some will not improve without the help of medication. The majority of them do not need to be euthanized. But there are treatment plans that can improve dog aggression. And they don't include fear-based punishment.

Anxious to provide others with the kind of information that would have sent me down a different path, I founded K9aggression.com over a decade ago with the support of a group of like minded dog owners. A year after that, I founded the K9aggression online support group on Yahoo which various volunteers have helped to run. Again, the goal was to help people to not feel isolated and possibly point them to some credible resources, or simply provide a place to vent.

But I came to understand that people still struggled. Many join the group in a crisis.   Many people write to us through the site.   Some of you feel you can't afford the cost of a veterinary behaviorist or even a trainer, and most of you can't afford to wait. You needed something you could do now.

In all cases, people were hungry for more information, even if it was simply a different take on the same thing so they could understand it and internalize it better. All too often people get really stuck. Sometimes, the understanding of a couple of key components and a little support is all it takes to make a difference.

From my perspective, I don't want anyone else getting hurt. An experience with an unknown dog during the writing of this book reminded me how traumatic and scarring aggression can be, not just to the victim, but also to those around them.

But I have never lost the feeling that aggression problems are not the dogs' fault. And over time, I came to see just how blind we are to dogs' plights in general and all the many ways we add to it.

And with all that in mind, this book was born.

REFERENCES

1 Benjamin L. Hart, Lynette A. Hart, Melissa Bain, *Canine and Feline Behavior,* Blackwell, 2006

2 Peters V, Sottiaux M, Appelboom J, Kahn A., "Posttraumatic stress disorder after dog bites in children," *J Pediatr.* 2004 Jan;144(1):121-2.

3 Mineur YS, Prasol DJ, Belzung C, CrusioWE "Agonistic behavior and unpredictable chronic mild stress in mice". *Behavior Genetics* (September 2003). 33(5): 513–519.

4 S Brammeier, J Brennan, S Brown, D Bryant, D Calnon, T Cole Stenson, G Colwin, S Dale, C Dominguez, D Dougherty, et al. "Good trainers: How to identify one and why this is important to your practice of veterinary medicine" *Journal of Veterinary Behavior: Clinical Applications and Research,* Volume 1, Issue 1, Pages 47-52

5 Gardner DE, Alley MR, Wyburn RS, et al. "Calcinosis circumscripta-like lesions in dogs associated with the use of choke chains," *N Z Vet J* 1975; 23:95-97.

6 Schilder, M.B.H., van der Borg, J.A.R.A.M., "Training dogs with help of the shock collar: short and long term behavioural effects, *Appl. Anim. Behav. Sci.* 85, 319–334. 2003

7 Beerda, B., Schilder, M.B.H., van Hooff, J.A.R.A.M., de Vries, H.W., Mol, J.A., 1998. "Behavioural, saliva cortisol and heart rate responses to different types of stimuli in dogs,"*Appl. Anim. Behav. Sci.* 58, 365–381.

8 E. Schalkea, J. Stichnotha, S. Otta, R. Jones-Baadeb, "Clinical signs caused by the use of electric training collars on dogs in everyday life situations", *Applied Animal Behavior Science* Vol. 105, Issue 4, July 2007, Pages 369–380

9 Schlereth T, Birklein F., "The sympathetic nervous system and pain," Neuromolecular Med. 2008;10(3):141-7. Epub 2007 Nov 8.

10 Yingjie Qi, Neng-Wei Hu and Michael J. Rowan, "Switching off LTP: mGlu and NMDA Receptor–Dependent Novelty Exploration–Induced Depotentiation in the Rat Hippocampus", *Cereb. Cortex* (2012)

11 Chih-Hao Yang Chiung-Chun Huang and Kuei-Sen Hsu "Novelty exploration elicits a reversal of acute stress-induced modulation of hippocampal synaptic plasticity in the rat,,, December 1, 2006 *The Journal of Physiology,* 577, 601-615.

12 Wichert, S., Wolf, O. T., & Schwabe, L."Reactivation, Interference, and Reconsolidation: Are Recent and Remote Memories Likewise Susceptible?" *Behavioral Neuroscience,* Oct;125(5):699-704.

13 Jennifer A. Obernier and Ransom L. Baldwin, "Establishing an Appropriate Period of Acclimatization Following Transportation of Laboratory Animals", *ILAR J.* 2006;47(4):364-9.

14 Bassett L. and H. Buchanan-Smith. 2007 "Effects of predictability on the welfare of captive animals." *Applied Animal Behavior Science* 102: 223-245.

15 Amanda C. Jones, , Robert A. Josephs, Interspecies hormonal interactions between man and the domestic dog (Canis familiaris), *Hormones and Behavior* Vol 50, Issue 3, Sep 2006, Pages 393–400

16 D J Menor-Campos, J M Molleda-Carbonell, R López-Rodríguez, "Effects of exercise and human contact on animal welfare in a dog shelter," *The Veterinary record* (2011) Vol 169, Issue: 15, Pages: 388

17 Eli Puterman, Jue Lin, Elizabeth Blackburn, Aoife O'Donovan, Nancy Adler, Elissa Epel, "The Power of Exercise: Buffering the Effect of Chronic Stress on Telomere Length", *PLoS ONE* 5(5): e10837. doi:10.1371/journal.pone.0010837 (2010)

18 KobiloT, LiuQR, GandhiK, MughalM, ShahamY, vanPraagH, "Running is the neurogenic and neurotrophic stimulus in environmental enrichment," *Learn Mem. 2011 Aug 30;18(9):605-9.*

19 Camilla Pastore, Federica Pirrone, Francesca Balzarotti, Massimo Faustini, Ludovica Pierantoni, Mariangela Albertini, "Evaluation of physiological and behavioral stress-dependent parameters in agility dogs," *Journal of Veterinary Behavior: Clinical Applications and Research*, Volume 6, Issue 3, May–June 2011, Pages 188-194

20 Norman Doidge, *The Brain that Changes Itself*, 2007, Penguin Books p. 165 – 176

21 Keng SL, Smoski MJ, Robins CJ, "Effects of mindfulness on psychological health: a review of empirical studies," *Clin Psychol Rev.* 2011 Aug;31(6):1041-56. Epub 2011 May 13.

22 Marchand WR., "Mindfulness-based stress reduction, mindfulness-based cognitive therapy, and zen meditation for depression, anxiety, pain, and psychological distress," *J Psychiatr Pract.* 2012 Jul;18(4):233-52.

23 Kang G, Oh S."[Effects of Mindfulness Meditation program on perceived stress, ways of coping, and stress response in breast cancer patients]," J *Korean Acad Nurs.* 2012 Apr;42(2):161-70

24 Smith WP, Compton WC, West WB."Meditation as an adjunct to a happiness enhancement program," *J Clin Psychol.* 1995 Mar;51(2):269-73.

25 Karen L. Overall, *Clinical Behavioral Medicine for Small Animals*, Mosby, 1997, p. 121

26 Alexandre Heeren, Hannah E. Reese, Richard J. McNally, Pierre Philippot, "Attention training toward and away from threat in social phobia: Effects on subjective, behavioral, and physiological measures of anxiety," *Behaviour Research and Therapy*, Volume 50, Issue 1, January 2012, Pages 30-39,

27 Kubinyi, E., Virányi, Zs., Miklósi, Á. "Comparative social cognition: From wolf and dog to humans." *Comparative Cognition & Behavior Reviews*, 2007. 2: 26-46.

28 Mariko Yamamoto, Nobuyo Ohtani, Mitsuaki Ohta, "The response of dogs to attentional focus of human beings: A comparison between guide dog candidates and other dog," *Journal of Veterinary Behavior* (2011) 6, 4-1

29 Karine Silva, Alexandra Ribeiro, Ana Magalhães, Alexandra Valongeiro, Liliana de Sousa «Are you looking at me? Dogs' responsiveness to human gaze" *Journal of Veterinary Behavior: Clinical Applications and Research*, January 2011 (volume 6 issue 1 Page 69

30 B.L. Deputte, A. Doll "Do dogs understand human facial expressions?" *Journal of Veterinary Behavior: Clinical Applications and Research*, 1 January 2011, volume 6 issue 1 Pages 78-79

31 Katalin Maros, Antal Dóka, Ádám Miklósi, "Behavioural correlation of heart rate changes in family dogs," *Applied Animal Behaviour Science*, Volume 109, Issue 2 , Pages 329-341, February 2008

32 Karen L. Overall, "Natural Animal Models of Human Psychiatric Conditions: Assessment of Mechanism and

Validity," *Prog Neuropsychopharmacol Biol Psychiatry*. 2000 Jul;24(5):727-76.

33 Kemp, A H, Guastella, A J, "The Role of Oxytocin in Human Affect; A Novel Hypothesis" *Current Directions in Psychological Science*, August 2011 vol. 20 no. 4222-231

34 Michael B Hennessy, Michael T. Williams, Deborah D Miller, Chet W Douglas, Victoria L Voith, "Influence of male and female petters on plasma cortisol and behaviour: can human interaction reduce the stress of dogs in a public animal shelter?," *Applied Animal Behaviour Science*, Volume 61, Issue 1, 14 December 1998, Pages 63-77

35 Crista L. Coppola, Temple Grandin, R. Mark Enns, "Human interaction and cortisol: Can human contact reduce stress for shelter dogs?," *Physiology & Behavior*, Volume 87, Issue 3, 30 March 2006, Pages 537-541

36 M. Cecilia Wendler, "Effects of Tellington Touch in Healthy Adults Awaiting Venipuncture", *Research in Nursing & Health*, 2003, 1-13

37 Mariko Yamamoto, Nobuyo Ohtani, Mitsuaki Ohta, "The response of dogs to attentional focus of human beings:A comparison between guide dog candidates and other dog", *Journal of Veterinary Behavior* (2011) 6, 4-1

38 Lisa Horn, Ludwig Huber, Friederike Range,"Dogs' (Canis familiaris) attention toward humans: does it depend on the relationship?" *Journal of Veterinary Behavior: Clinical Applications and Research,*January 2011 (volume 6 issue 1 Page 76)

39 Chiara Mariti, Beatrice Carlone, Silvana Borgognini-Tarli, Silvano Presciuttini, Ludovica Pierantoni, Angelo Gazzano, "Considering The Dog As Part Of The System: Studying The Attachment Bond Of Dogs Toward All Members Of The Fostering Family", *Journal of Veterinary Behavior*, Vol 6, No 1, January/February 2011

40 Lucscher, Andrew, U. "Sibling Rivalry", *Canine Aggression*, 2001published by Professional Animal Behavior Associatesand distributed at the Canine Behavioral Problems Symposiumfor attendees 2004, p. 21

41 "Environmental Enrichment", The Indoor Pet Initiative, College of Veterinary Medicine, The Ohio State University, 2008, http://indoorpet.osu.edu/dogs/environmental_enrichment_dogs/index.cfm

42 Martyn L. Gorman, Michael G. Mills, Jacobus P. Raath & John R. Speakman, "High hunting costs make African wild dogs vulnerable to kleptoparasitism by hyaenas", *Nature*, Vol 391, January 1998

43 Richard Norris, Douglas Carroll, Raymond Cochrane, "The effects of aerobic and anaerobic training on fitness, blood pressure, and psychological stress and well-being," *Journal of Psychosomatic Research*, Volume 34, Issue 4, 1990, Pages 367-375

44 Yigal Goldshtrom, Debra Korman, Iris Goldshtrom, Joyce Bendavid, "The effect of rhythmic exercises on cognition and behaviour of maltreated children: A pilot study," *Journal of Bodywork and Movement Therapies,*2011 Jul; 15(3):326-34.

Volume 15, Issue 3, July 2011, Pages 326-334, ISSN 1360-8592, 10.1016/j.jbmt.2010.06.006.

45 B Blakemore, "Fun and Play are Key to Survival for Bears, Dogs, Humans, Birds and Maybe Even Ants," *Nature and Environment*, Feb 5, 2012   http://abcnews.go.com/blogs/technology/2012/02/fun-and-play-are-key-to-survival-for-bears-dogs-humans-birds-and-maybe-even-ants/

46 Zsuzsánna Horváth, Antal Dóka, Ádám Miklósi, "Affiliative and disciplinary behavior of human handlers during play with their dog affects cortisol concentrations in opposite directions," *Hormones and Behavior*, Volume 54, Issue 1, June 2008, Pages 107-114

47 Lilla Tóth, Márta Gácsi, József Topál, Ádám Miklósi, "Playing styles and possible causative factors in dogs' behaviour when playing with humans" *Applied Animal Behaviour Science*, Volume 114, Issue 3 , Pages 473-484, 1 December 2008

48 Nicola J. Rooneya, fl, John W.S. Bradshawa, Ian H. Robinsonb, "Do dogs respond to play signals given by humans?" *Animal Behaviour*, Volume 61, Issue 4, April 2001, Pages 715–722

49 Erika Bauer, Camille Ward., Barbara Smuts, "Play like a puppy, play like a dog," *Journal of Veterinary Behavior: Clinical Applications and Research*, Volume 4, Issue 2 , Pages 68-69, March 2009

50 Alexandra Horowitz, *Inside of a Dog*, Scribner, 2009, p. 200-201

51 Patricia Simonet*, Donna Versteeg, Dan Storie, "Dog-laughter: Recorded playback reduces stress related behavior in shelter dogs" Proceedings of the 7th International Conference on Environmental Enrichment, July 31 – August 5, 2005

52 Nicola J Rooney, John W.S Bradshaw, Ian H Robinson, "A comparison of dog–dog and dog–human play behavior,,, *Applied Animal Behaviour Science*, Volume 66, Issue 3, 29 February 2000, Pages 235-248

53 Nicola J. Rooney, John W.S. Bradshaw, Ian H. Robinson, "Do dogs respond to play signals given by humans?", *Animal Behaviour*, Volume 61, Issue 4, April 2001, Pages 715-722

54 Anthony L. Podberscek, James A. Serpell, "Environmental influences on the expression of aggressive behaviour in English Cocker Spaniels,"*Applied Animal Behaviour Science*, Volume 52, Issues 3–4, April 1997, Pages 215-227

55 N J Rooney and J W S Bradshaw, "The effects of games on the dog-owner relationship", Anthrozoology Institute, University of Southampton, SO16 7PX. UK. E-mail:

njr@soton.ac.uk,http://www.leecharleskelley.com/images/play_study.pdf

56 N J Rooney, J. W. S Bradshaw, "An experimental study of the effects of play upon the dog-human relationship", *Applied Animal Behavior Science*, 75 (2002) 161-176

57 A. Grimmett, M.N. Sillence, "Calmatives for the excitable horse: A review of L-tryptophan", *The Veterinary Journal*, Volume 170, Issue 1, July 2005, Pages 24-32

58 DeNapoli JS, Dodman NH, Shuster L, Rand WM, Gross KL. "Effect of dietary protein content and tryptophan supplementation on dominance aggression, territorial aggression, and hyperactivity in dogs". *J Am Vet Med Assoc*. 2000 Aug 15;217(4):504-8.

59 Dodman NH, Reisner I, Shuster L, Rand W, Luescher UA, Robinson I, Houpt KA."Effect of dietary protein content on behavior in dogs". *J Am Vet Med Assoc*. 1996 Feb 1;208(3):376-9.

60 Guido Bosch, Bonne Beerda, Anton C. Beynen, Joanne A.M. van der Borg, Antonius F.B. van der Poel, Wouter H. Hendriks, ¿¿Dietary tryptophan supplementation in privately owned mildly anxious dogs," *Applied Animal Behaviour Science*, Volume 121, Issues 3–4, December 2009, Pages 197-205

61 Maki Kato, Kazuki Miyaji, Nobuyo Ohtani, Mitsuaki Ohta, "Effects of prescription diet on dealing with stressful situations and performance of anxiety-related behaviors in privately owned anxious dogs," *Journal of Veterinary Behavior: Clinical Applications and Research*, Volume 7, Issue 1, January–February 2012, Pages 21-26

62 Nicolas Violle, Michaël Messaoudi, Catherine Lefranc-Millot, Didier Desor, Amine Nejdi, Benoit Demagny, Henri Schroeder, "Ethological comparison of the effects of a bovine αs1-casein tryptic hydrolysate and diazepam

on the behaviour of rats in two models of anxiety," *Pharmacology Biochemistry and Behavior*, Volume 84, Issue 3, July 2006, Pages 517-523

63 V. Dramard, L. Kern, J. Hofmans, C. Halsberghe, C.A. Rème "Clinical efficacy of L-theanine tablets to reduce anxiety-related emotional disorders in cats: A pilot open-label clinical trial', *Journal of Veterinary Behavior: Clinical Applications and Research*, 1 May 2007 (volume 2 issue 3 Pages 85-86)

64 Joseph A. Araujo, Christina de Rivera, Jennifer L. Ethier, Gary M. Landsberg, Sagi Denenberg, Stephanie Arnold, Norton W. Milgram, "ANXITANE® tablets reduce fear of human beings in a laboratory model of anxiety-related behavior," *Journal of Veterinary Behavior: Clinical Applications and Research*, Volume 5, Issue 5, September–October 2010, Pages 268-275

65 Sinn N, Milte C, Howe PR. "Oiling the Brain: A Review of Randomized Controlled Trials of Omega-3 Fatty Acids in Psychopathology across the Lifespan", *Nutrients*. 2010 Feb;2(2):128-70. Epub 2010 Feb 9.

66 Re S, Zanoletti M, Emanuele E., "Aggressive dogs are characterized by low omega-3 polyunsaturated fatty acid status". *Vet Res Commun*. 2008 Mar;32(3):225-30. Epub 2007 Sep 19.

67 Fedorova I, Salem N Jr., "Omega-3 fatty acids and rodent behavior. "Prostaglandins, Leukotrienes, and Essential Fatty Acids (PLEFA)". 2006 Oct-Nov;75(4-5):271-89. Epub 2006 Sep 14.

68 G. Bosch, B. Beerda, W. H. Hendriks, A. F. B. van der Poel and M. W. A. Verstegen, "Impact of nutrition on canine behavior: current status and possible mechanisms", *Nutrition Research Reviews* (2007), 20, 180–19

69 Berns, Gregory, *Iconoclast*. 2010, Harvard Business Press, p7

70 Berns, Gregory, *Iconoclast*. 2010, Harvard Business Press, p22

71 Mark Muraven; Roy F. Baumeister and Dianne M. Tice (1999). "Longitudinal Improvement Of Self-Regulation Through Practice: Building Self-Control Strength Through Repeated Exercise", *Journal of Social Psychology*, 139(4), 446-458.

72 Long, Martyn, *The Psychology of Education*. Routledge.(2000) ISBN 0-415-23906-0.

73 Teresa M Edenfield, "Exercise and Mood: Exploring the Role of Exercise in Regulating Stress Reactivity in Bipolar Disorder"[unpublished doctoral dissertation], Fogler Library, The University of Main Digital Commons, http://digitalcommons.library.umaine.edu/cgi/viewcontent.cgi?article=1032&context=etd

74 M.Emanuela Albonetti, Francesca Farabollini, "Differential effects of restraint and novelty on the social behaviour of female rats," *Behavioural Processes*, Volume 37, Issues 2–3, September 1996, Pages 209-215

75 J. Riva, S.P. Marelli, V. Redaelli, E. Sforzini, F. Luzi, G.P. Bondiolotti, W. Di Mari, M. Verga, "Effect of training on behavioral reactivity and neurotransmitter levels in drug detection dogs," *Journal of Veterinary Behavior: Clinical Applications and Research*, 1 January 2010 (volume 5 issue 1 Pages 38-39

76 Thomas F. Denson, "Angry Rumination and the Self-Regulation of Aggression" In. J.P. Forgas, R.F. Baumeister, & D.M. Tice (Eds.) *The psychology nof self-regulation* (p. 233-247) New York, NY, US: Psychology Press, 2009

77 Ted Ruffman, Zara Morris-Trainor "Do dogs understand human emotional expressions?" *Journal of Veterinary Behavior: Clinical Applications and Research*"1 January 2011 (volume 6 issue 1 Pages 97-98

78 Philip Ogburn, Stephanie Crouse, Frank Martin, Katherine Houpt, "Comparison of behavioral and physiological

responses of dogs wearing two different types of collars", *Applied Animal Behaviour Science*, Volume 61, Issue 2, 28 December 1998, Pages 133-142

79 Wrubel KM, Moon-Fanelli AA, Maranda LS, Dodman NH., "Interdog household aggression: 38 cases (2006-2007)". *Am Vet Med Assoc.* 2011 Mar 15;238(6):731-40.

80 Friederike Range, Lisa Horn, Zso´ fia Viranyi, and Ludwig Huber, The absence of reward induces inequity aversion in dogs, Proceedings of the national Academy of Sciences of the United States of America

81 Karen L. Overall, *Clinical Behavioral Medicine for Small Animals*, Mosby, 1997, p. 441

82 Raisner, Ilana, "Tuesday's Pearl *"Reisner Veterinary Behavior & Consulting Services's Facebook page*, March 13, 2012 http://www.facebook.com/ReisnerVetBehavior

83 Karen L. Overall, *Clinical Behavioral Medicine for Small Animals*, Mosby, 1997 –p 429-431

84 Petr Řezáč, Petra Viziová, Michaela Dobešová, Zdeněk Havlíček, Dagmar Pospíšilová, "Factors affecting dog–dog interactions on walks with their owners, *Applied Animal Behaviour Science* 15 November 2011 (volume 134 issue 3 Pages 170-176

85 M. E. Albonetti' And F. Farabollini, "Effects of Single Restraint on the Defensive Behavior of Male and Female Rats," *Physiology & Behavior*, Vol. 57. No. 3, pp. 431-437, 1995

86 Petr Řezáč, Petra Viziová, Michaela Dobešová, Zdeněk Havlíček, Dagmar Pospíšilová, "Factors affecting dog–dog interactions on walks with their owners," *Applied Animal Behaviour Science* 15 November 2011 (volume 134 issue 3 Pages 170-176)

87 Petr Řezáč, Petra Viziová, Michaela Dobešová, Zdeněk Havlíček, Dagmar Pospíšilová, "Factors affecting dog–dog interactions on walks with their owners ," *Applied Animal Behaviour Science* 15 November 2011 (volume 134 issue 3 Pages 170-176

88 Dr. Ilana Resisner, "Tuesday Pearl ", *Reisner Veterinary Behavior & Consulting Services's Facebook page,* Jul 31, 2012, http://www.facebook.com/ReisnerVetBehavior

89 József Topál, György Gergely, Ágnes Erdo˝hegyi, Gergely Csibra, Ádám Miklósi, "Differential Sensitivity to Human Communication in Dogs, Wolves, and Human Infants," *Science*, Vol 325, 4 Sep 2009

90 ZsóWa Virányi · Márta Gácsi · Enikö Kubinyi · József Topál · Beatrix Belényi · Dorottya Ujfalussy · Ádám Miklósi, "Comprehension of human pointing gestures in young human-reared wolves (Canis lupus) and dogs (Canis familiaris)," *Anim Cogn* (2008) 11:373–387

91 József Topál, Márta Gácsi, Ádám Miklósi, Zsófia Virányi, Enikő Kubinyi, Vilmos Csányi, "Attachment to humans: a comparative study on hand-reared wolves and differently socialized dog puppies," *Animal Behaviour*, Volume 70, Issue 6, December 2005, Pages 1367-1375, ISSN 0003-3472, 10.1016/j.anbehav.2005.03.025. (http://www.sciencedirect.com/science/article/pii/S0003347205003155)

92 M. Gácsi, B. Gyri, Á. Miklósi, Zs. Virányi, E. Kubinyi, J. Topál, and V. Csányi, "Species-Specific Differences and Similarities in the Behavior of Hand Raised Dog and Wolf Puppies in Social Situations with Humans," *Developmental Psychobiology*, 2005, 47, p. 118

93 Tsuda, K, Kikkawa, Y, Yonekawa, H, Tanabe, Y, "Extensive interbreeding occurred among multiple matriarchal ancestors during the domestication of dogs: evidence from inter- and intraspecies polymorphisms in the D-loop

region of mitochondrial DNA between dogs and wolves," *Genes & Genetic Systems,* Vol 72, p 229-238, 1997

94 Sactre P, Lindberg J, Leonard JA, Olsson K, Pettersson U, Ellegren H, Bergström TF, Vilà C, Jazin E., "From wild wolf to domestic dog: gene expression changes in the brain," *Brain Res Mol Brain Res.* 2004 Jul 26;126(2):198-206.

95 Guo KG, Meints K, Hall C, Hall S, Mills D, "Left Gaze Bias in Humans, Rhesus Monkeys and Domestic Dogs", *Animal Cognition.,* 2009 12:409-418

96 Nicola J Rooney, John W.S Bradshaw, Ian H Robinson, "A comparison of dog–dog and dog–human play behaviour," *Applied Animal Behaviour Science,* Volume 66, Issue 3, 29 February 2000, Pages 235-248

97 Bekoff, Marc "Play Signals as Punctuation: The Structure of Social Play in Canids," *Behaviour,* (1995) 132 419-429.

98 Udell, M. A. R., Dorey, N. R. & Wynne, C. D. L. "Wolves outperform dogs in following human social cues," *Animal Behaviour,* 76, 1767-1773.] 2008

99 International Wolf Center "Learn – Communication,"

http://www.wolf.org/wolves/learn/basic/biology/communication.asp

100 John B. Theberge and Mary T. Theberge, "The Wolves of Algonquin Park: A 12 Year Ecological Study' *Department of Geography, University of Waterloo,* Waterloo, Ontario, Canada, 2004

101 Mech, L. David. "Alpha status, dominance, and division of labor in wolf packs." *Canadian Journal of Zoology* 1999. 77:1196-1203.

102 J.W.S. Bradshaw, "Conceptualizing The Domestic Dog – Should We Start Again?," *Journal of Veterinary Behavior,* Vol 6, No 1, January/February 2011

103 Enrique Font, "Spacing and social organization: Urban stray dogs revisited," *Applied Animal Behaviour Science*Volume 17, Issue 3 , Pages 319-328, June 1987

104 Roberto Bonanni, Simona Cafazzo, Paola Valsecchi &Eugenia Natoli, "Effect of group size, dominance rank and social bonding on leadership behaviour in feral dogs (Canis lupus familiaris)," Universita' Degli Studi Di Parma Dipartimento di Biologia Evolutiva e Funzionale, Dottorato di ricerca in Biologia del Comportamento, 2007-2008 http://dspace-unipr.cilea.it/bitstream/1889/1066/1/Tesi%20dottorato%203.pdf#page=43

105 McGeevy et al, "Overview of the dog-human dyad," *Journal of Veterinary Behavior,* Vol 7, No 2, Mar/Apr 2012

106 Angelica Steinker "Terminology Think Tank: Social dominance theory as it relates to dogs", *Journal of Veterinary Behavior: Clinical Applications and Research* 1 July 2007 (volume 2 issue 4 Pages 137-140 DOI: 10.1016/j.jveb.2007.07.004)

107 Drews, C., "The concept and definition of dominance in animal behavior," *Behaviour.* 125, 283-311993.

108 Packard, J.M., 2003. "Wolf behavior: reproductive, social and intelligent," In: Mech, L.D., Boitani, L. (Eds.), *Wolves: Behavior, Ecology and Conservation.* University of Chicago Press, Chicago, IL, pp. 35-65.

109 M. Wan, F.A. Champagne "Agreement among experts in ratings of emotion in dogs," *Journal of Veterinary Behavior: Clinical Applications and Research,* 1 January 2011 (volume 6 issue 1 Page 64 DOI: 10.1016/j.jveb.2010.09.046)

110 Karen L. Overall, "Behavior signals interpreted with body postures," *DVM Newsmagaine*, May 1, 2004

111 Bonne Beerda, Matthijs B.H. Schilder, Jan A.R.A.M. van Hooff, Hans W. de Vries, Jan A. Mol, "Behavioural, saliva cortisol and heart rate responses to different types of stimuli in dogs," *Applied Animal Behaviour Science* 58 1998 365–381

112 Jørn Våge1, Tina B Bønsdorff1, Ellen Arnet1, Aage Tverdal2 and Frode Lingaas1, "Differential gene expression in brain tissues of aggressive and non-aggressive dogs," *BMC Veterinary Research* 2010, 6:34 doi:10.1186/1746-6148-6-34

113 Lauriat TL, McInnes LA., "EAAT2 regulation and splicing: relevance to psychiatric and neurological disorders,". *Mol Psychiatry*. 2007 Dec;12(12):1065-78. Epub 2007 Aug 7.

114 Junko A. Arai1, Shaomin Li1, Dean M. Hartley2, and Larry A. Feig "Transgenerational Rescue of a Genetic Defect in Long-Term Potentiation and Memory Formation by Juvenile Enrichment," *The Journal of Neuroscience*, 4 February 2009, 29(5): 1496-1502

115 Tracey Clarke "Exploring breed diversity in behavior in the domestic dog (Canis familiaris)," *Journal of Veterinary Behavior: Clinical Applications and Research*, Volume 4, Issue 2 , Pages 101-102, March 2009

116 Deborah L. Duffy a, Yuying Hsu b, James A. Serpell , "Breed differences in canine aggression," *Applied Animal Behaviour Science*, Volume 114, Issues 3-4, 1 December 2008, Pages 441-460

117 Deborah L. Duffy a, Yuying Hsu b, James A. Serpell , "Breed differences in canine aggression," *Applied Animal Behaviour Science*, Volume 114, Issues 3-4, 1 December 2008, Pages 441-460

118 Pat Miller, *Positive Perspectives 2: Know Your Dog, Train Your Dog*, Dogwise Publishing, 2008, p 29-34

119 Gail Tamases Fisher, *The Thinking Dog: Crossover to Clicker Training*, p 51-55

120 Deborah A. Jones, "Crossover Dog Questions" *Whole Dog Journal*, http://www.k9infocus.com/questions.htm

121 Borbála Turcsán*, Eniko˝Kubinyi, Ádám Miklósi, "Trainability and boldness traits differ between dog breed clusters based on conventional breed categories and genetic relatedness", *Applied Animal Behaviour Science* 132 (2011) 61–70

122 J.P. Scott, J.L. Fuller, *Genetics and the Social behavior of the Dog*, The University of Chicago press, 1965, p79-80

123 Armstrong, Kevin R.1; Clark, Terri R.2; Peterson, Andmichael R., "Use of Corn-Husk Nesting Material to Reduce Aggression in Caged Mice," *Journal of the American Association for Laboratory Animal Science*, Volume 37, Number 4, July 1998 , pp. 64-66(3)

124 Chapillon P, Manneche C, Belzung C, Caston J "Rearing environmental enrichment in two inbred strains of mice: 1. Effects on emotional reactivity," *Behav Genet*(1999) 29(1): 41–46

125 Engellenner WJ, Goodlett CR, Burright RG, Donovick PJ "Environmental enrichment and restriction: effects on reactivity, exploration and maze learning in mice with septal lesions," *Physiol Behav*(1982) 29(5): 885–893

126 Hansen LT, Berthelsen H, "The effect of environmental enrichment on the behaviour of caged rabbits (Oryctolagus cuniculus),: *Appl Anim Behav Sci* (2000) 68(2): 163–178

127 Sharp J, Zammit T, Azar T, Lawson D "Stress-like responses to common procedures in individually and group-housed female rats," *Contemp Top Lab Anim Sci* (2003) 42(1): 9–18.

128 Chamove AS,„Cage design reduces emotionality in mice," *Lab Anim* (1989) 23(3): 215–219.

129 Van Loo PL, Van der Meer E, Kruitwagen CL, Koolhaas JM, Van Zutphen LF, et al. „Long-term effects of husbandry procedures on stress-related parameters in male mice of two strains," *Lab Anim* (2004) 38(2): 169–177.

130 Huang-Brown KM, Guhad FA "Chocolate, an effective means of oral drug delivery in rats," *Lab Anim* (NY)(2002) 31(10): 34–36.

131 Bennett EL, Diamond MC, Krech D, Rosenzweig "MR Chemical and Anatomical Plasticity Brain," *Science* (1964) 146: 610–619.

132 Kempermann G, Kuhn HG, Gage FH "More hippocampal neurons in adult mice living in an enriched environment," *Nature* (1997) 386(6624): 493–495

133 Patterson-Kane EG, Hunt M, Harper DN, "Behavioral indexes of poor welfare in laboratory rats," *J Appl Anim Welf Sci* 2(2): 97–110.(1999)

134 Ilin Y, Richter-Levin G "Enriched Environment Experience Overcomes Learning Deficits and Depressive-Like Behavior Induced by Juvenile Stress," PLoS ONE 4(1): e4329. (2009)

135 J. M. Koolhaas,* P. Meerlo, S. F. De Boer, J. H. Strubbe And B. Bohus, "The Temporal Dynamics of the Stress Response," *Neuroscience and Biobehavioral Reviews,* Vol. 21, No. 6, pp. 775–782, 1997

136 Melnick, Meredith, "Where Does Fear Come From? (Hint: It's Not the Creepy Basement)," *Time Healthland,* Dec 16, 2010,http://healthland.time.com/2010/12/16/where-does-fear-come-from-hint-its-not-the-creepy-basement/

137 Dr. Michael David, "Neurobiology of Fear, Anxiety and Extinction: Implications for Pyschotherapy", *MIT Video,*http://mitworld.mit.edu/video/576, April 14, 2008

138 Miguel Ibáñez Talegón and Bernadette Anzola Delgado (2011). Anxiety Disorders in Dogs, Anxiety Disorders, Vladimir Kalinin (Ed.), ISBN: 978-953-307-592-1, *InTech,* Available from:

http://www.intechopen.com/books/anxiety-disorders/anxiety-disorders-in-dogs1

139 Overall, K L. *Clinical Behavioral Medicine for Small Animals,* Mosby, 1997 –p215

140 Radley, Jason J. Morrison, John H.,„Repeated stress and structural plasticity in the brain,„, *Ageing Research Reviews,* 2005 (271-287)

141 de Kloet ER, Oitzl MS, Joels M "Stress and cognition: are corticosteroids good or bad guys?" *Trends Neurosci,* 1999,22(10): 422–426.

142 Kim JJ, Diamond DM (2002) "The stressed hippocampus, synaptic plasticity and lost memories," *Nat Rev Neurosci* 3(6): 453–462.

143   Roozendaal B "Stress and memory: opposing effects of glucocorticoids on memory consolidation and memory retrieval," *Neurobiol Learn Mem,* 200278(3): 578–595.

144 Gold PW, Chrousos GP (2002) "Organization of the stress system and its dysregulation in melancholic and atypical depression: high vs low CRH/NE states," *Mol Psychiatry* 7(3): 254–275.

145 Pittenger, Christopher, Duman, Ronald S "Stress, Depression, and Neuroplasticity: A Convergence of Mechanisms," *Neuropsychopharmacology* (2008) 33, 88–109

146 Reisner IR, Mann JJ, Stanley M, Huang YY, Houpt KA. „Comparison of cerebrospinal fluid monoamine metabolite levels in dominant-aggressive and non-aggressive dogs," *Brain Res.* 1996;714:57–64

147 King JN, Simpson BS, Overall KL, Appleby D, Pageat P, Ross C, et al. "Treatment of separation anxiety in dogs with clomipramine: results from a prospective, randomized, double-blind, placebo-controlled, parallel-group, multicenter clinical trial," *App. Anim. Behav. Sci.* 2000;67:255–275

148 Overall KL, Dunham AE, Frank D. "Frequency of nonspecific clinical signs in dogs with separation anxiety, thunderstorm phobia, and noise phobia, alone or in combination," *J. Am. Vet. Med. Assoc.* 2001;219:467–473

149 Seksel K, Lindeman MJ. "Use of clomipramine in treatment of obsessive-compulsive disorder, separation anxiety and noise phobia in dogs: a preliminary, clinical study," *Aust. Vet. J.* 2001;79:252–256

150 Overall K, Dunham AE. "Clinical features and outcome in dogs and cats with obsessive compulsive disorder: 126 cases (1989-2000)," *J. Am. Vet. Med. Assoc.* 2002;221:1445–1452

151 Riva J, Bondiolotti G, Michelazzi M, Marelli SP, Luzi F, Verga M. "Comparison of neurotransmitter levels and behaviors in drug detection dogs," *J. Vet. Behav.: Clin. Appl. Res.* 2007;2:86

152 Lars Schwabe, Marian Joëls, Benno Roozendaal, Oliver T. Wolf, Melly S. Oitzl , "Stress effects on memory: An update and integration," *Neuroscience and Biobehavioral Reviews*, Volume 36, Issue 7, August 2012, Pages 1740–1749

153 J. M. Koolhaas,* P. Meerlo, S. F. De Boer, J. H. Strubbe And B. Bohus, "The Temporal Dynamics of the Stress Response," *Neuroscience and Biobehavioral Reviews*, Vol. 21, No. 6, pp. 775–782, 1997

154 Våge J, Bønsdorff T B, Arnet E, Tverdal A and Lingaas F, "Differentialgene expression in brain tissues of aggressive and non-aggressive dogs," *BMC Veterinary Research* 2010, 6:34

155 Yvette I. Sheline, Deanna M. Barch Julie M. Donnelly John M. Ollinger Abraham Z. Snyder Mark A. Mintun, "Increased amygdala response to masked emotional faces in depressed subjects resolves with antidepressant treatment: an fMRI study," *Biological Psychiatry*, Volume 50, Issue 9 , Pages 651-658, 1 November 2001

156 Donegan et al.; Sanislow, CA; Blumberg, HP; Fulbright, RK; Lacadie, C; Skudlarski, P; Gore, JC; Olson, IR et al. (2003). "Amygdala hyperreactivity in borderline personality disorder: implications for emotional dysregulation," *Biological Psychiatry* 54 (11): 1284–1293.

157 Yvette I. Sheline, Deanna M. Barch Julie M. DonnellyJohn M. Ollinger Abraham Z. Snyder Mark A. Mintun, "Increased amygdala response to masked emotional faces in depressed subjects resolves with antidepressant treatment: an fMRI study,"*Biological Psychiatry* Volume 50, Issue 9, Pages 651-658, 1 November 2001

158 Karen L. Overall, *From Leashes to Neurons and Psychopharmacology,*IAABC 2007 Conference, http://www.youtube.com/watch?v=zxEkq2JVAbl

159 Norman Doidge, M.d., *The Brain that Changes Itself.* 2007, Penguin Books, p 240-241

160 Zetzsche T, Preuss UW, Frodl T, Schmitt G, Seifert D, Münchhausen E, Tabrizi S, Leinsinger G, Born C, Reiser M, Möller HJ, Meisenzahl EM., "Hippocampal volume reduction and history of aggressive behaviour in patients with borderline personality disorder," Psychiatry Res. 2007 Feb 28;154(2):157-70. Epub 2007 Feb 15.

161 Bremner, J., Randall, R., Scott, T., Bronen, R., Seibyl, J., Southwick, S., Delaney, R., McCarthy, G., Charney, D., Innis, R. (1995). "MRI-based measurement of hippocampal volume in patients with combat-related posttraumatic stress disorder," *American Journal of Psychiatry*, 152:973-981.

162 Bremner, J., Randall, P., Vermetten, E., Staib, L., Bronen, R., Mazure, C., Capelli, S., McCarthy, G., Innis, R.,

Charney, D. (1997). "Magnetic resonance imaging-based measurement of hippocampal volume in posttraumatic stress disorder related to childhood physical and sexual abuse: A preliminary report," *Biological Psychiatry*, 41:23-32.

163 Jessica D. Payne and Lynn Nadel, "Sleep, dreams, and memory consolidation: The role of the stress hormone cortisol," *Learn Mem.* 2004 November; 11(6): 671–678.

164 Siegel A, Victoroff J, "Understanding human aggression: New insights from neuroscience," *Int J Law Psychiatry*. 2009 Jul-Aug;32(4):209-15. Epub 2009 Jul 12.

165 Peremans, K., 2002. "Functional brain imaging in the dog. Single photon emission tomography as a research and clinical tool for the investigation of canine brain physiology and pathophysiology", PhD dissertation, Ghent University.

166 Allan Siegel, Thomas A.P. Roeling, Thomas R. Gregga, Menno R. Kruk, "Neuropharmacology of brain-stimulation-evoked aggression," *Neuroscience and Biobehavioral Reviews* 23 (1999) 359±389

167 Siegel A, Victoroff J. "Understanding human aggression: New insights from neuroscience," *Int J Law Psychiatry*. 2009 Jul-Aug;32(4):209-15. Epub 2009 Jul 12.

168 Dodman , Nicolas, "Medical Causes of Aggression In Dogs" *Pet Place*, http://www.petplace.com/dogs/medical-causes-of-aggression-in-dogs/page1.aspx

169 Francesca Benuzzi, Fausta Lui, Davide Duzzi, Paolo F. Nichelli and Carlo A. Porro, "Does It Look Painful or Disgusting? Ask Your Parietal and Cingulate Cortex," *The Journal of Neuroscience*, January 23, 2008 • 28(4):923–931

170 Ralph Adolphs, Hanna Damasio, Daniel Tranel, and Antonio R. Damasio, "Cortical Systems for the Recognition of Emotion in Facial Expressions," *The Journal of Neuroscience*, December 1, 1996, 16(23):7678 – 7687

171 Belén Rosado, Sylvia García-Belenguer, Marta León, Gema Chacón, Ainara Villegas, Jorge Palacio, ¿¿Blood concentrations of serotonin, cortisol and dehydroepiandrosterone in aggressive dogs," *Applied Animal Behaviour Science*, Volume 123, Issues 3–4, March 2010, Pages 124-130

172 Maria H. Couppis and Craig H. Kennedy, "The rewarding effect of aggression is reduced by nucleus accumbens dopamine receptor antagonism in mice" *Psychopharmacology*, Volume 197, Number 3 (2008), 449-456

173 Lu L, Bao G, Chen H, Xia P, Fan X, Zhang J, Pei G, Ma L., ¿¿Modification of hippocampal neurogenesis and neuroplasticity by social environments,"*Exp Neurol*. 2003 Oct;183(2):600-9.

174 Gould E, Tanapat P, McEwen BS, Flugge G, Fuchs E. "Proliferation of granule cell precursors in the dentate gyrus of adult monkeys is diminished by stress," *Proceedings of the National Academy of Science* USA. 1998;95:3168–3171.

175 Gould E, McEwen BS, Tanapat P, Galea LA, Fuchs E., "Neurogenesis in the dentate gyrus of the adult tree shrew is regulated by psychosocial stress and NMDA receptor activation," *J Neurosci*. 1997 Apr 1;17(7):2492-8.

176 Alexandre Heeren, Hannah E. Reese, Richard J. McNally, Pierre Philippot, "Attention training toward and away from threat in social phobia: Effects on subjective, behavioral, and physiological measures of anxiety," *Behaviour Research and Therapy*, Volume 50, Issue 1, January 2012, Pages 30-39

177 Stéphane D. Dandeneau, Mark W. Baldwin, Jodene R. Baccus, and Maya Sakellaropoulo, Jens C. Pruessner, "Cutting Stress Off at the Pass: Reducing Vigilance and Responsiveness to Social Threat by Manipulating Attention, Personality Processes And Individual Differences,,, *Journal Of Personality And Social Psychology* , 2007, vol. 93, no4, pp. 651-666 [16 page(s) (article)] (1 p.3/4)

178 M. Rosario Rueda, Michael I. Posner and Mary K. Rothbart, "The Development of Executive Attention: Contributions to the Emergence of Self-Regulation," *Developmental Neuropsychology*, 28(2), 573–594

179 Rebecca J Compton, Marie T Banich, Aprajita Mohanty, Michael P. Milham, John Herrington, Gregory A. Miller, Paige E. Scalf, Andrew Webb, And Wendy Heller, "Paying attention to emotion: An fMRI investigation of cognitive and emotional Stroop tasks," *Cognitive, Affective, & Behavioral Neuroscience* 2003, 3 (2), 81-96

180 Berns, Gregory,*Iconoclast*. 2010, Harvard Business Press, p7

181 Berns, Gregory,*Iconoclast*. 2010, Harvard Business Press, p22

182 Thomas F. Denson, "Angry Rumination and the Self-Regulation of Aggression" In. J.P. Forgas, R.F. Baumeister, & D.M. Tice (Eds.) The psychology nof self-regulation (p. 233-247) New York, NY, US: Psychology Press, 2009

183 Mead, N. L., Baumeister, R. F., Gino, F., Schweitzer, M. E., & Ariely, D. (2009). "Too tired to tell the truth: Self-control resource depletion and dishonesty," *Journal of Experimental Social Psychology*, 45,594-597.

184 Mark Muraven; Roy F. Baumeister and Dianne M. Tice , "Longitudinal Improvement Of Self-Regulation Through Practice: Building Self-Control Strength Through Repeated Exercise,"*Journal of Social Psychology*, (1999). 139(4), 446-458.

185 Roy F. Baumeister, Matthew Gailliot, C. Nathan DeWall, and Megan Oaten, "Self-Regulation and Personality: How Interventions Increase Regulatory Success, and How Depletion Moderates the Effects of Traits on Behavior,"J Pers. 2006 Dec;74(6):1773-801.

186 Karen L. Overall, "That Dog Is Smarter Than You Know: Advances in Understanding Canine Learning, Memory, and Cognition,,, *Companion Animal Medicine*, Volume 26, Issue 1, February 2011, Pages 2-9

187 Lars Schwabe, Marian Joëls, Benno Roozendaal, Oliver T. Wolf, Melly S. Oitzl , "Stress effects on memory: An update and integration,,,*Neuroscience and Biobehavioral Reviews* (2011) http://www.cog.psy.ruhr-uni-bochum.de/papers/2011/Schwabe_inpress_NBBR.pdf

188 Lally, P., van Jaarsveld, C. H. M., Potts, H. W. W. and Wardle, J. (2010), "How are habits formed: Modelling habit formation in the real world," *Eur. J. Soc. Psychol.*, 40: 998–1009. doi: 10.1002/ejsp.674

189 Emily D. Levine, Daniela Ramos, Daniel S. Mills, "A prospective study of two self-help CD based desensitization and counter-conditioning programmes with the use of Dog Appeasing Pheromone for the treatment of firework fears in dogs (Canis familiaris)," *Applied Animal Behaviour Science*, Volume 105, Issue 4, July 2007, Pages 311-329

190 "Principles of Behavior Modification and Treatment" *The Merck Veterinary Manual* , 2011; Merck Sharp & Dohme Corp., a subsidiary of Merck & Co., Inc.Whitehouse Station, NJ USA, http://www.merckvetmanual.com/mvm/index.jsp?cfile=htm/bc/140102.htm

191 Monika Sommer, Göran Hajak, Katrin Döhnel, Jörg Meinhardt, and Jürgen L. Müller, "Emotion-dependent

modulation of interference processes: an fMRI study," *Acta Neurobiol Exp* 2008, 68: 193–203

192 Maria H. Couppis and Craig H. Kennedy, "The rewarding effect of aggression is reduced by nucleus accumbens dopamine receptor antagonism in mice," *Psychopharmacology*, Volume 197, Number 3 (2008), 449-456, DOI: 10.1007/s00213-007-1054-y

193 Nicola Jane Rooney, Sarah Cowan, ,,Training methods and owner–dog interactions: Links with dog behaviour and learning ability," *Applied Animal Behaviour Science*, Volume 132, Issues 3–4, July 2011, Pages 169-177

194 J.Y. Kwan, ,,Owner Attachment and Problem Behaviors Related to Relinquishment and Training Techniques," 2011 ACVB/AVSAB scientific meeting

195 Lynch, James J., McCarthy, John F. "Social Responding in Dogs: Heart Rate Changes to a Person," *Psychophysiology*, Vol 4,1469-8936, 1969

196 Maier SF, Seligman MEP, "Learned Helplessness: Theory and Evidence," *Journal of Experimental Psychology*, 1976, Vol 105, No. 1, 3-46

197 Bonne Beerda, Matthijs B.H. Schilder, Jan A.R.A.M. van Hooff, Hans W. de Vries, Jan A. Mol, ,,Behavioural, saliva cortisol and heart rate responses to different types of stimuli in dogs,"*Applied Animal Behaviour Science* 58 1998 365–381

198 E. Schalke a,*, J. Stichnoth a, S. Ott a, R. Jones-Baade, "Clinical signs caused by the use of electric training collars on dogs in everyday life situations", *Applied Animal Behaviour Science* 105 (2007) 369–380

199 Berkowitz L, Cochran ST, Embree MC., "Physical pain and the goal of aversively stimulated aggression," *J Pers Soc Psychol.* 1981 Apr;40(4):687-700.

200 Berkowitz L. "Frustration-aggression hypothesis: examination and reformulation". *Psychol Bull.* 1989 Jul;106(1):59-73.

201 Gustafson R., "Human physical aggression as a function of magnitude of frustration: indirect support and a possible confounding influence," *Psychol Rep.* 1989 Apr;64(2):367-74.

202 Verona E, Sullivan EA., "Emotional catharsis and aggression revisited: heart rate reduction following aggressive responding," *Emotion.* 2008 Jun;8(3):331-40.

203 Miller, H C, Bender, C, "The breakfast effect: Dogs (Canis familiaris) search more accurately when thy are less hungry," *Behavior Processes*, Vol 91, Issue 3, Nov 2012, Pages 313-317

204 Overall, K L. *Clinical Behavioral Medicine for Small Animals*, Mosby, 1997 –p282

205 Karine Silva, Liliana de Sousa "Empathic dogs: theorizing about the possible domestication of emotional contagion" *Journal of Veterinary Behavior: Clinical Applications and Research* 1 January 2011 (volume 6 issue 1 Pages 69-70 DOI: 10.1016/j.jveb.2010.09.034)

206 Karen L. Overall, *Clinical Behavioral Medicine for Small Animals*, Mosby, 1997, p 215

207 Deepa Natarajan1, and Doretta Caramaschi, "Animal Violence Demystified," *Front Behav Neurosci.* 2010; 4: 9. Published online 2010 April 5. Prepublished online 2009 September 11

208 Benjamin L. Hart, Lynette A. Hart, Melissa Bain, *Canine and Feline Behavior Therapy*, 2006 Blackwell Publishing

209 Petra A. Mertens, , "The Concept of Dominance and the Treatment of Aggression in Multidog Homes: A

Comment on van Kerkhove's Commentary," *Journal Of Applied Animal Welfare Science,* 7(4), 287–291

210 Karen L. Overall, *Clinical Behavioral Medicine for Small Animals,* Mosby, 1997 - 544 pages

211 PETFAX behavior consultation can be accessed here as of the time of writing this
http://www.tufts.edu/vet/petfax/

212 Dodman NH, Smith A, Holmes D., "Comparison of the efficacy of remote consultations and personal consultations for the treatment of dogs which are aggressive towards their owners," *Vet Rec.* 2005 Feb 5;156(6):168-70.

213 Luescher, A. U., Flannigan, G., Frank, D., & Mertens, P. "The role and limitations of trainers in behavior treatment and therapy," *Journal of Veterinary Behavior: Clinical Applications and Research,* doi:10.1016/j.jveb.2006.12.004 (2007), 26-27

214 J. Shaw, "A Poll to Determine Veterinarians' Current Role Expectation of Dog Trainers," 2011 *ACVB/AVSAB Veterinary Behavior Symposium,*
http://www.avsabonline.org/avsabonline/images/stories/Meeting_Documents/2011_Meeting/2011%20acvb-avsab%20symposium%20proceedings.pdf

215 Anonymous, "The Irreverent Vet Speaks Out – What Veterinarians Don't Want You to Know,"
http://www.petplace.com/dogs/the-irreverent-vet-speaks-out--what-veterinarians-dont-want-you-to-know/page1.aspx

216 Dr. Karen Overall interview, http://youtu.be/6xIDl1bkomQ, posted Oct 20, 2011

217 Russell A. Powell, Diane G. Symbaluk, Suzanne E. MacDonald, *Introduction To Learning And Behavior,* Cengage Learning, 2008, p 427

218 Overall, KL., "Understanding How Dogs Learn: Importance In Training And Behavior Modification," *World Small Animal Veterinary Association World Congress Proceedings,* 2006

219 Alexandra Horowitz, "Disambiguating the "guilty look": Salient prompts to a familiar dog behaviour," *Behavioural Processes,* Volume 81, Issue 3, July 2009, Pages 447-452

220 Reisner, Ilana, "Tuesday's Pearl" *Reisner Veterinary Behavior & Consulting Services's Facebook page,* Aug 21, 2012, http://www.facebook.com/ReisnerVetBehavior

221 Kun Guo, Kerstin Meints, Charlotte Hall, Sophie Hall, Daniel Mills, "Left gaze bias in humans, rhesus monkeys and domestic dogs," 2009 *Anim Cogn* 12:409-418

222 Nicola J Rooney, John W.S Bradshaw, Ian H Robinson, "A comparison of dog–dog and dog–human play behaviour,,,*Applied Animal Behaviour Science,* Volume 66, Issue 3, 29 February 2000, Pages 235-248

223 Daniel Simon Millsa, Daniela Ramosa, Marta Gandia Estellesa, Claire Hargraveb, "A triple blind placebo-controlled investigation into the assessment of the effect of DogAppeasingPheromone (DAP) on anxiety related behaviour of problem dogs in the veterinary clinic," *Applied Animal Behaviour Science,* Volume 98, Issues 1–2, June 2006, Pages 114–126

224 G. Sheppard, BSc, RMN1 and D. S. Mills, BVSc, MRCVS1, "Evaluation of dog-appeasing pheromone as a potential treatment for dogs fearful of fireworks,"*Veterinary Record* 2003;152:432-436

225 Florian Mormann, Julien Dubois, Simon Kornblith, Milica Milosavljevic, Moran Cerf, Matias Ison, Naotsugu

Tsuchiya, Alexander Kraskov, Rodrigo Quian Quiroga, Ralph Adolphs, Itzhak Fried & Christof Koch, "A category-specific response to animals in the right human amygdala," *Nature Neuroscience,* Volume14 | Number 10 | October 2011

THE DOG AGGRESSION SYSTEM EVERY DOG OWNER NEEDS

21278732R00222